WILDERNESS SURVIVAL HANDBOOK

WILDERNESS SURVIVAL HANDBOOK

PRIMITIVE SKILLS FOR SHORT-TERM SURVIVAL AND LONG-TERM COMFORT

MICHAEL PEWTHERER

New York   Chicago   San Francisco   Lisbon   London   Madrid   Mexico City
Milan   New Delhi   San Juan   Seoul   Singapore   Sydney   Toronto

Library of Congress Cataloging-in-Publication Data

Pewtherer, Michael.
  Wilderness survival handbook : primitive skills for short-term survival and long-term comfort / Michael Pewtherer.
        p.   cm.
  Includes bibliographical references and index.
  ISBN 0-07-148467-1
  1. Wilderness survival.   2. Outdoor life.   I. Title.

GV200.5.P375   2010
613.6'9—dc22   2009049595

2 3 4 5 6 7 8 9 10 11 12 13 14 15 16   DOC/DOC 1 9 8 7 6 5 4 3 2 1

ISBN   978-0-07-148467-1
MHID   0-07-148467-1

McGraw-Hill books are available at special quantity discounts to use as premiums and sales promotions or for use in corporate training programs. To contact a representative, please e-mail us at bulksales@mcgraw-hill.com.

The information contained in this book is intended to provide helpful and informative material on the subject addressed. It is not intended to serve as a replacement for professional medical advice. A health-care professional should be consulted regarding your specific situation. Neither McGraw-Hill nor the author shall have any responsibility for any adverse effects that arise directly or indirectly as a result of the information provided in this book.

CONTENTS

PREFACE

We loped through the valley, two barefooted, suntanned boys, feeling a true levity of being. We stopped under the spreading branches of a large sycamore tree, and Sylvan reached up and snapped off a dead branch. Where it had broken was a split that he exploited with his knife to make a board of sorts. With another broken branch, a pine knot, some cordage, and a bow, he soon found his hand gliding back and forth with the new bow and drill set. In no time he had a coal glowing and smoking in a cedar tinder bundle that he dropped at my feet as it burst into flames. Collecting the bow and drill, he handed them to me with a joyful smile playing on his young face. I knelt down, determination fairly oozing from my pores. I was going to repeat the miracle I had just witnessed. Little did I know then that it would take two years of unguided determination and frustration before I would realize my goal. I was twelve years old.

With no books or teachers, I worked on that bow and drill, often becoming livid with anger and hurling the set into the woods or across my basement. For some reason I always stopped short of breaking the bow, and never did I leave the pieces of the set where I had thrown them. Instead, I listened to some inner wisdom suggesting that I collect them and leave them on the shelf.

Within two weeks, give or take, I would once again return to the set and another session of determined practice. Why I kept at it I do not know, but I knew that it was important; this determination has helped me ever since.

As a youngster, I only wanted to learn enough skills to survive. At least, that is what I told myself. But with the introduction of each new skill came a clear knowledge that there was so much more to learn. As my proficiency grew with a skill, I learned how little I actually knew; it was both depressing and heartening. Now I revel in the fact that I never will really master any of these skills. Even if I learn more than any other person on the planet, I will only be a master if I am graded on the curve. However, in relation to what there is to know of it, I will continue to be a student, and that is exciting.

What is the point in learning wilderness skills? Some people have a genuine interest in knowing how to interact and function in the wild, whether on a camping trip, taking an extended stay in the backcountry, or being unexpectedly stranded between populated areas. Others may expect to find themselves in a situation requiring these skills for the short term and want to be prepared. Still others want to know their place in the world or where their food comes from, and how to go without the benefits of the modern world. And there are those who, in combination with all of the above, merely enjoy knowledge.

The question of what gear to bring on a trip into the backcountry is not addressed in this book because of the constant changes in materials, styles, and techniques of employing said gear. How to modify clothing is covered, although it is recommended to get the right gear for a trip via an expedition outfitters or other knowledgeable organization.

Some people are happy in their preparedness with a purchased survival kit in their car, home, or pack, while others want to know what to do should they be stripped of all modern tools and amenities. Which group you fall into is the first step in learning survival skills, because knowing this will show you how best to proceed. It must be noted that modern survival skills and tools can be augmented by the skills of the past peoples of the world and vice versa. Use both to further your knowledge in whichever bent you follow. It is true that survival situations appear to arise infrequently, but the bulk of the ones that make the news end poorly or are close calls, while those that are averted through correct action seldom make the headlines.

I encourage all people to get out into the land and work on skills of survival, not because I believe that they will someday need them, but because we have become aliens on our own planet. We don't speak the language, we don't want to learn it, and we don't realize that our TVs, cell phones, tires, blenders, shoes, and countertops all come from the natural world. We as a species need to know how to take the pulse of our home. If we never take interest in its workings, we will continue to cause damage and forever change the world in which our children and grandchildren will dwell.

My hope is that those who can will not only visit the natural world but bring children and friends with them, building a reservoir of good memories and connections involving the outdoors.

If you wish to further pursue the skills of survival and/or primitive living, I urge you to learn from many schools, people, and books. All have something to offer, and the worst mistake that students can make is to cut themselves off from a source of knowledge. Form an allegiance with a source of knowledge if you will, but not to the exclusion of others.

Practice what you know. You do not need to be in the Alaskan wilderness to do this, because survival skills can serve you in any environment. Break a task, skill, or tool down to its simplest components so that you can come up with improvements on existing techniques plus rediscover those of old.

ACKNOWLEDGMENTS

Many people helped me to get on the path that I now walk. First and foremost, I would like to thank my wife, Diane, for her steady support and encouragement and for caring for our boys while I traveled to different parts of this continent in search of answers. Thanks to my two little men, Wyatt and Torrin, who didn't give their mother too hard of a time while Daddy was away. A special thanks to Mark Elbroch, who encouraged and advised me on this and other projects.

Many skilled people offered help in reviewing and editing parts of the manuscript, and they are among the very best, if not *the* best, in ensuring that solid information gets out to the public. To them, I send a profound thank you. They are: Matt Richards, Estabon Fire, Keith Badger, Craig Childs, Henry Glick, David Wescott, Steve Watts, Darren Wells, and Mors Kochanski.

Thanks to my parents for raising me in a rural area and giving me from dark until dark to roam the woods, and to my Grandpa Jack and my Uncle Jimmy Ferrigno for teaching me not only to fish, but to love it. Many others aided me in various ways for which I am grateful: Jonathan Talbott; Dana Stevens; Henry Glick; Paul-Ivan Derreumaux; Eric Muller; Raif Pomeroy; Ricardo Sierra; William Ward; my sisters, Alicia, Holly, and Kylie; my brother Galen; and Sylvan Incao, for getting me hooked on primitive technology.

Thanks to the folks at McGraw-Hill for their incredible amount of support, Jonathan Eaton for this opportunity, Bob Holtzman for his patience, and the editing team for their insightful recommendations that make this a better book than it might otherwise have been.

INTRODUCTION

The commonly accepted "survival situation" is one in which people are involuntarily detained in a potentially hazardous setting. A plane crash, a shipwreck, a broken-down vehicle far off the beaten path, or becoming injured or lost while hiking are just a few of the more common ways in which survival situations arise. These scenarios are usually resolved within a week—often in as little as three days—due to rescue or death.

"Wilderness living," on the other hand, implies a longer-term stay far outside of settled society, undertaken intentionally. Strictly construed, the term may differ from "camping" only in the duration of the stay, but to me, it has additional implications. It means relying upon natural resources and learned skills to satisfy all of your needs. It means avoiding modern camping and hunting gear like nylon tents, gas stoves, and rifles. It means the practice and appreciation of what are commonly called *primitive skills*—the skills practiced by aboriginal peoples of any part of the globe, from any period in history or prehistory.

This book is divided into two parts. Part I: Seven-Day Survival addresses the short-term needs of individuals who find themselves unintentionally stuck in the wilderness and looking to get out or get rescued as quickly as possible.

Because none of us know when we might encounter such a situation, this material is for anyone who ever travels beyond the borders of their city or rural residence.

Part II: Beyond Survival: Primitive Skills for Wilderness Living is for readers who have a deeper interest in the natural world and man's role within it. Although this section is not a camping manual, it will inevitably improve the outdoor skills of anyone who does camp, hike, hunt, or otherwise intentionally spend limited amounts of time in the wilderness. But it goes much beyond that in attempting to teach how to live a complete and comfortable material life not merely "off the grid" but out of sight and sound of the grid entirely. To gain, through these skills, an understanding of how aboriginal people lived is to gain a deeper appreciation for what it means to be human and a resident of the earth.

Wilderness survival and wilderness living overlap in many ways. The skills needed to survive in the short term can come into play when you are living for longer periods outside of society and vice versa. Regardless of your situation, man requires the same things to maintain comfort, health, and life.

While there are exceptions to every rule, the Rule of Threes is a good way to remember the priorities with regard to what the human body can handle in adverse wilderness settings: three minutes without air, three hours without shelter, three days without water, and three weeks without food. Sure, some people can hold their breath for more than three minutes, and three hours naked in the wilderness is not necessarily a death sentence. But step outside on cold day in winter with only your indoor clothes on and see how long it takes for you to lose the ability to touch your pinky fingertip to the thumb tip of the same hand. When you can't, say hello to the early stages of hypothermia!

Assuming, then, that you're not in imminent danger of drowning, the first and foremost need is to maintain your body temperature. This is done by providing an insulating barrier between the body and the elements, be they heat or cold in their various forms (wind, water, direct sun, etc.). Sometimes the insulation may be clothing; other times the protection is offered by the walls and roof of a building or other structure. Additionally, in warmer climates, nights can be cold, and the cumulative effect of trying to get all of your chores done at night or in the daylight when you are not sleeping will soon leave you exhausted and prone to accidents and miscalculations—with potentially deadly results. Among other things, shelter can keep you warm and dry, provide you with a place to sleep in comfort, and allow you to recover valuable energy.

Water is available in many ways. Our very surroundings are loaded with it, but knowing how to capture it and make it potable is critical, and you must be able to do this on a regular, ongoing basis.

Inserted into the Rule of Threes is the ability to make fire. In the right configurations, fire can act as a shelter against cold, it can prepare foods for easier digestion, and it can purify water. The heat can be applied to tools for fire hardening, or the coals can be used in direct contact to fell trees or shape wood. The power of fire to raise morale should not go unnoticed either, because that is of great importance if you are to survive.

It is possible for a healthy individual to last quite some time without food. Yet the idea of hunger often consumes us after missing our first meal. (People with diabetes or who have low blood sugar must keep much better track of what and when they eat as well as have ready access to food and are thus in a much more dangerous situation in any survival scenario.) Unless you hunt or harvest wild edibles as part of your lifestyle now, chances are that, if you were in a survival situation tomorrow, you would use far more energy in the pursuit of food than you would gain from what you found, if in fact you found anything. This is why I chose not to discuss food in Part I. For the short-term survival scenario, food should be lowest on the list of priorities, and actively seeking game or forage should be avoided.

That said, being ready to harvest or kill game that presents itself is something that I do advise. Whether you are sitting tight and waiting for rescue or trying to find your own way out of the wilderness, there is no harm in grabbing a couple of stones or rabbit sticks and keeping an eye out for a dinner guest or gathering easily accessible, edible plants, including fruit.

Regardless of where I am, I take note of all kinds of resources as I move over the land. These include food and water resources but also sites of available shelter and shelter-building materials, wood for tools and fires, and other useful raw materials like pitch, clay, certain types of stone, and natural fibers. Not only does this give me an idea of the frequency with which I can expect to encounter them, I can also go back and collect them when and if they are needed.

Through practice, I know how much time is required to construct a shelter in almost any situation. A warm and waterproof home in the pine forests of the U.S. Southwest takes me less than an hour to build; an igloo, when I am working under prime conditions, takes me three hours or less, depending on the snow-cutting tools I have at my disposal. If I am hoping for rescue, I'll still make a shelter just in case I'm not found before nightfall. If I am intent on staying out for a few weeks or more, I'll build a simple, temporary shelter to stay in while I'm building something more permanent. In any situation, simple shelters are better than no shelter, and in dire situations, they are the fastest and easiest to build.

Over the years, as I have pursued my love of wilderness survival along with primitive technology, I have been disturbed by the acrimonious relationships that seem to prevail between the different bents and different schools or programs. I hold knowledge above the petty allegiances to one instructor, book, or school and urge all people who are interested in these skills to read many books, attend different schools, and learn under a variety of instructors. We all have our prejudices, bad habits, gems of knowledge, and skills backgrounds. I believe that, from around 1500 A.D. back to the dawn of man, we have perhaps retained 10 percent of the myriad skills that we

developed. To me, this means that we should be collaborating to unearth many of these lost technologies and forge our way forward to the past.

No book on this subject can be truly complete. The skills that I have chosen to include were attained through much personal experience and consultation with many outdoor, wilderness, and primitive technology instructors, and they were informed by what readers of this type of book ask for in their reviews. In this book, it is assumed that you are dressed for the climate—and there is guidance on that subject in Chapter 1. Some skills will cover what to do if you have less, while other skills will require additional items; for example, orienteering requires a compass as well as a map of the area, and some fire-making techniques are greatly eased with a reliable cutting edge like a knife.

A topic that is covered to a lesser degree is that of wild edible plants. The reason for this is twofold. While I know about plants and their uses, I am not as well versed in this subject as would be necessary to give the plants their due diligence for *all* of North America. Second, there are a number of great books on the subject that I would be hard pressed to top, and these are listed in the Appendix. In a nod to the value of plants as part of a survival diet, I have included ten plants found widely in North America. These plants were chosen for two reasons: their widespread availability and their nutritional value, primarily their high content of vitamin C and carbohydrates.

WILDERNESS SURVIVAL HANDBOOK

PART I

SEVEN-DAY SURVIVAL

CHAPTER 1

PREPARING TO SURVIVE

Camping equipment, cookstoves, tents, sleeping bags, and the like are not addressed in this book because, well, then it would be a book on camping. If you practice surviving only with a tent, a sleeping bag, and all of your other camping amenities, then you will suffer if you find yourself without one or more of these items. If you prepare for the worst, then anything short of that is a bonus. Clothing, however, *is* covered, because most people don't leave home without it, and if you are putting together a survival kit for your car, boat, plane, pack, or home or are venturing into areas in which any of the aforementioned survival situations is a possibility, then dressing appropriately is a wise move. Whether I'm in an arctic or a desert environment, with a car or on foot, I make sure that I have clothing, including footwear, that is sufficient for dealing with local weather should the need arise.

CLOTHING

Different climates and weather conditions call for a great variety of clothing. It is to this end that I strongly recommend that you pack for any excursion, short or long, with the most severe weather the region can offer in mind. It may be warm now, but what will the temperature drop to at 2:00 or 3:00 A.M.? Or at seven thousand feet? Do you have enough clothing to change into if you become soaked? Are you prepared for any eventuality? Keep these questions in mind as you prepare for a trip.

For colder weather, this includes an outer shell that effectively blocks the wind and repels the rain and an inner layer (or layers) that creates plenty of dead air space that can be heated effectively by your body. In cool weather, just the outer shell may be all that is required, but as the temperature drops, more of the insulating layer is called for in order to slow the heat exchange with the outside air.

In warmer areas, the outer shell is called for, but this time it is to protect your skin from the sun. The insulating layer used in cold-weather garments will provide no benefit here, because the goal is to promote heat exchange. Thus, loose-fitting outerwear is the name of the game. In excessively hot and humid climates, forgoing underwear is sometimes a good idea, as jock itch and heat rash can become issues.

I have been surprised, when spending extended periods of time in hot climates, at how quickly my body has adjusted to the high temperatures. While living in Australia's western deserts, I seldom wore short pants and instead preferred to go in jeans, a long-sleeve, button-front shirt, and a wide-brimmed hat unless the thermometer hit 52°C (125°F) in the shade; then shorts were nice and water was necessary.

The clothing options available for today's outdoor enthusiasts easily outstrip those of the past, so I'll touch on some basic rules and describe how to improve inadequate clothing if that is all you have.

A common expression in outdoor apparel is "cotton kills." Why? Because cotton loses its insulating qualities when it is wet and holds moisture next to your skin. Water pulls heat from your body twenty times faster than air, so between that and cooling through evaporation, it should be clear that cotton is only a fair-weather friend. Wool, on the other hand, retains heat when it is wet, and while this may be uncomfortable, it is certainly preferably to developing hypothermia.

Layering

There are places on this fine planet of ours where shelter is not to be had, the ground is too hard to dig into, there is little or no vegetation, and no loose stone is available with which to create even a simple windbreak. The likelihood of getting stranded with nothing in such a place is nonexistent for the bulk of the population, and I cannot imagine the scenario that would place anyone in it. Adventure racers regularly traverse extreme terrain with little in the way of supplies, but most are carefully watched and teams are closely scrutinized before being allowed to participate. While accidents do happen out in the field, others happen in the planning stage—inadequate clothing, poor route planning, or no emergency plan.

Clothing is easy to carry and can offer protection when the environment cannot. Keep clothing clean for better insulation and to avoid odors when you are hunting. Many thinner layers are preferable to a few thick ones. Even in subzero weather, a moderate amount of activity can get a person sweating. This causes the clothing to become moist (even with a wicking layer next to the skin, the moisture will freeze in your clothes before it makes it to the outside) and often results in dangerous cooling of the body. The key to maintaining the viability of the insulation provided by your clothing is to keep it clean and dry. Therefore, as you increase your aerobic activity, take off layers to prevent overheating and excessive perspiration. Mountaineering suits come with plenty of closable vents but sport a pretty high price tag, and for rigorous activities like building snow shelters or snowshoeing, the vents of these suits are often inadequate.

Covering Your Body

For cooler climates, I wear one to three pairs of thin wool or polypropylene (poly-pro) long underwear with a couple of fleeces—either wool or synthetic—over them. A jacket and/or a windbreaker up top and snow or ski pants below leave me well prepared for anything from about 75°F down to -40°F. Large boots that allow for at least two pairs of wool socks to be worn at a time keep feet warm and blister free. Mors Kochanski (see the Appendix) recommends wearing three pairs of thick wool socks inside boots. Coats with a tie at the hem and at kidney level (like the U.S. Army coats) can make a great difference in maintaining warmth, because they prevent cold air from coming in and hot air from going out as movement creates a bellows effect inside your coat. As you

Clothing Modifications

I went out hunting one early winter day and was wearing cotton army pants with the tie at the ankles and the cargo pockets on the thigh. The temperature dropped from the mid-forties (Fahrenheit) into the low thirties, and it started drizzling. My choices were to head home and scrap the hunt or make some clothing modifications and stick it out. I opted for the latter and headed for a somewhat sheltered rock outcropping where I collected a bunch of leaves and stuffed them into my pant legs. They were scratchy and uncomfortable and made stalking game impossible, because the leaves made quite a lot of noise. They also shifted down lower, requiring me to add more and more leaves. However, when I was still, my legs were warm. I am not sure that the awkwardness in moving or the fact that I looked and felt like Popeye with the spinach gone to my legs was worth the trouble, but it was clear that this could help in extreme situations. With this in mind, I sewed two sweatshirts, one inside the other, stitching the cuffs and waistbands together but leaving the collars separate. I then stuffed the space between the shirts with leaves and cattail down. It was better—not great—but it worked, provided I didn't move too much and end up with a lumpy wad around my waist. Filling the space between the shirts to such an extent that the insulation stayed where I wanted it left something to be desired when it came to ease of movement, but in a pinch, it proved beneficial.

heat up due to activity, you can doff layers until you are able to maintain a comfortable working temperature. Remember to start putting layers back on once you cease your activity, because cooling happens fast and can cause you to become chilled.

In desert climates, I found that once I was acclimatized, wearing boxers, long pants, loose, button-front shirts, socks, and cowboy boots as well as a wide-brimmed hat kept me the most comfortable while doing moderate work, even as the temperature rose past 110°F and into the 120s. The long pants protected my legs from the prickly desert foliage, and the boots made me feel better about snake strikes. (The trade-offs with cowboy boots are the lack of tread on the sole and lousy ankle support.) Exposure to the sun is an important consideration, because sunburn can be debilitating and cause sickness or even death. Evaporation of moisture from your skin also must be taken seriously. I can remember sweating with no moisture perceivable on my skin—just the slow growth of salt crystals on my cheeks and in my eyebrows. A pair of jeans just out of the wash dried completely in less than fifteen minutes—a third of what it takes in a dryer! The point is: don't strip down and expose your skin directly to the sun if you want to cool off.

Head and Hands

We use our head and hands for everything, not only in survival, but in day-to-day living as well. Hats are vital in most cases, whether they protect us from the sun or the cold. In high heat, a wide-brimmed hat with a crown is advisable, although baseball-type hats with tails in the back can provide adequate protection. To improvise, use a handkerchief or other cloth draped over your neck and hold it in place with a cap.

In colder climates, a snug hat that covers your head, neck, and ears is advisable, and hoods can

Head covering

be of tremendous value especially if they are deep, because they provide shelter from all but a direct head wind. Additionally, hoods greatly reduce the heat that is lost through the collar of your coat.

Mittens are the way to go in cold climates. I use a pair with a fleece insert and a pad for wiping my nose on the thumb . . . a great perk. Mittens keep all of your fingers (except the thumb) in the same compartment, making it easier to keep your digits warm. The trade-off is a loss of dexterity unless you remove the mittens, which, depending on the task at hand, could be no big deal or something that must be done between hand-warming sessions. Wool or synthetics are good options, because they will keep your hands warm even when they are wet. I like to have a spare set of liners at the least but prefer to carry two pairs of mittens if I can.

If you plan a trip or think that you might, get the clothing you want and try it out. Note what works and what does not, and make the appropriate corrections. The knowledge that you gain in practice can save you trouble down the road. Just

because a clothing item is "rated to -60°F" or "waterproof" does not mean that you should take the manufacturer's word for it. Test it out!

Footwear

Determining what footwear works for you is an individual process, because some people have easily warmed or cooled feet, dry or sweaty feet, and a number of other individual characteristics. Women tend to hold their heat in their torso and often suffer from cold feet, thus spurring the production of sleeping bags with extra insulation at the feet for women. In really cold climates, I'll wear two pairs of wool socks inside my insulated boots, making sure that my feet are not too cramped (thus reducing circulation and making it impossible to keep my feet warm). If I have a pair of new leather boots, I'll wear them in water (or in the shower) in the morning and walk them dry. After such treatment, I never suffer blisters or any discomfort, because the softened leather stretches and conforms to my foot. From then on, I'll treat them with oil to keep the leather supple and waterproof. New synthetic boots should be worn and broken in prior to any trip. I cannot count the times I have seen hikers with debilitating blisters due to new boots. In a survival situation, blisters can herald a death sentence . . . if you can't move, you can't support yourself, and if the blisters become infected, then the clock is really ticking.

SURVIVAL KITS

Survival and first-aid kits can be purchased almost anywhere from gas stations to Internet sites that specialize in the emergency preparedness market. They are available in all colors and sizes and contain everything from Band-Aids to blimp puncture kits. However, with all of the options, you would be hard pressed to find the kit that fully meets your precise needs. Often the store-bought kits sit in some corner of the car or rattle around under a seat with the owner unaware of the contents, which is why it is a good idea to build your own. I do *not* recommend starting with a store-bought kit and building on it. I once purchased an emergency kit for my wife's car when we lived in Montana; the quality of the gear in the crappy bag was utter junk. The flashlight was fragile and broke when it was dropped, the tow strap was never intended to pull a kid in a wagon let alone a vehicle, and the tools were molded in what can only have been a sand mold. If you start from scratch, you can choose the quality of the items included and will not be disappointed when you need them. You also will become very familiar with the contents and will know immediately what is needed and where it is when an emergency situation arises.

There are so many little items you can take with you on a hike that will provide a backup for just about any system you are likely to have with you. Fire starters abound in camping stores, water-treatment options grow with new filtration systems showing up all the time, shelter options with space-age materials are folding up smaller than ever before (although my money says that you can't get them back to the size they were when you purchased them), and high-energy foods are being condensed into ever smaller, multimeal bricks. So which ones do you take with you and which ones do you leave behind?

I keep my kits quite simple, and, depending on the trip, I may add or remove something. Consider all of the following items, then personalize the kit to fit your needs and your environment. After each trip, remember to replace items that you have used or that get worn out.

A good survival kit should include:

- First-aid kit
- A sheath knife with a full tang. This is the heaviest item, but the thick, full tang on my knife is shaped like the handle, and even if the wood rotted off, I would still have a completely functional knife.
- A lighter with an adjustable flame and with childproofing removed. You need to be able to use it effortlessly, especially when the temperature is especially cold and your dexterity is decreased.
- Matches in a film canister with the striker glued to the outside of the lid. The striker gets worn and needs to be replaced or carefully packed to avoid wear.
- A metal match is good to have as a standby. Also known as a Swedish FireSteel, it is a rod composed of ferrocerium, iron, and magnesium and is scraped to produce very hot showers of sparks.
- A film canister with four petroleum-jelly-impregnated cotton balls. I really knead the jelly into the cotton, which means that these take up more space. If you want more fire starters, do not add as much jelly and you will be able to squeeze a few more of them into the container. I have inserted these balls into a prebuilt tipi fire, after burning for eight minutes, and they still had enough flame to get the fire going with no fussing. They catch easily and are a godsend in cold, wet, dire situations. See Chapter 4 for basic fire-making techniques.

Survival kit

- A Mini Maglite flashlight with the spare bulb in the end cap is worth getting. I have left mine out in the woods for more than a year, and it still worked when I picked it up. I have also used it under water with no leakage.
- Spare batteries labeled with the date they were added to the kit. In truth, every time I go on a trip, I replace them, or, failing that, I change them out every three months and use them around the house.
- One-gallon Ziploc bags—great for holding water.
- A Space Blanket. I used a bag version of one of these when I was camping in the Rockies on the Canadian border one February. It was wickedly cold (around -30°F), and my sleeping bag was not doing the trick. The Space Bag worked, although the noise was pretty impressive, and the condensation that collected on the inside and consequently wet the outside of my sleeping bag was a little concerning. I did sleep that night, so even though I could not get that silver devil back into its container, I was happy to have thrown it in my bag. The blanket poses a challenge when you try to keep it on top of yourself. Placing pebbles in the corners with the material bunched around each corner and tying it with cord works well as a way to anchor the blanket. Beware of sharp rocks, because they will tear the material.
- Parachute cord—the real stuff with a core made up of multiple smaller strings. These smaller, inner cords can be pulled out and used individually for tasks that do not require the strength of the full cord.
- A signal mirror. This takes a little practice to use (see the sidebar) but can be visible from miles away, so try it out where you will not alarm or irritate anyone.

Using a Signal Mirror

Signal mirrors come with or without sighting holes. The two styles require different techniques when you use them.

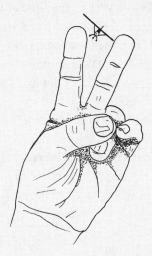

Signal mirror use

To use a mirror with no sighting hole:

1. With the mirror near your face, point it toward your intended target with one hand.
2. Raise your other hand at arm's length in front of the mirror, and manipulate the mirror until the reflected light hits your outstretched hand.
3. Create a V-notch sight by making the "victory" sign with your outstretched hand, and focus the brightest point of light on your palm at the base of the V.
4. Raise the light up until it just touches both fingers at the base of the V. In this way, the brightest light is being shown between the fingers.
5. Turning your body as a unit, move until the target can be seen through the V notch. Move back and forth slightly to paint the target many times; in this way, anyone at the target location or in the target vehicle will see bright flashes of light.

If you have no specific target, flash as much of the horizon as you can (there are any number of issues that will limit your range, such as the location of the sun in relation to your intended target, hills, trees, etc.).

To use a signal mirror that has a clear aiming hole surrounded by a grid or square mesh:

1. Hold the mirror up to your eye.
2. Look through the sight at a nearby surface or your hand.
3. Locate the reflection on the surface or on your hand, and you will see a bright spot in the mesh.
4. Carefully tilt the mirror to your target while keeping the spot within the mesh.
5. Locate your target in the clear spot in the middle of the grid.
6. Move the spot by tilting the mirror until the spot hits your target in the middle of the clear sight hole.
7. Practice.

- A candy bar or Power Bar. I prefer the Three Musketeers bar over the Power Bar, because I can actually bite through the candy, while the Power Bar provides a challenge. Kidding aside, the Power Bar has more substance and has a longer shelf life, but the candy provides quick energy and tastes good, too. Carry at least two Power Bars with you.
- A wallet magnifying glass. This cheap, light-weight little guy is easy to carry and provides yet another way in which you can get a fire started. With a prebuilt fire and a tinder bundle ready to go, place the lens between the sun and the tinder. Move the lens from a few feet away ever nearer to the tinder, and watch the area of brighter light coalesce and form a small pinprick of brilliant white light (do not look directly at the light spot; it can damage your eyes). Hold the lens in place, and watch the smoke curl up from the tinder. With practice or observation, you will learn when the tinder is smoldering and can be blown into flame.
- A large garbage bag. Good for collecting rain-water, wearing as a poncho, or keeping a treated wound dry, among other uses.
- Tweezers
- Bandanna
- Tourniquet
- Compass
- Topographical maps
- Cell phone
- Emergency transponder
- Sewing kit

There are many items usually found in commercial kits that I take or leave, depending on the trip I'm taking. These include:

- Wire saw. The saws included in kits today are junk; if you needed to cut down a tree to survive, I can't imagine doing so with these "tools."
- Fishing line and hooks. Unless you have practiced fishing with a hand line or with a pole that has no reel, you may find yourself challenged more than you want. Even so, they add little weight and take up almost no space; you make the call. (See Chapter 10 for fishing techniques.)
- Emergency whistles. These carry farther than your voice with less effort, add little weight, and often have an attachment ring or string. I prefer the whistles marketed to scuba divers, some of which work underwater and all of which work when they are wet. Again, you make the call.

If you are not careful, your survival kit will get so big that it will become part of your primary-use gear. Being prepared is not having a backup for every item you bring; it is having the knowledge and experience to know what to bring, knowing how to stretch those items in an emergency, and learning to pack backups of those items that you cannot do without.

It is also a matter of weighing the possibilities of something going wrong. For example, the possibility of getting a flat tire is reasonably high, as is the chance that your spare has issues (my new truck's spare release was rusted beyond use after four years), especially when compared to going down over wilderness in an airliner, surviving the crash, and having no one know where you are for weeks. If you are traveling through country like North Dakota or parts of Canada, for example, and you get a flat tire driving back from town one

January night, with the temperature at -40°F along with wind, what are you going to do? Maybe you could let the vehicle idle, but for how long? And what happens when you're out of fuel? Given these two examples, where would you pack a few extra goodies—in your carry-on or in your vehicle? If you have the space and don't mind the extra weight, add items that you *could* get by without but that would make life a lot easier if you had them. Obviously, a five-pound kit with a wool blanket will have much more impact on the weight and space in a pack than it will in a car.

CHAPTER 2
SHELTER

There are many ways in which shelter is found, built, or otherwise created, but the primary purpose of having shelter is simply to allow our bodies to maintain a core temperature of approximately 98.6°F with minimum energy expenditure. With no clothes, in subfreezing weather, it is possible to keep warm if you engage in vigorous aerobic activity such as jumping jacks. The problem with this method of warming yourself is that the amount of energy expended is excessive and the activity cannot be maintained. Therefore, instead of just freezing to death, you now get tired and sweaty first, then freeze to death. Clothes are often sufficient shelter for temperate climates provided you maintain some small level of physical activity such as walking. Desert climates are another matter altogether and pose some interesting dilemmas: extreme heat in the day coupled with cool nights (although this is not a given). Many cultures from desert and tropical regions cease vigorous activity from late morning to midafternoon and avoid the taxing nature of the hottest part of the day.

Shelter is basically a somewhat permeable barrier between your skin and the environment that dampens the loss or gain of heat. It can also protect against windburn, sunburn, and direct-contact injuries. Different environments might require different kinds of "shelter." A wet suit not only keeps a diver warm but protects against jellyfish stings, just as the primary purpose of work gloves is to protect the hands against injury rather than to keep the hands warm. In temperatures below 98.6°F, the goal is to create dead air space—pockets of air that are heated by your body and not easily cooled or replaced through the action of wind or water. A case in point is a jacket made of goose down. Heat from the wearer passes through the breathable lining and warms the air pockets between the feathers. The windproof shell and feathers slow the departure of warmed air to such an extent that the wearer risks becoming overheated if too much activity is undertaken, even in subzero weather. (When down is wet, however, it loses all of its insulating qualities, as the feathers stick together in clumps and thus eliminate the dead air space or air pockets.) Some materials transfer heat or cold quickly, such as the metal in a steel-toed boot. This can cause very real problems in cold climates by transferring cold from the outside directly to your digits—something to be avoided for obvious reasons. A wet suit is another great example. Water flows into the suit via the ankles, the wrists, and the neck, forming a thin layer that is trapped between the suit and your skin. The water is quickly heated by your body and can escape only via the five points of entry, greatly slowing the loss of heated water.

In hot climates, temperature regulation is also imperative, because heat exhaustion and other heat-related illnesses can be not only debilitating but can kill you. The methodology behind desert shelters differs surprisingly little from those of colder climates; again, the desire is to slow or stop the exchange of the interior climate with that of the exterior. When I was in the western deserts of Australia, sheep with two years' worth of wool on them did fine in 120+°F; however, some died within minutes of being shorn. Their ability to keep their body temperature steady required some time for adjustment, and losing their thermal-regulating wool in three minutes was not always a sufficient amount of time.

Of course, the length of time that you plan on spending in a shelter, the climate you're in, and the potential weather determine much when deciding what type of shelter to seek or build. For example, if you got stranded somewhere in New Mexico and had left your detailed travel plans with a friend, you wouldn't build an involved and long-lasting adobe structure. Instead, you'd make something far simpler, such as a lean-to or a wick-iup (a small, often tipi-like structure made from branches, brush, or other organic material to create shade and cut the wind), to keep you in fine condition until aid arrived.

LOCATION, LOCATION, LOCATION

Regardless of the shelter type, location is paramount. Many drainages, washes, arroyos, draws, wadis, or whatever you wish to call them, have great ground for digging yet pose significant risk of flash flooding in most desert areas. There are plenty of places that do flood but that are not subject to *flash* floods, or they may flood only once every three years or so. I have made shelters in sands deposited by spring floods in areas where flooding occurred only after prolonged (days of) heavy rain. In such cases, when you seek shelter for a day or two, these spots can work. If you are not sure if the area you are in is flash-flood prone, find a spot on higher ground. I have stood in the desert sun and seen torrents of water roar through a "dry" arroyo. Cloudbursts out of sight and up canyon can deposit enough water to kill the unwary hiker. Take into account the following things when you are selecting a shelter site:

- Is it safe from flash flooding?
- Where would water come from, and what path would it take if a downpour rolled in?
- Are there any dead trees or limbs that could fall and land in the shelter area?
- Is there a potential for an avalanche or rocks and debris to slide down?
- Are there obvious signs of large carnivore activity nearby? This could be in the form of trails, worn ground, lots of scat, a den, dead animals, or a bear tying a napkin under his chin while drooling and leering at you. Smaller critters like ground-dwelling hornets, ants, scorpions, snakes, and spiders and large amounts of bat or mouse scat are also nature's way of suggesting that you find an alternate shelter location.
- Are there enough materials with which to build a shelter and to sustain you in the way of water and firewood?
- Are you visible to potential rescuers?

- Does the sun work in your favor? (In cooler climates in the Northern Hemisphere, having plenty of southern exposure is desirable, because it means a maximum amount of sun. In desert climates, a little eastern exposure can be welcome in the cool of the morning, but too much of a good thing can be problematic.)

One of the first orders of business is finding a suitable location. After all, "a good shelter in a bad location is a bad shelter." So consider the following characteristics of your potential shelter site:

- **Materials:** An area without leaf litter, wood, or brush will provide a challenge when it comes to building a shelter, because you will have to bring materials from another location in order to build it. (Doing this even with the aid of a tarp is a waste of energy.) Look for areas with lots of building materials, such as flat areas in mixed-wood forests.
- **Grade:** Sleeping on a slight incline may prove to be a lesson in frustration. Anything beyond even the slightest incline can leave you cramped and somewhat crumpled on the downhill side of your shelter. Look for a flat area on which to build.
- **Drainage:** The beautiful, grassy meadow near the creek is quite likely a floodplain. Find some higher ground on which to stay. Look at your proposed shelter area, and try to imagine where water will run in a torrential downpour. Even if no rain is expected, river valleys can get chilly. This is not an issue when you are sleeping, but upon waking, things are likely to be damp and cold, and the valley bottom will get the sun later than other areas.

- **Widow-makers or deadfalls:** Always check the areas both overhead and upslope from your shelter. Are there big dead branches or trees that may fall and injure you, or large rocks that could roll when the soil below them is eroded by rain and squish you in your shelter? Remember, your goal is to survive.

Last tip: don't waste too much time searching for the perfect spot; practice building shelters in different locations, and you'll soon be able to tell how difficult a given location will be.

TYPES OF SHELTER

I break shelters into one of three broad categories or a combination of them.

- **Portable surface shelters:** tents, clothes, and tarp/hide-covered shelters.
- **Stationary surface shelters:** lean-tos, snow-built structures, debris huts, wickiups, simple shelters like the lee side of a boulder, and the like (this would include tree shelters).
- **Subsurface shelters:** caves (existing or dug in snow or sand) and covered pits.

If you have no blankets or a sleeping bag, some shelters—like lean-tos, longhouses, and any shelter that has no specific sleeping compartment—rely on a heat source in addition to the human body; i.e., they require an internal or external fire or the use of heated rocks placed in the floor and covered with sand so that a comfortable temperature can be maintained. The drawbacks of such shelters include the following:

- They are not easily transportable.
- They require time and effort to erect.
- They require maintenance to varying degrees (continuous fire tending, reheating rocks each night).

The advantages include:

- They provide sheltered space in which to work.
- They provide protected storage space.
- Their "hominess" serves as a morale booster—a function frequently overlooked but very valuable.

Other shelters, like debris huts, squirrel nests, and bedding-filled, pit-type shelters, need no heat source other than the occupant. The drawbacks of such shelters include the following:

- They often lack work and storage space (although this is easily remedied with an awning).
- They may (read: *definitely will*) take a few nights to get used to.

The advantages include:

- They need little to no maintenance depending upon length of stay.
- They can be readily constructed in most environments.
- They require relatively little time to construct.
- They need no heat source.

The shelters discussed in this chapter are all "expedient" ones; they are relatively quick to construct and are suitable for survival situations of a week or less, though their use can be stretched to last weeks or even months if you are not too picky. For more comfortable shelters that are suitable for long-term wilderness living, see Chapter 7.

FINDING SHELTER

The quality of shelter for which you are looking will vary greatly depending upon your situation. Are you looking for temporary relief from rain or wind? In such a case, simply hunkering down under a hemlock or pine tree or moving to the lee side of a hill will do the job. But suppose you find yourself stranded in the rising heat of the Sonoran Desert, or you are lost as darkness arrives and it is both rainy and cold. What then? Sometimes a good shelter can be found with little effort, while other times it would be more expedient to build one with the materials available.

When I was hitchhiking through Germany as a teen, I found myself out in the south German countryside at midnight. There were no cars or visible towns, so I walked a ways looking for a haystack to crawl into. Well, farming had changed from what I had read about it in a World War I–era book, and no welcoming haystacks beckoned. Hell, I would have settled for an unfriendly one at that point. Eventually, I got so tired I crawled into some weeds and quickly crawled out, brushing my stinging cheeks with my sleeve in an effort to ease the nettle's rebuke. I did find some shrubs and was amazed at what we, as humans, will settle for if we are exhausted enough. This lesson would be reiterated in the military, where I learned that it is, in fact, possible to sleep standing up in the chow line.

Over the years, I have taken shelter under rock overhangs and still-leafy fallen trees, in caves, under glaciers, in shrubs, beneath small trees, and under a variety of found man-made objects. Most of these shelters have pros and cons and, in some cases, real hazards associated with them. Rock overhangs may provide great dry spots from which to make a signal fire, yet they could have loose rock that could fall for no perceivable reason. Fallen trees can offer great protection from wind and, with some modification, from rain, but they may be unstable or have dead and hanging limbs above them. Caves, especially those with small, sheltered openings, can be great for shelter; however, some can be subject to flash flooding and be home to poisonous reptiles and insects and large mammals—not to mention the viruses that can be in the dust and present a danger when they are inhaled. The ground below glaciers is usually muddy and can be unstable, not to mention treacherous. Venturing into ice fields and caves should be left to those who have the technical knowledge and equipment to do so safely. Shrubs—well, they're shrubs—what can you expect . . . some modifications can go a long way. Found objects such as boards or large pieces of bark can provide shelter to one degree or another.

It is very easy to simply lament your predicament and whine your wishes to the surrounding countryside, but that gets you nowhere fast. So act! It is one thing to suffer the cold when your jacket zipper is busted and you're running over to the neighbors, because relief is close at hand. Out in the wild places, if you do not act, you may die. It's as simple as that. No one's going to hand you a blanket and a cup of cocoa—not unless you have filled out a detailed trip plan and distributed it to local rangers and friends, or you have a magic lamp in your pack with at least one good rub left in it.

I say it all the time: if you want the skills, practice them. *Then* you can quickly spring to the correct actions at the moment they are required.

WOODLAND SHELTERS

Creating simple shelters in areas with plenty of leaf litter, sticks, and other forest debris is quite easy and fast, provided you have the willingness to get down and dirty. The materials are all there, but significant quantities need to be gathered if you aim to be warm and dry. The learning curve is steep if you are willing to spend three or four nights in a row in a given shelter. This is to say that, in practice, if you are to have faith in a shelter's ability to do its job, I strongly urge you to commit to four nights or more in a row in the shelter of your choice. Typically, the following process is what happens to people who are trying to learn how to build shelters:

1. On night one, you crawl into the shelter and quickly discover that it is nothing like your bed, and your resolve tends to dwindle as you get cold and tired. You wish that you had made an extra pile of leaves near the door or that you had completed the shelter.
2. You finally acknowledge that morning has come. You are crabby, tired, and cold as you curse me and the horse I rode in on. You rally and add material to the shelter, making it bombproof. On night two, you are leery about the coming night, yet fatigue helps you sleep better. Your work during the day pays off; you are warmer at

first but begin to wake in the wee hours of the morning as cold creeps in.

3. Feeling slightly better about the shelter's potential to live up to the title of "shelter," you add yet more insulation the next day. On night three, because of improvements to the shelter and fatigue, you sleep well the whole night through, and in the morning you have faith in the shelter. When rains come, more adjustments are needed to prevent drips, but after the first night of rainy forays to correct leaks, your shelter is dry. You now have not only the knowledge to prevent many of these discomforts in future shelters, you also have faith that this shelter will help you to survive.

As a kid, I was stranded on the bank of a river during a canoe trip. It was pouring rain and getting dark. My friend and I had no tent, tarps, or food; we had only a canoe and some very wet sleeping bags. I knew that we should build a shelter with the leaves all around us, but I was cold and wet and had no faith in the ability of leaves to keep us warm for the night. My experience with shelter was as described above, yet without the resolve to fix my first shelter. I spent the night shivering in a soaking sleeping bag. Had I followed the above three steps, I could have been warm, though admittedly soggy, within half an hour. It is important that you practice this skill if you hope to employ it effectively in the future.

Squirrel Nests

If you don't have the time to make a "real" shelter, then a simple pile of leaves will suffice, provided it is large enough for the type of weather in the area; i.e., a larger pile for cold weather and a smaller pile for warm weather. There are some finer points, however, when you are mounding and sleeping in a pile of leaves.

The first time I tried it was when I was working for a wilderness survival program and all participants were building debris-type huts (discussed in the next section). I was too lazy to build yet another shelter for two nights of accommodation and therefore waited until the last minute before I scraped a rather pathetic pile together. That night I made a trough in the leaves, lay down, and pulled the leaves over me. It was great! I was toasty even as the temperature fell into the forties. Around 2:00 A.M., I awoke cold as hell and glanced around to figure out why. There, glinting in the moonlight, and lying on my shoulder as still as could be, was the reason—one single, solitary oak leaf. That lonely little leaf, while perhaps well intentioned, was wholly inadequate for the task of keeping me warm. Thus, I learned that moving (to include heavy breathing) in a squirrel shelter was to be avoided at all costs. Hence, the following innovations were born.

The first technique I used was to learn how to sleep in one position. I did this by sleeping on a bench made up of two seven-inch-diameter logs placed side by side with two other logs laid crossways beneath them. The first few nights were less than great, but then, as is always the case, I adapted and slept well. In the squirrel nest, this translated to lying down, getting situated and covered, and falling asleep. Waking in the morning after not having moved left me with little desire to lie in bed, and I would promptly exit the leaves, well rested.

The other method I used was to situate my leaf pile next to an object, such as a fallen tree, a rock outcropping, or a berm, and create a second containment object for the other side. This was quite

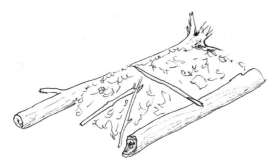

Squirrel nest

effective in keeping the leaves around me while allowing for a little movement. Such a bed can be put together in minutes and has other applications. I have, upon being surprised by a cloudburst or thunderstorm, gathered a pile of leaves or grasses, shucked my clothes, buried them beneath the pile, and squatted atop it—a king on my own little kingdom or a wet, naked guy squatting on a pile of damp leaves in the woods. Your choice, but either way, when the rain stopped I had dry togs to put on.

Any improvements beyond this "shelter" and you move into the realm of the debris hut.

Debris Huts

Squirrel shelters are to a debris hut as a pile of wool is to a sweater.

There are many ways of building shelters and many environments in which to build them. The woodland shelter described here is called the debris hut, popularized by Tom Brown Jr. It is a small, easily constructed, snug little "burrow" in which you can keep warm and dry if you build it correctly.

The debris hut is nothing more than a framework of sticks filled and covered with leaves and other forest debris. The value of leaves is similar to that of wool. By creating an area of dead air space around you, it is possible for your body to heat it up, and if adequately stuffed, it will keep you warm (even when wet). Once you have your spot picked out, the initial construction goes pretty quickly. Following are guidelines for the construction of a one-person debris hut.

1. A ridgepole needs to be located. It should be longer than you are tall by at least two feet and strong enough to hold your weight. Make sure that there are no ants or other critters already using it as a home.

2. Find something about waist height with which to support one end, such as a fork in a tree, a branch, or a rock. Or, you can construct something using a Y stick or two. (Be careful; I know of one fellow who broke his arm when his improperly secured support collapsed.)

3. Your ridgepole should run from your support to the ground. When you lie down underneath it on your back, your toes should be a couple of inches below the ridgepole at the lower end. It is also a good idea to check for roots or rocks that may be uncomfortable to sleep on. To measure the height of the upper end, roll onto your side. Your upper shoulder should be one hand's length from the bottom of the ridgepole. These measurements are for cold weather. In warmer times, I make my shelters more spacious inside and use less insulation outside.

4. Once the pole is set, start placing your ribbing against it, creating an A-frame shape. The ribbing is merely a bunch of sticks from thumb thickness to wrist thickness that are laid against the ridgepole. It is

important that your ridgepole does not extend too far beyond the support and that the ribbing does not protrude more than three or four inches above the ridgepole. This prevents water from running down the ribbing or ridgepole and into your shelter. At the shoulders, the ribbing should be one hand's length away on either side. To measure, lie on your back, centered under the ridgepole, and with your right hand, reach across your chest and put a twig into the ground one hand's length away from your shoulder. Repeat for the left side. As the ribbing is applied, it can taper in toward your feet. Until you have built a good number of shelters, it would be wise to periodically get in and check it for size. If you can't breathe without moving the shelter's frame, you might want to enlarge it. If you have enough room for a social event, you ought to downsize.

5. At this point, you should have something resembling a wooden tent with one open end. Place ribs over one-half of the open end; the other half will serve as your doorway. Another option is to completely block off the end and remove a few of the ribs from the side for a doorway. Different situations require different types of "doors." More on doors later.

6. Small, brushy material like the thin, upper branches of fallen dead trees is now laid in a crosshatch manner over the ribbing. The purpose is to keep the soon-to-be-applied debris from falling down into the shelter and your eyes.

With the frame complete, it's time to collect leaves for insulation. I use the "digging dog" technique. Start well away from your shelter and, using your fingers as a rake, move backward, flinging the leaves between your legs and toward the shelter. In very short order you should have a big pile of leaves (check them for ants before putting them on your shelter). Start gathering leaves . . . lots and lots of leaves. Keep gathering leaves; do not stop. Cover the entire shelter with

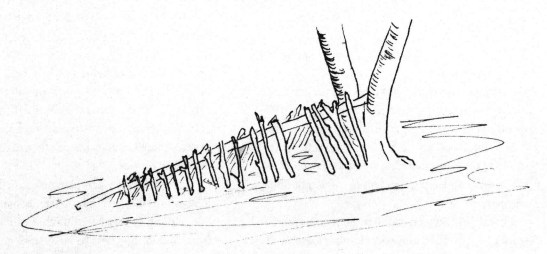

Debris hut skeleton

mounds of leaves, and then pack them down. The most effective packing technique I have found is to actually slide the leaves down along the ribs. Basically, I reach up to the top of the pile and bring my hands downward in the same direction as the ribbing. It is shockingly disappointing to see how far leaves will compact in this manner. Continue with the piling and packing until the leaf layer is about four feet thick. In summer, an arm's length seems to do the trick. You can't cheat here. You could loosely pile leaves to four feet and then freeze all night—not the greatest idea in the world. Once the shelter is covered, lay loose bark or dead branches over it to keep the leaves from blowing away.

Now it's time to stuff the inside! Some people like to be picky here and remove all of the sticks and other lumpy debris from their leaf pile before they stuff their shelter to bulging with it. Others pick out the undesirables as they find them while attempting sleep. Once the inside is packed properly, you should have trouble getting into your shelter the first time due to the quantity of leaves. I always start barefoot and slowly worm my way

in until I am all the way into the shelter. I then begin rolling around to pack the leaves, giving me more space for—you guessed it—stuffing with more leaves! I also use my legs to push and compress the leaves into the shelter as much as possible. It is amazing how compressed those leaves become in a short period of time. It's better to gather more than you think you will need while in leaf-gathering mode than at 1:00 A.M. when you're too cold to sleep. In cold weather, this step is vital, so do it right and don't skimp.

It is a good idea to keep your eyes closed as you enter and exit the shelter. This way, you can avoid any falling debris. I also give the ridgepole a good kick before entering; this knocks most of the loose material out of the "ceiling" and decreases the chance of having it fall in my eyes.

There are a number of ways to construct a door for this type of shelter, the first of which is the plug. This door type consists of two disks, usually made by loosely "weaving" green branches, fashioned in the shape of the door opening. Leaves are sandwiched between the two (like an Oreo cookie), and then they are lashed

Completed debris hut

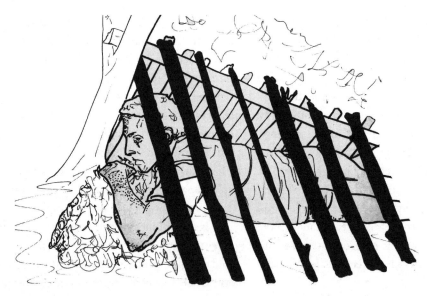

Door with leaves

together with more green branches or cordage. When you crawl backward into the shelter, the plug is pulled into the opening (it should be a tight fit) and left for the night.

Another option, one that I prefer, is to have a "door pile"—a heap of leaves that I compress with my arms and pull in after me. Once pressure is released, the pile of leaves expands, nicely filling the opening.

I have never slept as well as the nights I've spent in my debris huts, but I must warn you that your first few nights may not be restful. Leaves do not immediately offer the same security that we associate with blankets. However, after a night or two, you might find the leaves preferable.

There is no end to how elaborate a debris hut you can make. I'll often settle for the basic hut with an awning over the door, or maybe a little area in which I can crouch and work on rainy days. If I'm in a bit of a rush, I'll just pile some leaves together and burrow in.

Debris Hut Hints

I recommend that you have a *big* pile of spare leaves outside your shelter; this way, in the event of a leak, you have the patching material ready. You will also find that, after a stay of a few weeks in one shelter, the bedding leaves will be pulverized into powder. You'll need to periodically pull out the leaves, heap them on top of the hut, and get fresh ones for the inside.

For your first attempt, you may want to substitute a sleeping bag for the bedding leaves. This will allow you to become familiar with sleeping inside the debris hut. Then you can move on to using just leaves. Please understand that exposure is a real danger in the outdoors. Shelter building should be done in warm weather with backups until you have a firm grasp and understanding of the chosen type of shelter. Good luck and sweet dreams.

Ponderosa Forest Shelters
(Pine Needle Shelters)

When traveling, I often ask myself survival questions like: Where would I get liquid if I needed it now? What would I do for shelter tonight? During many a cross-country trip, I wondered what I would do for shelter in the ponderosa and other pine forests. These forests of central and western North America are extensive and can be found from southern Canada south into Mexico and from the Pacific Coast east to Oklahoma and Nebraska. Given their widespread occurrence, it seemed only fitting to address shelter in such places. While any pine needles can be used in the making of a shelter, some trees, like the ponderosa pine, build up thick layers of needles under their branches while others do not. The latter require significantly more work to collect and put to use.

The greatest asset from a shelter standpoint regarding ponderosa forests has to be the thick thatch of long needles beneath the branches of the trees. Following this are the remains of the trees themselves. Often with the inside rotted out, boards are much of what's left after a tree has fallen. In some areas, wood can be a little scarce, so you may have to settle for a simpler shelter—

more along the lines of the squirrel nest. With no scouting and no rush, I have easily constructed a needle shelter in forty-five minutes. Knowing what to do is only a bit of the battle; motivating yourself to get busy is the rest of it.

Look for an area with a good supply of building materials, ideally an area with a few dead pines in the vicinity as well as live ones for their dropped needles. The ponderosas often have a thick mat of needles under their branches.

Place two logs or bundles of sticks (the walls) parallel to each other and wide enough apart to accommodate your body comfortably. Build the walls tall enough so that you can fit under a branch placed across both walls.

Lay wooden crosspieces spanning the walls at both ends in place of a headboard and footboard on a conventional bed. These should be far enough apart to allow your body to fit between them lengthwise (feet at one end and head at the other), plus you should have an additional foot at your feet and another foot at your head (i.e., your body plus two feet). Gather needles from under the surrounding trees by sliding one hand, palm up and flat, under the thatch. Place your other hand over the palm of the first hand and lift the "plate" up. Fill the area outlined by the walls and crosspieces you have just made with needles. Do not skimp; it

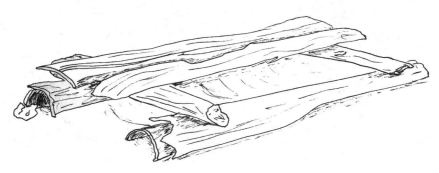

Pine woods frame

is far easier to remove needles when you are hot and tired than it is to get up and gather them when you are cold and tired!

If long pieces of dead tree trunk are available, lay these over the crosspieces lengthwise until you have a complete roof. If only short wood is available, continue laying them across the walls. (Note: I have been able to find wood in lengths exceeding my requirements by any number of feet. By allowing these pieces to overhang the entrance end, I create an awning under which I can keep clothes or other items dry. This works well if the roof is flat or has enough needles on top of it to prevent rain from running down the wood to the

interior. Even so, if you look at the bright side, it would only leak when it rains; the rest of the time it would be fine.)

Gather lots of needle plates and cover the shelter completely. If there is a chance of rain and you don't want to get wet, add a solid arm's length (about thirty inches) of needles or get more wood and place it over the shelter. You can do this shingle style, or you can lean pieces against it, A-frame style, down the whole length. Any wood that is exposed to the sky will help get water to the ground in ways other than through your shelter, provided it is angled correctly. It may make for a prickly bed if you are wearing thin clothes, but when you are cold and tired, it is a small price to pay for warmth and shelter.

The best recommendation I can offer is to practice. Do not wait until you need a shelter and then try to read up on it! Make many different types of shelters, mix and match them, and see what works and how. Then, if you ever have need of a shelter, you will be prepared to take action.

Completed pine woods shelter

Bark or wood slab shingling

Group Shelters

There are a great number of group-shelter possibilities, some more practical than others depending on your situation. Many group shelters found in books are made for the long term and require a lot of know-how, materials, and time. Hasty shelters, group or otherwise, are not generally classified as "shelters" because of their lack of form and peoples' inability to think of a shelter as something without any real structure or ability to stand on its own. The longhouses of museums and the past are seldom practical given the amount of green bark needed for the construction and the lack of large trees.

Almost any shelter type can be modified into a group shelter; for example, debris huts can be built in close proximity to one another and awnings constructed between them. Thatch can be used to protect a large area, and wind-packed snow can be excavated to accommodate large numbers as well. Additionally, shelter combinations can provide some of the creature comforts we love and miss when we are in the wilds. A lean-to can provide a great sheltered work space but needs an ongoing fire to keep the occupants warm, so why not make a squirrel nest in the back? You can burrow in and allow yourself a full night's sleep with no waste of wood or constant fire tending.

When creating group shelters, be aware that, as with so many things, your imagination is your only limitation. The ideas put forth here can be improved upon, altered, or discarded altogether, and new ones can be born. The only principles to which you must adhere are those of shelter, because the body's need to maintain 98.6°F does not change. If you are constructing a shelter, pay careful attention to the structural integrity of the design and materials. Arms have been broken through shoddy construction and poorly thought-out designs. Rotten wood, the weight of water-logged leaves and snow, and the size and placement of the fire pit and smoke hole all factor into the construction of a survival shelter. Remember, the goal is to survive, not to get crushed, burned, or smoked like a piece of venison. Dry and warm will suffice.

SNOW SHELTERS

Snow is a great insulator and can provide you with a fine shelter in short order. The different types of snow shelters are many, but the principles are similar. Snow shelters can be divided into two basic categories: those that are excavated from a large snowbank or mound, and those that are constructed using blocks of wind or manually packed snow. Your abilities and the materials present will dictate the type you build. I have seen an igloo constructed in little time—less than an hour—and have built them unassisted in less than three hours. (With more practice I know that the time could be cut by half.) I recommend that you take a look at the documentary *Nanook of the North* for a great demonstration of igloo building. Snow caves are great and can be as simple as a hollowed-out tube for sleeping or more elaborate with group areas, sleeping compartments, etc.

The three main issues with snow shelters are that they are airtight, require that the occupant be sufficiently insulated from the snow, and blend in with the environment, making it difficult for rescuers to locate them.

In order to vent out the stale air, create a ventilation hole near the highest point of each room near the upper portion of the wall above the level where you will normally have your head. Do not make this a vertical hole, but a horizontal one. In this way, you will avoid blockage from blowing or falling snow. However, heat will also be lost.

Carbon dioxide will not leave via a high vent but must be trapped in a sink (a pit that is lower than the floor of the living space), or it must have access to a lower vent. Carbon monoxide is produced by camp stoves and is lighter than oxygen but only slightly (its specific gravity is .96; that of oxygen is 1.00); therefore, it will not sink like the carbon dioxide, nor will it rise. Rather, it will spread through the shelter and will not vent easily unless you are willing to sacrifice *all* of your heat. Do not use a gas stove in your shelter! A seal-oil *kudlik*, in the style of the Inuit, may produce less carbon monoxide at a slower rate but should still be used sparingly.

If you have ski poles, one can be shoved through the roof handle first, from above. To maintain the vent, wiggle the pole around, especially if it is snowing. As warm air is vented out, it can enlarge the vent hole and cause excessive heat loss, so it must be partially blocked periodically. In good conditions (15°F and cooler), the warm air cools somewhat as it passes through the snow, slowing or even halting this problem. A stick can be substituted for the pole, but do whatever is necessary to ensure that fresh air comes in and stale air goes out.

Avalanche Safety

While we were tracking in Montana, my wife and I ventured to the edge of a lake. The land beyond dropped sharply about fifteen to twenty feet, and a significant drift had formed with a bit of an overhang. Beyond it the land was flat. We walked to the edge, and with a grin at my wife, I stamped my foot. Chaos! The mini-snowfall left me no frame of reference with which to orient myself as I tumbled, but it did give me just a peek into what it might be like to be caught in an avalanche and how little control I would have.

Avalanches are a very real threat in steep terrain, and to the uninitiated, danger is often not recognized until the snow begins to fall with tremendous power and awe-inspiring results. If you live in or visit an area prone to avalanches, take a course on avalanche forecasting and seek the advice of local forest service, park, or rescue personnel.

Having or getting material with which you can insulate yourself from the snow is crucial. Without it, the snow or ground on which you are in contact will leach the heat right out of you. I like to use conifer boughs due to their springy nature, but sticks with all of their branches removed and laid parallel to one another work too. Grasses, hides, leaves, brush, or anything else that will keep you off of the snow or ground without wicking water up to you will help. If I can afford the materials and time, I put on an eight-inch layer of boughs (not compressed) with another eight-inch layer of grasses on top. Often, this option will not be available and you will have one without the other. Shifting around in your sleep can soon have your hip nestled into the snow—something that is best avoided.

Maybe you don't want to be rescued, but if you do, colorful spare clothing or other man-made colored objects need to be staked to the outside of the shelter and cleaned of new snow periodically so that rescuers have an easier time spotting your shelter.

Other considerations are those that go along with all campsites and shelter locations. Be alert for snags, dead branches, and trees nearby that could fall on you. Watch out for loose rocks, the potential for avalanches, floods, and other hazards. Use your head to determine a good spot.

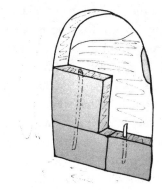

Blocking off excavation opening

Snow Caves and Trenches

A snow cave may be built anywhere snow collects in quantities sufficient to accommodate the desired interior space—especially on the lee side of objects such as hills, berms, hedgerows, stone walls, and slopes.

Creating a snow cave can be fun, but in a survival situation, the goal is to get out of the weather ASAP! Your shelter needs to be big enough to comfortably accommodate your body so that blood flow is not restricted and cramping is prevented. (Each occupant should be able to lie down completely without having to keep any part of the body bent and should be able to sit or kneel without having to hunch over.) Remember, though—the larger the area, the more it takes to heat it. A sleeping tube branching off of a larger work or storage space allows you to access your gear and change clothes without having to get out into the elements. Include an air hole and some insulation (branches, grasses, leaves) to lie on or sit on, and you're all set.

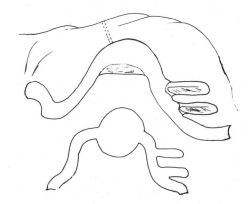

Floor plan and elevation view of a shelter

The entry should be lower than both the work area and the sleeping area to prevent warmed interior air from flowing out while cold outside air comes in and to give the carbon dioxide a place in which to sink. This does not mean, however, that all the snow to be excavated must come out through the tiny entry tunnel. Removal of so much snow in this manner is labor intensive and time consuming, and it requires that you are in direct contact with the snow for extended periods of time. This may cause your clothes to become moist with both snowmelt and sweat. Instead, create an opening or two (excavation ports) that are larger than the finished door will be to promote easy snow removal. These ports can be filled in later with snow blocks if conditions allow, or you may have to make a lattice with sticks to hold loose snow piled against it until it hardens. Use a shovel, stick, or anything that can move snow efficiently. Make sure to maintain an air vent. The same method is used in making the entry for a quinzhee, described in the next section.

Many variations are possible with snow caves. Use your imagination and remember the function of a shelter—to protect you from the wind and weather and allow heat to build up beyond that of the outside air. You may envision a grand series of rooms with vaulted ceilings when all you need to do is to burrow under a conifer with spreading branches that have created a cave as the snow built up around them. As a kid in upstate New York, I used to wander through the woods and build forts where white pines and birch saplings were bent, their tips to the ground from the weight of the snow. Even in windy weather, these little caves were warmer than being out in the open.

One useful variation on the snow cave is the snow trench. If conditions are conducive to cutting igloo blocks, excavate a trough that is three or four feet deep. Make it long enough and wide enough to accommodate your body as you lie down. The bottom can be covered with boughs for insulation from the ground. A flat or A-frame roof can be placed over it with snow slabs and a vent hole poked into the roof. The interior volume should not be so great it will be hard to heat with your body or a candle. A sloping ramp or a step will lead down to the door—usually a block of snow. Doors that are inside the shelter and pushed into the opening from inside are fine, but they require more interior space, while doors that are pulled into the opening after you enter can be tricky to place precisely. Whichever entry you choose, make sure that your digging stick, snow knife, or other tool is inside with you, because the door block can freeze to the shelter and make your exit tougher than your entry. These short-term, expedient emergency shelters can be very effective in a pinch.

Quinzhees

The quinzhee is, in essence, a snow cave for those times when no naturally occurring drifts are found or when snow quality is such that igloo construction is tricky due to warmer temperatures (15°F and warmer) and poor-quality snow (granular, powder, wet, or loose), and you need a shelter within three to four hours. Here are the steps to build a quinzhee:

1. Lay out a floor plan of the interior, keeping in mind that the smaller the volume, the more easily the shelter is heated. Additionally, a shelter that is too small will not be able to accommodate you for obvious reasons. The most reliable technique is to lie down and mark out an area that is slightly larger than each person. Another option is to break a stick that is as tall as the tallest member of your party and another that's a little wider than this person's shoulders. Use these measuring sticks to lay out the interior. If necessary, include a little space for gear.

2. Pile snow into a mound (do not hard pack it) or dome that is larger than the footprint or floor plan by at least a foot on the radius. Make sure that the dome is tall enough so that you can kneel, then add two feet. The

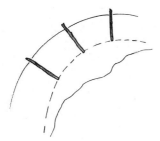

Cross section of a quinzhee wall with ten-inch sticks

two-foot size increase not only allows for the settling of the snow but also for a raised floor (six to eight inches insulate you well from the ground) and a thick roof. One option is to pile gear together and cover it with snow, and when you burrow in, remove it for easy excavation.

3. Insert pencil-thick twigs that are about ten inches long all over the mound at one-foot or greater intervals. These will act as thickness gauges when you are excavating the inside. When you expose the end of a twig, stop excavating that area.

4. Let the pile sit for no more than one and one-half to two hours. During this time, the snow will harden enough to allow for excavation. If the snow sits for too long, it can get really hard and make excavation a real bear of a task.

5. Excavate the pile not only by way of the intended door but also through one or two large openings elsewhere on the shelter. (Excavation tools can be anything from emergency shovels to a slab of wood, a stone, bone, shell, or anything else that will aid in scraping or otherwise removing snow.) These openings can be refilled later and will greatly cut down on the time required to complete the shelter. They also will minimize the time you spend crawling around *in* the snow. Depending on the snow, you may be able to fill in the excavation doors with blocks of snow, or you may need to create a crude latticework of sticks to help hold looser snow until it can harden. As in number 3 above, use the ten-inch twigs as guides for thickness; once a twig end is exposed on the inside of the shelter, stop digging there.

6. Make sure to leave a good six to eight inches or more of snow on the ground where you will be sleeping. This not only insulates you from the ground but also

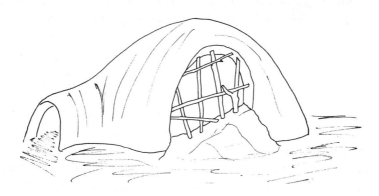

Excavated quinzhee with ports partially filled in

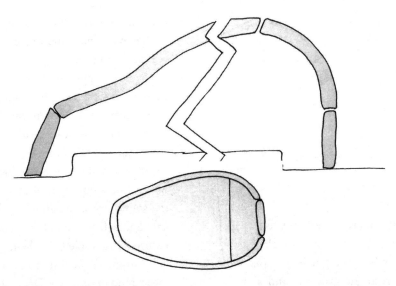

Floor plan and elevation view of a shelter

allows the area around the entry to be lower, creating a trap or cold sink for the colder air. In addition, it puts you closer to the ceiling where the warmer air is trapped.

7. Prior to closing things up, you may want to put some of your supplies such as boughs for bedding into the shelter rather than drag them through the small doorway.

8. A block of snow, a backpack, or other gear can be used to close the door once you are inside.

9. Add a vent.

Igloos

Igloos are good shelters for open, windy areas, although they can be built anywhere that conditions allow. Two moderately experienced people can expect to build an igloo in less than two hours, and one person can build one in less than three hours, provided it is not their first attempt. Nanook (of the North) of documentary fame built a huge one in about an hour.

Prime conditions for igloo building are +15°F and colder with wind-packed snow that dents slightly and squeaks like Styrofoam when you walk on it and when conditions have not ranged above freezing.

This is not to say that igloos cannot be constructed in other conditions, just that they take more work, may be weaker initially, and may not be as practical for a survival shelter as perhaps a quinzhee or snow cave. If you are hell-bent on building an igloo and the snow is not packed, simply make a long mound about three feet high, pack it well, and let it sit overnight. The next day it will be ready for igloo blocks if the temperature has remained below freezing.

To build an igloo, you will need a snow-cutting tool. Saws and machetes work beautifully; a wooden snow knife works well but requires more effort to use.

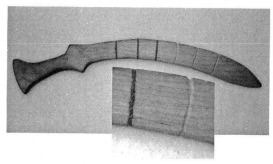

Wooden snow knife

To determine, to some degree, the quality of the snow in the area you intend to build, slide your snow knife into the snow, paying attention to the resistance that the snow puts up. Often, when I'm looking for a good snow cave spot, I find great snow, stiff and squeaky, only to slide my snow knife in and suddenly feel almost no resistance two or three inches below the surface. This is great for snow caves but not for cutting blocks for igloos. The lack of resistance is due to powder or granular snow that has not been wind or otherwise packed and will not be suitable for building as it is. As snow falls, it forms layers; you will find some variation in the levels and layers. Some are made of hard-packed snow, while others may be fine or granular and loose. Just because the top layer is no good does not mean that the next layer down is also inadequate.

Another way to determine snow quality is to cut out a small block and check it out. It should be able to withstand some abuse, like dropping on the ground with little or no breakage, under prime conditions, although igloos can be built with borderline fragile snow.

Each occupant should be able to lie down without having to bend his or her knees to fit. Lie down and mark your head and feet, then draw a circle that encompasses these marks and leave an extra foot on either end to accommodate sleeping bag ends, blankets, footgear, hats, etc. Look at your diagram and note that all occupants will be on a sleeping platform; therefore, you must allow some space for the entry area. (One six-foot person would require an eight-foot-diameter igloo.)

The size of the blocks you use is determined by your ability to move them into place (at least initially). The blocks I have used were usually about eight inches thick and two and a half feet tall on the first row, with smaller sizes following. When snow is more brittle (granular; warmer conditions), large blocks do not survive the handling well; thus, smaller blocks are used. In most situations, I have found that cutting vertical blocks is not the best, because as snow falls and weather factors in with warming and cooling, plus with the varying types of snow, natural layering will occur. It is between these different types of snow that the block will naturally want to separate. It has been my experience, meager as it may be, that horizontal blocks are often easier to quarry successfully. Cut out a rectangular block, and cut downward from the surface. The first block may be wasted, as removing it can be tricky, so make it a small one. The second block, once it is cut from above, can be freed from the snow beneath it by sliding the snow knife parallel to the surface about eight inches down. I found that some natural layering gave me two-inch-thick slabs separated by a layer of fluffy snow. Below that were eight-inch slabs. Situations will vary. Some people recommend cutting horizontally first, then vertically. This gives an audible "thunk" when the block breaks as the vertical cuts are made and the block drops the width of your cutting blade. With a thicker snow knife, like the wooden one pictured above, the blocks would

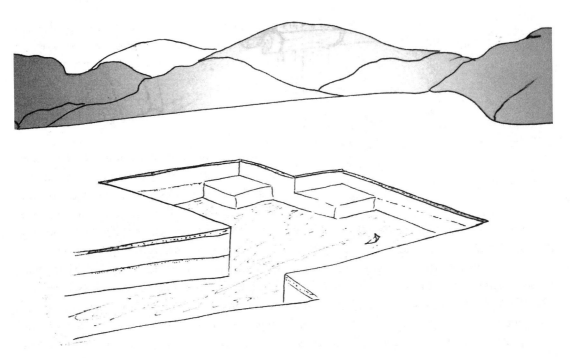

Snow quarry

break irregularly if I made the horizontal cut before cutting from above.

Most descriptions with which I am familiar suggest cutting blocks from inside the igloo area, but I have found this to be counterproductive for the lone igloo builder for two reasons: (1) by removing the floor, it can be difficult to reach the ceiling; and (2) making the sleeping platform and the cold sink can be done simultaneously by removing part of the floor in blocks to create the elevated sleeping platform.

Lay a row of blocks around the whole circle. Where they butt up against one another will be a wedge-shaped void, as only the upper corners will touch. This void can be eliminated by removing the corners with your snow knife, allowing full-surface contact between all block ends and thus providing stronger walls and better insulation.

Blocks are laid in a spiral pattern, which adds strength to the igloo. This is easier than building concentric tiers of blocks. Six inches above the bottom corner of a given block, make a mark. From this mark, draw an ascending line to the top corner of the fourth block from the mark or about one-quarter of the way around the igloo. Cut along the line and remove the snow.

For the first two rows, I work from outside the igloo, after which the inward slope of the wall requires me to be inside. Right-handed builders will want to spiral up to the right as viewed from outside the igloo; lefties will go in the opposite direction.

The second row of blocks begins on top of the block whose lowest end has just been cut to six inches. Prep your blocks by giving a concave cut to the bottom and side that will butt up to the

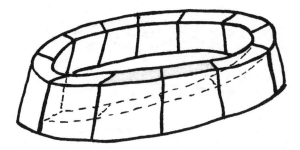

First row whole, then a line showing snow removed

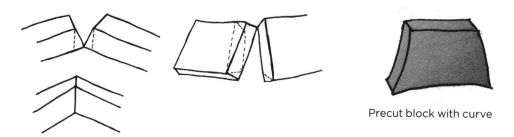

Precut block with curve

A bird's-eye view of a wedge and the correct cut

most recently placed blocks. When they are placed on top of the blocks below and butted up to the neighboring blocks only the bottom corners and one top corner will make contact with the igloo wall. The advantage of this is to eliminate rocking and precariously perched blocks that may well set you up for drama later. Once the block is in place you can "settle" it by sliding your snow knife up and down the vertical joint while pushing the blocks together, ever-tightening the seam. The same can then be done for the horizontal seam. Slide the knife back and forth, and the block will settle onto the block below, reducing the need for chinking later on. The igloo pictured is in optimal conditions—no chinking.

Before you begin the third row, the top edge of the second row needs to be beveled such that if a long spear were lain on it pointing into the igloo,

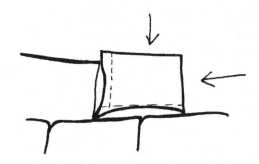

Settling the block

the point would hit the center of the floor. If you are building solo, you will need to cut an entry hole. Choose a spot, preferably under a large block, that will allow you to make an opening that is large enough for access but that will not expose a seam above. This doorway can be enlarged later. If you are building with a partner, now is the time for one of you to get into the igloo before the wall gets too high.

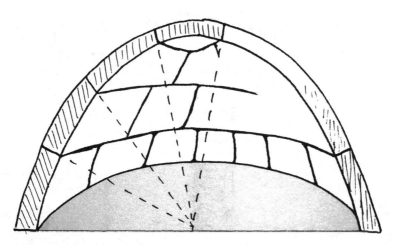

Bevel of the top surface of the wall in relation to the center of the shelter

The next set of blocks is be pretrimmed to trapezoids, put in place, and adjusted to fit. It is important to angle the blocks inward enough so that the shape of the dome is round, not flat nor pointy. Mors Kochanski, author of *Bush Craft* (Lone Pine, 1987), showed me some of what he knows about igloos. He explained that new builders tend to construct their igloos like the pointy end of an egg, when the goal is the broader end. Sure enough, my first igloo looked like the pointy end of a stove-in egg. Step out of the igloo periodically and look at the shape. If it is too pointy, *Backtrack!* Do it right the first time and avoid problems later on. It is easy to underestimate the friction that quickly becomes a weld between two blocks of snow. The goal is a dome, and the last row of blocks is almost horizontal. Be gentle and thin out the blocks to four inches to make them more manageable.

Just like a stone archway with its keystone, the igloo becomes incredibly strong the moment that the "key block" is put in place. Cut the key block to the approximate shape, but make it slightly larger than the opening. From inside the igloo, slide the key block through the opening sideways (this is impossible if the opening is truly round; don't worry, it won't be) and place it over the hole. Slide your snow knife up along the edge of the opening, trimming the key block on all sides so that it settles into place.

It is vital that all holes and cracks be filled if the igloo is to be effective as a shelter. Your skill level, the tools at your disposal, and the snow conditions will dictate how much chinking you have to do. In warmer areas with wetter snow, the cracks can be easily filled by packing loose snow into them. With more granular snow, it can get tricky, because the loose snow won't pack and will stay loose. Therefore, you have to place any piece of snow crust you can find into the openings and then wait for the snow to harden—sometimes a half hour and other times overnight. In optimal conditions, chunks of snow can be cut to fit each hole. When you cut them into wedge-like shapes, they can be forced into openings where they will immediately weld to the rest of the igloo. Small

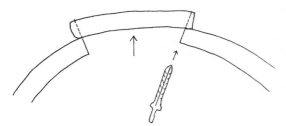

Trimming and installing the last piece

Igloo on Rock Lake, Alberta

cracks can be smeared over with another block of snow to completely windproof the structure. A quick look from the inside will light up all of the thin areas and holes. Once all the chinks are filled, smooth the outside of the igloo to a degree so that the wind has no edges to work on.

The entry should be perpendicular to prevailing winds (if it is on the lee side, a drift will form in the protected area directly in front of the door opening) and have the floor cut down into the snow below, providing space enough to allow you to move through hunched over. Walls of snow one block high (two feet) can be built on the edge of the excavated entry with snow slabs placed across it. At the outer end of the entry tunnel, stop short of the outside when you are excavating the tunnel floor so as to leave a small opening to the outside world. Skins often made the actual door if one was used at all and were placed at the entry to the tunnel and the igloo living area. I use a snow block pushed into place from the inside and keep my snow knife in the shelter to aid in my departure the following morning.

The sleeping platform allows the occupants to sleep at a level above that of the highest part of the door opening. This keeps them in the warmest part of the shelter where temperatures can rise into the fifties. The area next to the sleeping platform is called a cold sink and provides a place for

any cold air entering the igloo to go without having any adverse effects on the occupants. The platform can be created by excavating into the snowpack if there is enough snow and removing everything that will not comprise the sleeping platform. Another option is to build up the platform with snow blocks.

Bedding traditionally consisted of three caribou hides, one fur-side down on the sleeping platform, a second on top of that one, fur-side up, and a third as a blanket. Soapstone lamps were used for cooking, heating, and lighting inside. Given that few people carry three caribou hides in their back pockets these days, you will likely use boughs from evergreens as an insulating "pad" (I use the word *very* loosely). It has been my experience that green boughs contain moisture and therefore absorb more body heat than dead boughs (a nonissue if your clothes are well insulated), so the best choice is the dead material. Of course there are exceptions. White pine is far too brittle when it is dead to be very comfortable, so bunches of pencil-thick sticks have to be used. Or, you can go green and enjoy the comfort of the flexible green boughs, although you risk getting

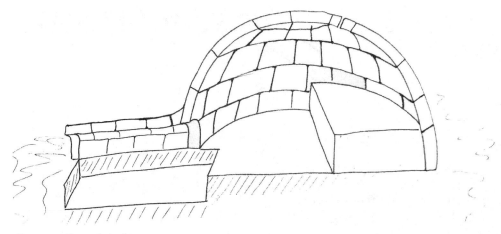

Cross section of shelter

sticky from the sap. Spruce trees have very stiff, sharp needles that fall off of the branch after it dies, yet the wood retains some flexibility and in such a state makes a fine mattress. Grasses, if available, are far more comfortable, but they compress quickly. In many parks and other public and private lands, cutting live trees or boughs is against the law; however, do what you must if you are in a true survival situation, or make sure that harvesting green wood is permitted.

It is of utmost importance that an airhole be bored through the upper part of the dome to

Heating an Igloo

Heat in an igloo seems like an oxymoron, yet temperatures of 60°F have been reached and maintained. The inner wall melts and ices up, while the curve of the dome allows the water to run down the walls and not fall from the ceiling onto the bed or living area. You do not need to try to attain such high temperatures, because acclimatization needs to be factored in. I can remember being numb with cold at +45°F in Australia and sweating bullets at 0°F in Montana. So if you step out of the wind in subzero weather and enter an igloo heated only with an oil lamp, you will find yourself doffing gear and luxuriating in the thirty-degree weather. Body heat of the occupants, a candle, or a primitive lamp (see "Stone Lamps" in Chapter 16) can generate enough heat for the shelter to offer a welcome reprieve from the cold wind outside. Carbon monoxide precludes the use of modern cooking stoves inside enclosed areas, but a well-ventilated area open to the outside can provide enough shelter to allow for the preparation of meals or hot water while not subjecting the cook to the dangers of carbon monoxide.

allow fresh air in and stale air out. Carbon dioxide will collect in the cold sink or can be vented out of a lower vent hole in the cold sink. The size of the holes that I have used in caves and other snow shelters is about two inches in diameter and is placed on the lee side of the structure. Check it now and then to ensure that it does not get filled with falling or windblown snow.

After an igloo has stood in the cold for a few hours, it is capable of holding quite some weight. I have climbed on mine within a few hours of completing it and not fallen through. Use your judgment, though, and climb on it just before you depart.

DESERT SHELTERS

While I was on the Sonoran Desert one July, I measured the temperature on the ground; it was 136°F. Four feet above the same spot, the temperature was cooler at 121°F. Working at a slow pace for about half an hour, I collected enough saguaro ribs from the surrounding desert to create a shade shelter by leaning them up tipi-style against a paloverde tree. Once the hot layer of sand had been scraped away, the temperature inside was a crisp 93°F!

The value of a bit of shade in which to wait out the heat of the day is immeasurable, and while it is preferable to build when it is cooler (early morning or night), many areas provide easy access to building materials, making it possible to build in the heat of the day without overtaxing the healthy survivalist. Conversely, many areas have very little with which to build; it is, after all, a desert. It also must be noted that deserts, when compared to most nondesert environments, are, for the most

part, uninhabited. Or, more precisely, the flora and fauna are often much smaller and/or fewer and farther between. This is not to say that long-term survival within a desert is impossible, merely that it requires a somewhat more refined set of skills and offers fewer choices in everything from diet to shelter type and location. When I'm at places like the Kelso Dunes in the Mojave Desert, I see no point in constructing a shelter. Sure, I could dig a pit shelter, support it with dead wood (not abundant in the dunes), and then laboriously trek out to find water at one of the seasonal springs. Blacktail jackrabbits are plentiful, as evidenced by many tracks and the number of kit fox kills found in the few tree islands visible from most spots on the dunes, indicating a source of food. However, the work involved in residing in such a place can be overly taxing to the human body.

There are exceptions of course. Along rivers there is often plenty of vegetation with which to build a shelter, but you will have to be creative and versatile. Take note as you move along where water sources are, if there are any, and whether they're seasonal or reliable year-round. Pay attention to where shelter building locations might be good. If you spend a lot of time outdoors, you will get pretty good at noting items and their locations that could save your life as you move through the landscape. Talk to locals, rangers, and other people who spend a lot of time outdoors in the area. Cars break down, ankles twist, and help may be a long time coming if you are not prepared. A case in point:

While driving in Australia's western deserts one Sunday night, I was startled by an aboriginal fellow who dashed out of the bush into the road waving his arms. I had little choice but to stop and, after inquiring about his health, was told that his family had been traveling to a friend's place when they got a flat tire early in the morning. Having no jack with which to lift the car, they had unsuccessfully attempted to dig a hollow beneath the deflated tire. The family, which included a toddler and two older children, had spent the day sitting in the desert near their car. Rather than lamenting their situation, they had a large shade cloth strung up and a fire going and were quite at their ease, ready and prepared to remain the night. A few minutes with my jack and they were on their way. They were prepared in one way, but not in another.

The deserts I have experienced, while having some characteristic that defines them to the through traveler (the saguaro cacti of the Sonoran Desert, for example, or the Joshua tree of the Mojave Desert), are really quite varied in their diversity and terrain. This means that one valley may have plenty of shelter material and the valley over the next rise may have none. Understand this: There are no hard and fast recipes for survival in the desert; there *are* wise and rather general guidelines that in most cases will help you last longer than you would if you went blindly traipsing off in some random direction, hoping to stumble upon a man with air-conditioning and a glass of cold water. It is easy to tell you to stay cool, stay hydrated, and keep out of the sun. Yet what are those words worth if they are not fleshed out with more specific advice and practice?

Shade Shelters

Shade shelters are great when you wish to sit out the heat of the day either as a pause in your trekking or while you wait for rescue. I once fell asleep at seven thousand feet in the Utah sun while wearing shorts. Temperatures were cool, but I was beet red and hurting when I finally awoke. If you find yourself needing such a shelter in the cooler part of the day, great! Build even if you expect to be rescued prior to needing it. Not only does it give you something to do, which is good for morale, it also helps you preserve yourself. If you are already in the high heat, look for existing shade or a situation that will require minimal modifications to make it suitable. These modifications can be as simple as hanging a blanket or placing some brush or branches against a rocky outcrop or shrub. The goal is to expend as little energy as possible and minimize water loss through sweating.

First, of course, you must locate a site. I look for something that already provides some shade, like a plant or rock structure. Remember, if you are in the midday heat and you need to build a shelter, think before you act; wandering around looking for the perfect situation will waste water, energy, and potentially your life. Do not mess around. Get the shelter up, get out of the sun, and rest! Improvements can be made later when it cools off.

Next, clear debris out of the area that will make up the interior. Do this carefully with your feet, or better yet, use a stick. I have been stung by scorpions doing this with my bare hands. In severe heat, this step should wait until the materials for the shelter have been gathered to avoid heating the newly exposed ground.

Collect materials—anything that will keep the sun from getting to you and that you can place, lean, or otherwise suspend will suffice. Again, be cautious when you're collecting wood or vegetation, as local venomous inhabitants may be a little miffed at being unceremoniously evicted. If I have

Shade shelter, Sonoran Desert

boots on, I'll give wood a good kick to jog loose any scorpions or spiders; otherwise, I'll use a stick to give it a rap. Grasses and leafy branches also get the stick rustled through them. Whether you opt to build the shelter as you collect each piece of material, or you make a big pile of supplies then build it all at once, is up to you.

Stack the materials against the tree, shrub, rock, or what have you, and keep adding them until no sun spots remain on the floor of the shelter. If the ground inside is hot, scrape it out or put something else in on which to sit. Remember the object? Keeping cool.

The entrance ought not to face west. I prefer facing to the east, because the sun can take off the night's chill first thing, and by the time it starts to get really hot, the sun is too high to shine into the shelter. Using an awning or having the door to the north can also reduce the time the sun has access to the shelter.

This shelter is not set up to be waterproof, although it will shed differing amounts of rain depending on what materials were used and how exactly it was constructed.

Wikiups and Brush Shelters

The wikiup is, quite simply, a conical skeleton of sticks and sotol (similar to yucca) or saguaro ribs with a thatchlike covering of grasses or leafy branches. (See Chapter 7 for more on thatched structures.) More weatherproof than the shade shelter, the wikiup is a better shelter for extended stays in desert areas, although it can be used in other climates. While it takes more work to construct than a brush shelter, it will last longer and will usually provide better protection. Size is dictated by your needs and the availability of materials. For one person, a small shelter about five feet high with a four-foot diameter can do the trick, although there is value to the ability to fully stretch out for a restful sleep. As the shelters get bigger, they require longer skeleton poles—a "tall" order in some areas. It has been my experience that, for a group, it is easier to build a few smaller shelters than one large one.

To build a wickiup:

1. Create a tripod with three sturdy sticks; if a forked stick can be found, use it and lay the other two in the fork, then spread the bases out to form an equilateral triangle. Keep in mind that the steeper the pitch, the better the shelter will shed rain. If no forked sticks are available, I like to pound a yucca leaf, as if I were preparing it for cordage (see Chapter 15), then I use it as a tie to lash the poles together. David Alloway takes it a step further in his book *Desert Survival Skills*, where he mentions *pita*, a flexible and strong material for lashing made by heating the yucca leaf in preparation for tying. I have tried it and found it

Frame for a wikiup

comparable to beating the leaf, but if a fire is safely and easily produced, it is faster.

2. Dig the butts of the poles into the ground about six inches if it's not too hard, or brace rocks against the outside of each of the three main poles. I have built these without digging in or using rocks to anchor the structure with no ill effects. However, if you want to sleep well in areas prone to high winds, it is advisable to use one or both techniques; all it takes is a quick downburst to flip over a small shelter.

3. Add poles between those of the tripod. I prefer to space them about an arm's length apart (about two feet) at the base. Do not allow the support poles to extend more than six inches beyond the top of the shelter. Rain will hit them and will run down inside, dripping at various points between the top and the bottom.

4. Gather long, flexible branches of willow or, in a pinch, use cottonwood. Cottonwood breaks more easily and needs babying. Lash these pieces horizontally around the poles. The first row should be about eighteen inches above the ground (if materials are readily available, I like to have a ground-level row as well, because it keeps the more flexible coverings from sagging into the shelter), and each row thereafter should be the same distance above the previous row. This distance really hinges upon the length of the materials you have available for thatching. I make the distance two-thirds to three-fourths of the length of my thatch, which allows for decent overlap.

5. Gather thatching materials, grasses, or leafy branches, and form them into bundles that can be just grasped with one hand. The stems or thick ends are oriented

Wickiup

upward with the tops pointing at the ground when they are in place on the shelter.

6. Using willow shoots or yucca leaves (pounded as for cordage), tie on the thatch bundles tightly in next to each other, starting on the bottom level. When the entire lower rung has been thatched, minus an area for the door, move up to the next rung, and so on, until you are done.

In desert areas, torrential downpours do occur no matter how short-lived they are, but things tend to dry out pretty quickly. (I have had bedsheets dry before I could get the second clothespin to hold it on the line and jeans bone dry even in the darkest recesses of the watch pocket in fifteen minutes.) However, if you want to go for a watertight shelter, the top can be tough. Here are some tips to help reduce the amount of water that will get in:

- Tie cordage around the pole, leaving a tail where you want any water that has managed to infiltrate the thatch to drip. Much of it will run down the poles, hit the cordage, and run down the tail and drop.
- Wad up any grasses or plant matter you can find and wedge it in the gaps where the poles meet.

Brush shelters, and I use the word "shelter" loosely, are very similar to shade shelters and

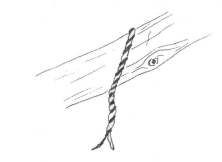

Cordage rain drip

wikiups but much more crude in their construction and used where organic matter is scarce and less substantial (no trees, primarily sparse scrub). A short-term, expedient way to get out of the sun, they are merely a few sticks balanced against each other, leaning in forks or simply tied with some cordage or pounded yucca leaf. Brush and grass are then thrown on the sunward side and over the top. Not much attention to detail with these; the goal is just to create some shade. Wind can be an issue depending on your location, the time of year, and the local weather, so keep off of southern slopes and on the leeward side of slopes, boulders, or other windbreaks.

More Tips on Shelters

- With heat, even cold-weather shelters can be made fit for kings. Rocks heated in a fire can be buried in the ground within your shelter, and as long as they are sufficiently buried (four to six inches), you should have a cozy night with the ground still toasty in the morning. If you shift around a lot in the night and have buried your hot rocks too shallowly, you may suffer a burn or a fire. Be careful.

- Sometimes damp or cold areas cannot be avoided, and sleeping on the ground is not desirable. Such was the case while I was on a training exercise with my unit and the slow soldiers to arrive at the platoon tent were left with a puddle in which to sleep. This was not appealing but was quickly remedied with a load of kindling wood from the pile outside the tent. In such instances, making a "mattress" of sticks or boughs can provide enough separation from the offending surface.

- Think about the energy required to construct and maintain the shelter and its heat source. A lean-to may seem like a good idea, but it requires a tarp or, missing that, almost as much work as a debris hut. It also requires a fire. A debris hut properly constructed will keep you warm and dry with no fire. If you're sick, you do not need to gather wood to stay warm; you can sleep through the night without having to wake and tend the fire. You can stay in the same location and not have to worry about the wood supply as much, because you only need fire for cooking and working. A lean-to, however, makes a great work area, whereas a debris hut by itself is really just a sleeping bag. Weigh your options and think through your shelter decisions.

- If you make primitive shelters, then you *will* have failures! The key is to practice before you need the shelter so that when do, you can build one correctly and without hesitation. Learn why you failed, think through the path the water took from the outside into your shelter, or how the wind managed to fill it with smoke from your fire. Understanding these lessons is what makes the difference in the field.

- Remember the "Six Ps: **P**roper **P**lanning and **P**ractice **P**revent **P**oor **P**erformance." If you really want to *know* these skills, then *do* them!

CHAPTER 3

WATER

Water is a high priority for life. It's what scientists at NASA search for in their quest for life on other planets. Without it, we will begin to fade in two or three days, when, debilitated by dehydration, our mind will swim as our head pounds and our tongue, thick and sticky, begs our salivary glands to produce a drop of precious moisture. With a failing ability to make sense of our world as hallucinations play out in our thirsty mind, we will fall and perish. This happens. Sometimes the body is found with water in a container. Why? Rationing water is not always the best option, nor is fooling your body with the pebble under the tongue. The best action to take in any environment, desert or otherwise, is to drink water. Store water in your belly where it is available for use as needed. I have been so parched at times that when I finally drank, I swear the first gulp was absorbed by my mouth before it could hit my stomach. Liquids are utilized by the body to flush out the system. When we urinate and the smell is strong and the color dark, the waste-to-water ratio is off; a higher percentage of waste in our urine makes it darker and more odoriferous. The two primary reasons for this are illness and dehydration. Use this as a message telling you to drink more water and slow the water loss from your body.

FINDING WATER

If you were thirsty while out in the wild, where would you find a drink? In most places, it is too easy to become sick from drinking polluted water; therefore, it is very important to find a clean source of liquid or a reliable purification system.

You need water now; where can it be found? In order to answer this question, let's look at a few simple rules that water follows.

- It runs downhill.
- If exposed to heat, it evaporates.
- It comes to the surface via precipitation, or springs.
- It remains on the surface if the material below is nonpermeable and/or new water arrives faster than, or as fast as, water leaves.

Next time you are on a walk or hike, see if you can describe where the water goes when it rains in your specific location. Is the soil absorbent? How long must it rain for water to run off and form rivulets? Once the rain stops, where could you find catchments, and how long would the water remain in them? These are just some of the questions you want to have in your consciousness as you keep an eye out for water. When I was on the Sonoran and Mojave deserts, I looked for water sans map and quickly realized that country this big does not afford the uninformed many second chances. So, before you head across the valley to the far ridge in search of water, you may want to see some evidence of a water source.

Sometimes water sources are obvious, such as a patch of brightly colored greenery when all around it is only dull tans and muted greens. Other times, the spring or catchment is in a ravine hidden in some nook and cannot be seen from more than a few feet away. A small consolation in this area, however, is that it can be smelled for a long way or, more accurately, the rotting vegetation in it can be smelled. The downside is that sometimes all you can find is a rank, soggy patch of ground. One of the reasons why deserts pose the risks to the traveler that they do is because seldom can a spring be recognized from any great distance. Additionally, some "springs" are not springs at all, but catchments, where water collects after running off surrounding rocks that have also filled with sand and gravel. Some of these basins have one or more exit points at or near the surface where, if they contain water, it can be seen seeping or trickling out. Such subterranean basins may hold anywhere from a few cups to thousands of gallons and may drain in a few days or over the course of months.

Just because a map shows a spring, stream, or other water source at a certain location does not mean that it is a *reliable* water source. Nor does the lack of a marked water source mean that no water is to be had. I have had the pleasure of drinking from desert springs that were so constant, nettles grew around them. I have also had the lesson of thirst after reaching a spring that had nothing to offer. But counting on a spring to refill your water containers because it is marked on a map is not wise. If you want to travel through unfamiliar terrain, desert or otherwise, check maps, talk to local authorities, or, if you are planning a group trek, go scout out some of the water sources you want to visit on your trip. Be safe when you can, and push the envelope only when you have to.

PURIFYING WATER

Streams, ponds, and other surface water may be dangerous to drink untreated. Filters to remove sediment and other larger debris can be made with grass, charcoal, and sand, but boiling is what ensures that water is safe to drink. According to the National Ski Patrol, water needs only to be brought to a boil in order to kill almost all harmful viruses, protozoa, and bacteria. At elevations from sea level to 6,500 feet, the Centers for Disease Control and Prevention advises bringing water to a rolling boil for one minute, then allowing it to cool to ambient temperature. Above 6,500 feet, it is suggested that the water maintain a rolling boil for three minutes. (See "Rock Boiling" in Chapter 9.) If you *must* drink untreated water from a stream, do so from an area that has a good, steady flow, such as from near the bottom of rapids or riffles.

SPRINGS

Springs come in many forms. I have found seeps to be the most common. Often only a small, moist area, they can be dug out into a shallow depression and allowed to fill. Once the sediment has settled, water can be collected. Sometimes the only sign of a seep is a patch of green moss or vegetation that is thicker than the surrounding area. Other times, insect activity can be the clue that tips you off.

In the Southeast, I have found hillsides where holes the size of quarters spout clean water in wet times and seep in dry times. A local man showed me that, by folding a rhododendron leaf lengthwise into a U shape (with the stem and midrib making the bottom of the U) and sticking it into a hillside seep, clean water soon runs down the leaf, providing an easy drink. Some springs are extreme, like fossil springs in Arizona. There, holes that a man can fit into gush drinkable water out of the ground at such a rate that it is almost impossible to force your body in against the current.

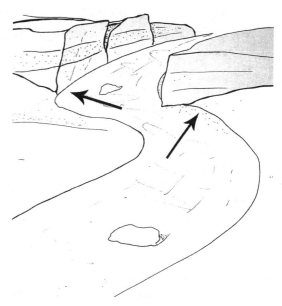

A riverbed showing dig areas

DIGGING

Digging is sometimes the best way of securing water. There are a number of situations in which making a shallow hole (seep hole) and allowing it to fill with water is the easiest option. Even though the ground is a great filter, boiling is still advised.

- In dry creek beds, water can be just below the surface. Good places to dig are on the inside of bends where the water has cut deepest into the bank and can form a pocket that holds water. You will, however, have to dig through the sand and gravel that has also collected there. The bases of cliffs with plenty of greenery like cattails and areas with wetland trees (willows, basswoods, cottonwoods, and syca-

mores, to name a few) are generally good places to investigate for water.

- In deserts, such wetland trees may take up water in the early hours of the day and release it only once the cool of early evening has come. Pay attention to areas that look as if they have held water recently, because water may still be close to the surface. Additionally, as the tree releases the water, then you may not have to dig at all, as the level can rise above grade. Craig Childs mentions in his book, *The Secret Knowledge of Water* (Back Bay Books, 2000), streams that flowed only at night and disappeared with the rising sun.

- Near swamps, lakes, or moving water, digging a seep hole and allowing the nearby swamp water to seep in is a good way to acquire somewhat filtered water.

- Along the coast, where salt water is abundant and fresh water is harder to find, dig a seep hole that is well inland from the high-tide line (at least one dune inland). Low-lying areas with plenty of vegetation are prime locations. In sandy ground with little vegetation, the hole must either be lined with whatever is on hand or dug to such a width that the collapsing sand near the edges does not affect the middle of the seep.

- Coyotes and other animals will also dig holes for water, and you can use the holes for water collection. If you have the luxury of being squeamish, these holes can at least serve as indicators of where to dig your own hole and how deep it will have to be. This is not an automatic water source. I know people who have made concerted efforts to dig such wells without success. Mark Elbroch, a tracker and friend, first found coyote-dug wells in eastern Massachusetts while collecting data for his book, *Mammal Tracks & Sign* (Stackpole Books, 2003).

DEW GATHERING AND CATCHMENTS

Dew does not always fall and should not be counted on as a reliable way to replenish your water supply. However, there are times when dew-collecting techniques would benefit you, especially if you currently or soon expect to need water and this source is available to you.

Clothing can be used to soak up dew by dragging it or brushing it over grasses and then wringing it out into a container. Let the water stand, skim off anything floating on the surface, and carefully pour off the water without disturbing any sediment on the bottom. At this point, the water may look clean, but boiling it is still a good idea. Dew is only as clean as what it touches; therefore, if you use your T-shirt, it will impart its own flavor to your drink.

Catchments can be made from bark or clothing to secure rainwater. Tarps, ponchos, and other waterproof items can be used as a funnel, i.e., a large surface to catch raindrops and direct them to a container. Absorbent material can be used to catch and hold water and then be wrung out and treated.

SOLAR STILLS

The purpose of a solar still is to promote evaporation of moisture, condense water vapor, and collect the drinkable product. I must say that, as a survival tool, the solar still is greatly overrated. I have set up stills from the northeastern United States to the Sonoran, Mojave, and Great Basin deserts. The Sonoran and Mojave typically gave me next to nothing after twenty-four hours, while the Great Basin provided somewhere between nothing and barely enough to cover the bottom of a two-cup measuring cup. The most I have ever gotten from a solar still, even with adding cactus pulp, urine, and foul water, was about one-half cup in twenty-four hours. I could have collected more with a larger still, but how much plastic is one to carry, and how much digging can be expected of a dehydrated person in the desert? Given the amount of work required to install a still (even with a shovel), the materials you must have with you for it, and the fact that you must stay put for some time before you can hope to gain any benefit from it, I recommend making great preparations to avoid a situation that might have you killing yourself in an effort to make solar

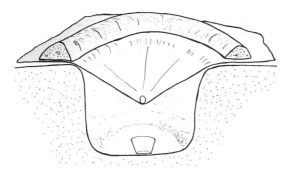

Solar still cross section

stills. That said, here is how they are typically made.

Pit Stills

You will need one piece of plastic that is sixty inches by sixty inches, a wide-mouthed water container, a digging stick (see Chapter 16), an egg-sized rock, and, for the deluxe model, a thirty-inch piece of flexible tubing and a stopper or cork to fit it.

In a spot receiving maximum sunlight, dig a hole that is thirty or more inches in diameter and about twenty or more inches deep. Put the soil from the hole in a pile nearby and run the digging stick around the rim of the hole to knock free any loose soil. In some areas there is a layer of fine dust a few inches thick on the surface that should scraped away from the edge of the hole. Place the water container in the middle of the hole. Place the plastic over the hole and weigh down the four corners with stones or handfuls of earth. Place the egg-sized rock in the center of the plastic and move the corners in toward the hole until the rock hangs about ten inches below grade. Cover the edge of the plastic sheet completely, using soil removed from the hole, and pack it down.

When the sun strikes the still, the air and the dirt inside heat up, causing any moisture in the soil to evaporate. The rising water vapor hits the plastic and condenses. Running down the plastic to the rock, it drips into the water container. When you are thirsty, you must open the still in order to retrieve the water.

For the deluxe model, lay one end of the tubing inside the water container, hammer a stake into the bottom of the hole, and tie the tubing to it; this will prevent accidental removal of the tube. Make sure that the tubing extends from the water container to beyond the edge of the plastic sheet. It is a good idea to carve a cork or otherwise protect the upper end of the tube to prevent debris and/or critters from entering. Finish the still as above. To drink, simply remove the cork and suck on the tubing.

In dry climates, green plant matter, foul water, salt water, or urine can be put inside the still (be careful not to contaminate your drinking tube or water container) either directly on the bottom of the hole or in a container of their own. When the moisture evaporates, it leaves behind any impurities, providing you with clean drinking water.

The Quick Still or Transpiration Bag

The quick still requires one plastic bag, a pebble, and bit of cordage.

The bag is placed over the end of a branch with green leaves and is exposed to the sun. A pebble is placed in one corner to create a low spot, or the bag can usually be manipulated to do the same sans pebble. The bag is tied shut, blocking any flow of air in or out of the bag.

Water will evaporate out of the leaves, condense on the bag, and run down to the low spot. To improve this slightly, more green matter (slices

Transpiration bag

of cactus, grass, etc.) can be draped over the branch prior to covering with the bag. To collect the water, untie the bag and tilt the low spot with the pebble up, allowing the water to run out of the bag and into a water container. Be warned that the water collected in this manner is actually tea and, depending on the taste of the plant, can be quite nasty to drink.

I have found clear plastic to be more effective in making stills than black plastic. I believe that this is a result of the sun being able to pass through the clear plastic and heat the soil directly—something not possible with black plastic.

SAP GATHERING

In the spring and fall, during times when it freezes at night and warms up during the day, sap is run-

Barrel Cactus

The barrel cactus of spaghetti western fame is often touted as a barrel of water just waiting for someone to shove a spigot through its wall and turn it on. I can tell you from firsthand experience that the barrel cactus *is* full of moist pulp, and the deeper you dig within it, the wetter it gets. I can also tell you that the liquid so readily available (at least once you get the top of the cactus off, which is a challenge with anything but a chainsaw) is more likely to make you vomit up valuable liquid than it is to quench your thirst. In an emergency, if a commercial filter was available, you could get valuable liquid from these long-lived cacti; otherwise they should be left alone and admired from the outside.

Barrel cactus and pulp

ning in the trees, and it is possible to collect more than a gallon of sap a day from a single tree by tapping it. Late-fall tapping of trees can be done, although the sap output in the fall is about half of what it is in the spring and, in the case of the sugar maple, with considerably less sugar content. Fresh sap from some trees is delicious and safe to drink.

Any of the maple, walnut, and black birch trees can be tapped in the following manner:

1. On the side of the tree that is exposed to the sun, carve, chop, or abrade a vertical channel through the bark and into the cambium layer (green wood).
2. At the bottom, bore a hole that is deep enough to hold a twig or stick in such a way that it slopes gently downward.
3. Add channels radiating out from the center channel at an upward angle.
4. Place a container at the base of the tree, under the lower end of the stick, to catch the sap.

Tree tap

As the sap moves in the tree, it will flow into the grooves and into the central channel. From there, it will move to the twig, where it will drip off the end into the collecting container.

Boiling the sap down will give you ever thicker and sweeter syrup as the water evaporates, leaving behind the sugars and other flavors. The unboiled sap, however, is quite delicious and safe to drink. Forty gallons of sugar maple sap will provide one gallon of syrup—twice that is required for birch.

Grapevines can be cut and the sap collected in the spring and fall in the method described below:

1. Cut a grapevine three feet above the ground.
2. Bend the vine over, and, if necessary, tie it so that the fast-dripping sap falls into a container.
3. Recut the end of the vine every day or so to maintain a flow. Otherwise the plant will heal enough to stop the flow altogether.

If you try this when the sap is no longer running, all you will get for your efforts is some clear jelly, something for which I have as yet found no use.

Heat is applied to dry wood or tinder. At around 300°F, it begins to smoke as some of the cellulose begins to decompose, and it emits often visible, volatile gases. The wood left behind is converted to charcoal and ash, the former being almost pure carbon and the latter being the unburnable minerals contained in the wood. As the temperature rises to about 500°F, the gases combust and, as long as there is a supply of fuel to continue this process, a fire will burn.

The trick is in applying heat to wood or tinder, usually by one of these approaches:

- Through direct application of something already alight or exceptionally hot, such as rocks pulled from a fire, or focusing sunlight with a magnifier of some sort. (When I was grinding acorns to flour, I smelled something burning and discovered that the sun was being reflected, satellite-dish style, off of the inside wall of the metal bowl containing the flour and had actually ignited the flour.)
- By converting energy from your body through motion to friction between two woody materials, thus generating heat that is simultaneously transferred to small particles of wood pulled from their parent pieces and deposited in a specific location. Here, they glom together and burn flamelessly in the form of a coal.

The simple goal with a fire is to have dry fuel balanced with oxygen. Too much of one can prevent the desired result or at best make for a very inefficient fire.

The methods in this chapter are generally well suited to short-term survival situations. For more advanced fire-making skills suitable to long-term wilderness living, see Chapter 8.

MATERIALS

The following components are needed to build a fire:

- **Tinder.** True tinder consists of any dry, thin, flammable material that, when nested around a coal, can be blown into a flame. Some kinds of tinder are: the outer bark of red cedars; the inner bark of any dead poplar, basswood, or maple tree; dry grasses; cattail down; cottonwood cotton; and milkweed fibers and down. Dead agave stalks make great coal carriers, as

Fuels and a fire set

- **First wood.** First wood should be from pencil thickness to wrist thickness and helps ignite the firewood.
- **Firewood.** Finally, firewood is wrist thickness and larger and is used to keep a fire burning for extended periods of time.

Dry wood burns far better than wet or green wood and is *necessary* for starting fires. Wood on the ground tends to absorb moisture, so try to use dead branches from trees, alive or dead, that are still standing. Check with local authorities about regulations regarding the harvesting of wood. Even during wet weather, branches on trees are surrounded by air and dried by the wind. Even if the branches are wet on the outside, the insides are usually dry. If you are in doubt, break a piece of wood. If it snaps in two without much bending, it should be good.

A broken branch can be held against the upper lip, which is very sensitive to moisture, as another "dry test." When you are collecting firewood, keep in mind that it is not necessary to break it all into eighteen-inch lengths. Let the fire work for you and burn longer logs in half. Caution: be very aware of fire danger in your area, and be sure to keep fire contained within your fire pit.

their inner "wood" becomes incredibly soft and can almost be lit with flint and steel. Tinder fungus, found on birch trees, can be broken or cut open and the pithy inner material used as tinder (it works best when it is live, although if it is dried slowly it can still be used). These are all good for your tinder bundle. The downy materials mentioned, as well as polypore (a type of shelf fungus often found on trees or rotting logs), are good additives but do not make very good tinder on their own. The other tinders should be buffed or rubbed briskly between the hands to separate the fibers. This promotes brisk burning when the tinder is ignited.

Some tinder requires a flame, as opposed to a coal, in order to ignite. So-called "flame tinders" include dry pine needles (which can also be used with a coal in a pinch), birch bark, freshly dried strips of pine bark cambium, the smallest of branches, and other woody materials. Dead hemlock branch ends are also superb, as well as dried flood debris from along streams.

- **Kindling.** Thin, dry branches and plant stalks up to pencil thickness make great kindling to get the fire going.

TIPI FIRES

How do you build a fire that can be lit with only one match or a coal in any weather? A fire built in the form of a tipi is the best design for this task. A well-built tipi fire can burn with no attention for extended periods of time, because as it burns, it collapses inward, thus feeding itself. In wet weather, the wood making up the tipi fire begins drying the moment the tinder is ignited, because as the heat rises, it passes around the wood. In addition, the outer firewood protects the flame from severe weather, be it snow, rain, or wind.

To build a tipi fire, take a handful of twelve-inch-long fire tinder and kindling in both hands, thumbs down, and bend or break them in the middle (they need not separate). Place them in your fire pit and form them into a rough tipi or triangular shape while using your thumbs to ensure that a doorway and open area are inside for the tinder. Face the opening to the wind to help spread the fire into the tipi. Next, lay on more kindling and first wood, starting with smaller pieces and building up until you have a tipi of a size required for your needs. Practice making fires of different sizes in a safe location, such as a riverbed, to determine what size is adequate for your various needs. Set aside some wood of all sizes, and cover your door once the tinder is lit and placed inside. If you are using a coal to start your fire, you can either ignite your tinder and place it in the tipi or place the smoking tinder bundle into the tipi just prior to ignition, then give it a final breath of air once it is in place. Now just cover the door and sit back. The fire should need no tinkering for some time.

Common Mistakes to Avoid

- Many times, I have watched people build tiny fires in the rain, light their birch bark, and wait to see if the wood will catch. Then, when it looks promising, they furiously add more wood, only to have the fire die. The recently added wood did not have enough time in the heat to dry to the point of combustion. Build the entire tipi and *then* light it!
- Some people spend a lot of time painstakingly building their tipi as if to enter it in a beauty contest. After you have built a few, construction should take no more than thirty seconds to one minute if you have already collected the materials.
- A huge cavity, or "door," and a little bit of tinder result in the tinder burning up and the flames hardly touching the kindling or first wood. Whereas . . .
- Packing your tinder too tightly into the tipi will not allow the flame to spread well and often ends with a little whiff of smoke and no heat. Therefore, your tinder should be fluffed to fill the space evenly and just come in contact with the tipi structure.

FIRE PITS AND RINGS

Fire pits serve a number of purposes and to varying degrees. Some pits are no more than a simple ring of rocks, while others are more elaborate with drying racks, an oven, and frying rocks.

What is the purpose of fire pits?

- They contain the fire by providing an unburnable barrier between the fire and other combustible materials around the fire, such as shelters, duff, grasses, leaves, etc.
- They help the fire burn evenly due to wind protection as well as concentrate the heat and light by reflecting them back into the fire.
- They help us direct fire for specific uses such as cooking in different ways (roasting, frying, baking), drying foods, and making tools (for

example, burning logs down to a size that is suitable for ax handles or fire-hardening a spear point and tips for digging sticks).

To make a basic fire pit, dig into the ground to a depth of about six inches, and form it like a half sphere, with the excavated dirt acting as a fire ring and reflector around the pit. This pit acts something like a satellite dish and reflects the light and heat up above the fire. Fire pits lined with rocks will hold heat longer and will protect against fire leaving the fire area.

A fire ring is quite simply a ring of stone to contain fire and provide minimal wind protection. A word of caution on stones and fire: although I regularly use stones directly from the stream for heating in fires, it must be noted that

small cavities within the rock can slowly, over the years, acquire moisture; when heated, this water will boil, often resulting in the rock breaking, usually with a small creak or pop. Some rocks, however (quartz in particular), will explode with quite some force and should be avoided.

The keyhole pit is one of the more versatile pits I have used. Dug in the shape of an old-fashioned keyhole, this pit allows for all kinds of cooking.

The round portion is good for general use, like working tools, providing light and heat, and cooking fish and ashcakes. (Ashcakes are a dough of flour and water, spread into a round disk. Berries are added in the middle, and then the dough is folded in half and pinched shut, closing the berries inside. This ashcake is then placed in the

Fire pit with extras

hot ashes near the coals to cook. The ash acts as a leavening agent and can be blown off the ashcake once cooked.)

The box or smaller rectangular section can be used for a variety of tasks. For roasting, use Y sticks on either side to hold a spit. A rock can be placed over the top, heated slowly, and used to fry food. Coals can be raked into the box until the rocks are hot and then removed. Meat or veggies put inside are baked in the residual heat from the stones.

Rocks for rock boiling are easier to remove from the fire when the area is smaller, because you spend less time hunting around for them. A flat stone leaned against the back of the box can be used for drying mashed berries or other foods (see "Preserving Food" in Chapter 9).

When you leave camp for the day, heap the coals together in the box and cover them with ash, where they will last for a day or more. In the case of bonfires, a rainfall wetting the top few inches of ash can seal in the coals, keeping out the drafts and allowing a very slow burning of fuel. In this case, fire can be coaxed from them for days afterward.

Be mindful of the fire danger in your area. Leaving a fire unattended or in a windy area can be risky. Always be on the lookout for overhanging branches and flammable debris nearby. Lining a fire pit with stones, clay, mud, or a mixture of any of these can prevent the fire from traveling along dead roots underground. Keeping a container of water or soil nearby is handy for dowsing or smothering a runaway fire.

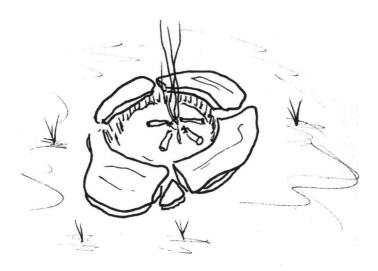

Fire pit

CHAPTER 5

NAVIGATION

I don't get lost, but sometimes I become temporarily unsure of my current location in relation to a known point.

Navigation in a wilderness area is tricky even for the experienced traveler. With the Global Positioning System (GPS) accurate to ten feet or less and the size of a folding cell phone, almost anyone can venture into the unknown wilds of any remote wilderness area. The confidence such a device offers, however, is dangerous. The batteries may not last, and spare batteries can get lost or wet and lose their charge, leaving the hiker with little more than a memory of the terrain as seen through the GPS screen.

Better-prepared trekkers carry backup systems or maps and a compass, although if you do not have the knowledge required to read such instruments, they are next to useless. If you have a GPS, use it as a backup or to check your assessment of your current location. If you take a map and compass, learn how they are used and practice. Navigating unfamiliar terrain by using a topographical map and a compass may look simple on paper, but the translation to the field takes practice.

WHAT TO DO IF LOST

What if your navigation aids fail or get lost? Or perhaps your vehicle breaks down on a seasonal road and you have no map or compass and you have no choice but to move. How do you proceed? The Six Ps come into play again here—Proper Planning and Practice Prevent Poor Performance. If you are going through remote terrain, take a minute to look at a map, noting the peaks and prominent valleys. What direction must you walk to find a major road, and how far off of your intended route is it? Road atlas maps will have peaks and major rivers listed but will not show cliffs or severe changes in elevation. A stream on a road map may, in fact, be a canyon that is 400 feet deep and one mile across, or it may be a dry wash. I don't expect everyone to purchase topographical maps of every area they drive through, pass over on flights, or hike into, but knowing roughly that a highway is due north and about twenty miles away is valuable information.

A stationary person is easier to find than someone who is moving, and if you must move, leave indicators as to your presence, including a note about your direction of travel (an arrow at least), your health, and your intentions. If at all possible, leave indicators that can be seen from the air by rescue aircraft.

When I was north of the Arctic Circle, I was struck with the realization that I could walk for hundreds of miles and not see a soul before coming to the Arctic Ocean. Having this experience of remoteness is very refreshing for some and scary for others. Many environments do not need to be trackless wilderness areas to kill the unwary traveler, and those folks who aimlessly wander with no rational reason for choosing one direction over another are courting death. Many instances of people getting lost and dying as a result occur within a mile of help—although the victim usually does not know how close he or she is. It's difficult to imagine realistic situations that would require traveling long distances far from any inhabited area in the lower forty-eight states with no map or compass, but I can imagine four wilderness situations in which, even if you have lost your navigational tools, you should move rather than stay put:

- Your current location is dangerous and/or cannot meet your needs (forest fire approaching; flash-flood area; steep, unstable ground; no water; etc.).
- You expect no rescue, because people do not know where you are and you failed to mention or changed your plans.
- You have an injured person in your party and someone must seek medical aid. This can be tricky in that medical professionals are not much help if you can't take them back to the victim.
- You are familiar with the area and know how to get out safely.

Failing any of these scenarios, once you find yourself in an area that can support you for a time with water and opportunities for shelter, you should set up camp and make yourself as comfortable and safe as possible. If the weather is not severe and you are healthy, begin exploring the immediate area around your camp, bringing along necessities such as water, a knife, and matches if you have them. Walk a little ways off, stop, turn, and consciously look back, noting landmarks, trees, tracks, etc. If I head out, day or night, I make it a point to look at my back trail— not just a quick glance over my shoulder but actually turning around and memorizing what the way back looks like. I pay special attention to the trees and branches above as well. This way, if I return in the dark, I can still see the silhouettes against the sky. This is not as difficult as it sounds, but it does take practice.

I am not recommending night travel for most scenarios, but some situations may call for it. If you are in doubt, make marks as you walk; be sure that they are signs you will recognize and that they cannot be easily removed. In areas of low flora, it is sometimes possible to erect something that stands above the surrounding scrub. It is surprising how quickly we can forget where camp is. Even in fairly open desert, cars can go unnoticed when they are relatively close. The number of times an off-trail hiker turns left or right to circumvent an obstacle is pretty high, so imagine traveling in thick chaparral or a spruce forest and trying to maintain a heading, even with a compass. On the other hand, there are areas where you can see a peak or a series of peaks many miles away, and walking a straight line is simple in clear weather.

If you are truly lost without a clue as to the direction of the nearest human habitation, all is not lost. Man leaves signs. At night, light pollution can be seen from more than thirty miles away, and on slightly overcast nights, if the cloud ceiling is not too low, the lights of towns reflecting off the clouds make for a rather prominent beacon. Highways, trains, and low-flying aircraft also create noise that can be heard from great distances. These signs are clearly valuable to the lost, but they give no indication of what terrain lies between you and them. Rivers are a widely accepted goal to lost travelers, as their banks are often populated at one point or another. Be warned, however, that the banks of waterways are not always the most hiker-friendly places; vegetation can be thick, the terrain steep and unstable, and the water may not be safe to swim in.

E-W line

BASIC DIRECTION FINDING

In the absence of a map and compass, here are a few aids that may help you find your way, if, for example, you happen to know that a major feature lies roughly eighty-five miles south of your current location.

- With the sun out, find a straight stick, orient it vertically, and drive or push one end into the ground. Find the tip of the shadow and mark it with a stone or scrape mark in the ground. Wait an hour or until the shadow has moved about six inches and mark the spot to where the tip of the shadow has moved. Imagine or draw a line between the two marks; this is the east-west line, and the first mark indicates west. Another option is to observe the shadow's movement as you hike, thereby always being aware of the cardinal directions. In the

Northern Hemisphere, shadows move northwest to northeast through the day.

- To use your watch in determining your directions, hold your watch level, and turn until the hour hand points at the sun. Holding the watch still, imagine that a line bisects the angle between the hour hand and twelve o'clock. This line points south. If you have a digital watch, you just need to imagine the face of a conventional watch in its place or simply draw it out on paper or the ground.
- It's possible to improvise a compass from some common materials. See the sidebar "Improvising a Compass" in this chapter.

If you know your cardinal directions, and you know in what direction you need to move, there is still plenty of room for error, especially if your target destination is small, isolated, and not connected to rail lines or major roads (as in some areas in Alaska) or has no major airport.

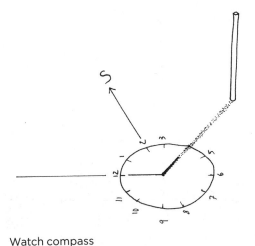

Watch compass

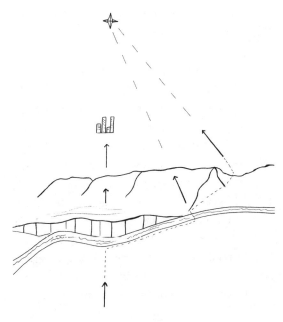

Issues with celestial navigation

For example, let's say that you are trying to get to a town due north of your location and you are using the North Star as your guide. When you set out, you are traveling north. Then you come to a cliff and travel five miles in an easterly direction before taking your bearing on the North Star again. Will you miss the town? You have now moved about five miles laterally, but this shift will not show up in your view of the star. Counting steps is unreliable over long distances, because terrain, fatigue, and other factors will create inconsistencies in your stride. If you have a good view of the terrain ahead, the best option is to locate two or three landmarks in a northerly line beyond your obstacle or anywhere along your direction of travel as long as they will be visible once you have overcome said obstacle. This way, after swinging five miles to the east and around the obstacle, you can move back to the west until the previously viewed objects once again line up and you can continue on your northerly heading (see the illustration showing lined-up landmarks in this chapter). Sometimes your view is obstructed and you have to choose landmarks

that are much closer in proximity to you. It is definitely a hassle to constantly check your heading this way, but losing patience and trusting your sense of direction is foolhardy and can be costly.

Clearly, navigation poses some interesting questions; it is more complicated when you have no compass or map. The best thing to do is to practice, or better yet, prepare before you enter an unfamiliar area. I know people who wander all over backwoods areas in which they have never been. I'm guilty of it myself, but the more wilderness traveling you do, the better you get at noting landscape features, the sun's position, etc. It is these things that make up the "sense of direction" people claim to have, not an inner compass. Learning how to navigate can be fun, and there are groups all over the country that hold competitions using a variety of navigational aids. Have fun with it and enjoy learning.

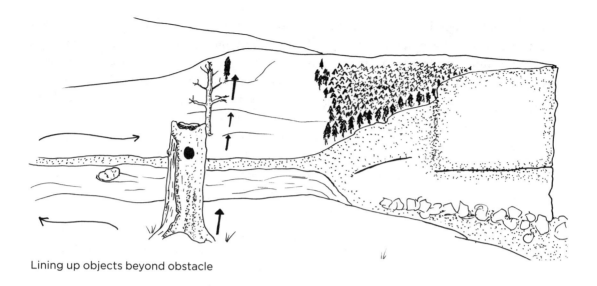

Lining up objects beyond obstacle

Basic Land Navigation Terms

Back Bearing: The direction opposite your direction of travel. If you are heading 360°, your back bearing is 180°.

Back Trail: The trail you have already covered.

Bearing: The horizontal line or direction from your location to a specific point or landmark as it relates to the 360° of a circle.

Declination: The angle between the terrestrial North Pole and magnetic north. This varies depending on your location and can be found on topographical maps.

Lateral Drift: The unintentional lateral or sideways travel that builds up as objects are circumvented.

Magnetic North: The point on the Earth to which a compass needle points (not the North Pole).

Terrestrial North: The North Pole, the point from which all northern ends of longitudinal lines come. Also known as true north.

MAP AND COMPASS

Finding your way through unfamiliar terrain is greatly eased with the aid of a compass and is almost pleasurable if a map of the area is also available. It's valuable to know how to use them separately as well as together.

Map Basics

A map is a representation of the Earth's surface in whole or part, showing how land features are related to each other with regard to direction, distance, and size. Different types of maps show these and sometimes other (elevation) features to varying degrees and thus offer more or less precise information.

Types of maps include the following:

- Topographical or *topo* maps are two-dimensional renderings of three-dimensional landscapes. They show elevation in relation to sea level through the use of contour lines that are a fixed vertical distance from sea level and one another (the contour interval). Horizontal distances are also easily determined by use of the scale at the bottom of the map. Other indicators show the directions.

- Geologic maps indicate the different types of rock found on the surface and are used primarily by geologists to find certain mineral deposits, although builders of structures and roads also reference them in preparation for construction.
- Biographic maps show the home habitats of plants and animals as well as the migration routes of the latter.
- Environmental maps show physiological features, including woodlands, grasslands, and ocean floors, as well as human activity (primarily in urban areas). Meteorological maps also fit in this category, as they cover—among other meteorological factors—climate, weather, and prevailing winds.
- Planimetric maps, by definition, show no relief; a road atlas is full of such maps and merely shows where roads, cities, towns, parks, and waterways or bodies of water lie. Mountain peaks and chains may be indicated, with the heights of more significant features listed, but no contour lines are used.

READING A MAP. For camping and hiking, the map of choice is the topographical map, and from this point on, we will concern ourselves only with this type.

In the margin around the printed map is what, to many, seems a confusing cluster of symbols, numbers, and type. This is the *legend*, and it effectively provides the reader with the code for deciphering the map. Daunting at first, the sym-

bols make logical sense; most novices can quickly remember their meaning. On Canadian maps, the entire legend is printed, whereas on U.S. maps, you are likely to find some information missing and need to get the "Topographical Map Symbols" pamphlet; it is free from any U.S. Geological Survey (USGS) office or can be downloaded and printed from their website.

Below is a description of what you will find on these maps.

- **Scale**. This is usually found centrally located in the lower margin. The USGS has mapped most of the lower forty-eight states in a scale of 1:24,000 (1 in = 2,000 ft/1 cm = 240 M). This means that each inch on the map represents 2,000 feet on land. Some states are mapped at 1:25,000 (1 in = 2,083 ft/1 cm = 250 M). Alaska is mapped primarily at 1:63,360 (1 in = 1 mile/1 cm = 633.6 M). Canadian maps seem to be predominantly 1:50,000 (1 in = 4,166 ft/1 cm = 500 M). Both the United States and Canada also use 1:250,000 (1 in = 4 mi/1 cm = 2.5 K). While there are other scales, those mentioned here are what you are most likely to encounter.
- **Scale Bars**. These bars make it possible to measure point to point on the map and then convert easily to feet/meters and miles/kilometers. (Note that on USGS quads, the scale bar is actually two miles from end to end.)
- **Declination Scale (also known as Declination Diagram)**. Found at the base of topo maps, this scale shows a representation of the angle of declination and gives it in degrees.
- **Grid North**. North as defined by the vertical grid lines on a map. This north does not always coincide with terrestrial north, because the grid lines on small topographical maps

run parallel to one another, whereas the lines of longitude are lines on a sphere that all begin at one point and end at a second point; thus, they cannot be parallel.

- **Terrestrial North or True North**. The direction of a meridian of longitude that converges on the North Pole.
- **Magnetic North**. The direction indicated by a magnetic compass. Magnetic north moves slowly, on average two to three minutes a year (60 minutes = 1°), with a variable rate. Currently, it is approximately 250 nautical miles (290 statute miles/465 kilometers) west of northern Axel Heiberg Island in Canada.

NAVIGATING WITH ONLY A MAP. A map by itself is a very helpful tool, especially if the landscape has easily distinguishable features such as hills or mountains. Flatlands, brushy areas, and forests are among some of the harder types of terrain to navigate through without the aid of a compass. If you are heading out from a known point, keeping track of your location on a map is far easier than figuring out where you are within the mapped area.

To determine your location if you get lost but you do have a map of the area in your possession, match up your surroundings with their symbolic twins on the map. Of course, this is easier said than done. The map is the view from above, while you are somewhere on the surface. This requires some careful observation of both the landscape and the map.

MAP CARE. Maps get dirty easily, become illegible, and tear along fold lines. Be careful when you are packing your map for a trip.

Use a map case with a clear plastic window that allows you to read the map, rain or shine,

without removing and unfolding it, if possible. This requires you to look at your overall trip and fold the map accordingly so that a good bit of your day's travel is visible at one time. The following day, you need to remove the map and fold it so that the coming section of your trip is viewable. Folding and handling your map once a day with dry, clean hands is far better than pulling it out of your pack or a pocket and unfolding it at every bend in the trail.

Tape the seams or fold lines with a clear, thin tape. This will prevent the excessive wear that maps usually suffer, causing map markings near the fold to be marred or obliterated. If you are using a map only, or have adjusted your map as described in the sidebar "Modifying the Map for Declination" (later in this chapter), then the following is an option. On a flat surface, cut the map along the fold lines and separate the pieces by an inch. Make sure that each map piece has some of the margin visible for orienting the map. Place a piece of clear packing tape over the inch-wide seam to reconnect the map pieces (but maintaining the one-inch gap), and repeat on the other side. Your map, when laid out, will be a series of map sections connected by the clear tape. In effect, you have created a hinge at all of the fold points. This allows for repetition, as in the case of practicing or teaching children on the same terrain. Warning: This method results in a map that is often off by a few degrees or more unless the utmost care is taken in placing the pieces of the map together to ensure that they all are oriented in the exact same way. When you are orienting such a map, use the margin of the piece representing your current location, because it may not jive with the other sections around it. Another method to help in accuracy, but only if you are using a compass in conjunction with such a map, is to alter the map as indicated in step 6 of the section "Orienting the Map and Factoring in Declination," found later in this chapter. By and large, this method is best suited for when your position can be verified by clear landmarks.

Compass Basics

A compass is not a GPS. It will not teleport you out of a jam or point you to the nearest water, shelter, or rescuer. It *is* a tool that can help you follow a specific heading or travel out from a point and return to that point. With a map, it can assist you, if you are lost, in orienting yourself to a known point or landmark. Just like any other tool, great things can be done with a compass in the hands of a competent person.

There are several types of compasses available in stores. These include the following:

- The Lensatic or military compass is a type of card compass in which the needle is attached to the underside of a nonmagnetic card that has the cardinal directions and the degrees of a circle printed directly on it. In such compasses, the whole card rotates rather than just the needle.
- A base-plate or orienteering compass is designed specifically for use with a map and has a number of features built into it for that

Various compasses

Lensatic compass

purpose. (Of course, it can be used by itself as well.) The bezel, a movable ring, encircles the needle and has the cardinal directions as well as the 360° of a circle printed on it. Some compasses have marks every two to four degrees rather than every degree.

- Other compasses are available; some are meant for boats or aircraft or for very specific purposes like surveying. The goals of this book with regard to terrestrial navigation can be met using the first two compasses mentioned above.

The base of a base-plate compass is imprinted with a bearing arrow (also known as a heading or direction-of-travel arrow.) This is key to taking a bearing—i.e., finding the compass direction to an object. With both forearms braced horizontally against your sides, and your compass held level in your upturned palm, turn toward a landmark or object you wish to go toward so that the bearing

Base-plate compass

Improvising a Compass

A needle, a pin, or a piece of wire like a twist tie used for closing bread products or garbage bags all work as a compass if they are allowed to rotate freely. Magnetizing is seldom really necessary; however, the "needle" may need more time to find north. Rubbing a needle with a magnet or a piece of silk in one direction will also magnetize a needle. This is best accomplished by allowing it to float in an open container of water. Place the needle in the middle of a small square of toilet paper that is the same length as the needle. Lift the paper by opposite edges so that the needle is slung between them, and gently lower it to the surface of the water. Let go. The paper will saturate and slowly sink, leaving the needle floating on the surface, supported by surface tension. It is now free to rotate.

Depending on how magnetic it is, the time required for it to point north will vary from rapid to almost imperceptible. If your water container is small (three to four inches across), the needle may be pulled to the edge as it slides along the surface. To determine which end of the needle is pointing north, remember that in the Northern Hemisphere, the sun travels a path from east to west and that this arc does not travel directly overhead, but to the south. As you near the equator, of course, you would have to take note of the direction the sun is moving to indicate west.

A small piece of buoyant material (dry wood, cork) can be used to support the needle, provided it is not too large. Hanging the needle from a thread is not as reliable: the thread easily influences the direction the needle points, as does any breeze.

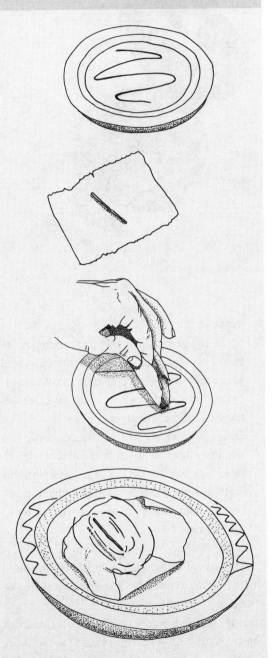

Improvising a compass

arrow points toward it. (Another method is to hold your index fingers along the sides of the base plate with your thumbs hooked behind the compass and your other fingers folded beneath it for support (see the illustration "Sighting with a baseplate compass," later in this chapter). By pulling both hands back against your stomach, you have a well-braced compass. Holding the base plate stationary, turn the bezel until the orienting arrow aligns with the north end of the compass

Compass Terminology

Bezel. The movable ring encircling the compass needle; in many cases, the directions are printed on it. Also known as the compass housing or turntable. It is found on both baseplate and Lensatic compasses. In the Lensatic compass, however, the bezel has a few lines on its face that extend onto the clear face of the compass over the compass card, but it does not have the degrees of the circle on it.

Card. A nonmagnetic disk on Lensatic compasses with the directions printed on it and to which the magnetic needle is affixed. This causes the whole card to align with magnetic north.

Marker Line. A mark on a compass base parallel with the direction-of-travel arrow and under the bezel that remains in place and allows an observer to see exactly what point of the compass is in line with the direction of travel.

Orienting Arrow or the Shed. On a base-plate or orienteering compass, this is the outline of an arrow printed on the bottom of the bezel, below the needle. The orienting arrow turns with the bezel.

eedle. Look at the direction-of-travel arrow and the bearing it indicates.

NAVIGATING WITH A COMPASS. The value of a compass sans map is often underestimated, and while it may not hold a candle to having a map, too, it can still be of great use.

To take a bearing is to determine the position of one object as it relates laterally to another (this could be you and a distant hilltop). Depending on the type of compass used, the method varies a bit.

To take a bearing using a Lensatic compass:

1. Fold the metal loop under the upright compass, and place the thumb of your dominant hand through it.
2. Fold the dominant index finger around the compass so that the tip rests on the hinge.
3. Form an L with your other thumb and index finger, and place the finger opposite the first and the thumb over the one in the loop in the same manner as illustrated with the base plate compass.
4. Fold the lid of the compass up 90° and the eyepiece about 60° (this will need to be adjusted for your vision).
5. Hold the compass up to your eye while you are closing the other one, and brace your elbows against your sides while resting your thumb against your face. This gives you a sturdy platform from which to read your bearing.
6. Sight through the slit above the eyepiece lens, and line up the wire with your target.
7. Without moving, look down through the lens (adjust it so that you can see the com-

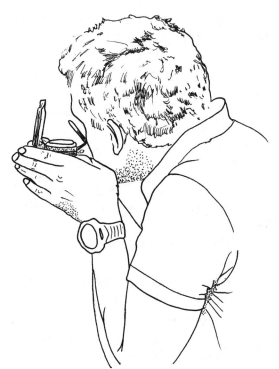

Sighting with a Lensatic compass

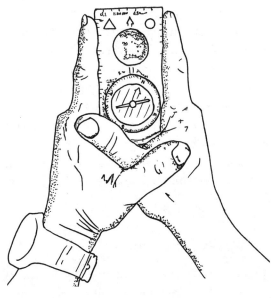

Sighting with a base-plate compass

pass dial clearly), and read the number of degrees on the far side of the dial.

8. This is your heading or bearing.

The procedure is different if you're using a base-plate compass:

1. Make an L with your nondominant thumb and index finger, and hold the compass so that the tips of both fingers are at opposite corners.
2. Do the same with the dominant hand, placing the thumb atop the first.
3. At about waist level, pull your hands back until they rest against your stomach and your arms are braced by your sides. Turn your whole body until the direction-of-travel arrow is pointing directly at your next goal or landmark.
4. With your thumb, rotate the bezel until the orienting arrow is directly underneath and in line with the red (north) end of the needle. The (rather silly) mnemonic for this is *Red Fred in the Shed*.
5. Look at where your direction-of-travel arrow intersects with your bezel and read the degrees. This is your bearing.

USING MAP AND COMPASS TOGETHER

When a topo map and a compass are used together, it is much easier to put yourself on the map and, as you move, to maintain a bird's-eye view of where you are on the landscape. This knowledge allows you to make informed decisions about which direction to go and when to alter your immediate course to avoid a significant obstacle like a lake or steep cliffs. If you are hiking in trailless areas, it is important to start using your map and compass while you still know where you are. Don't wait until you become lost.

To do this, take the following steps:

1. Place the map on the ground and orient it to true north, as described in steps 2 and 3 in the section "Orienting the Map and Factoring in Declination," later in this chapter.

2. Look at your planned route on the map, and take a bearing from your current location to the end of the first leg.

3. View your direction of travel, and, if the landscape allows (growth is not too dense), find a landmark toward which to head and note the lay of the land. If the area is thick with vegetation and your view is limited, look at your map for easily definable features, such as drainages, streams, cliffs, etc., that are large or long and close enough that you can find them even if you are a few degrees off course.

4. Take a back bearing and find a landmark to aid in your return or if you lose sight of your forward landmark. This back landmark can aid you in determining your location on the map.

5. Set out toward your landmark, and, upon reaching it, take another bearing to your next landmark until you reach the next leg.

Before you begin on the second leg of your route, consult your map to verify your position.

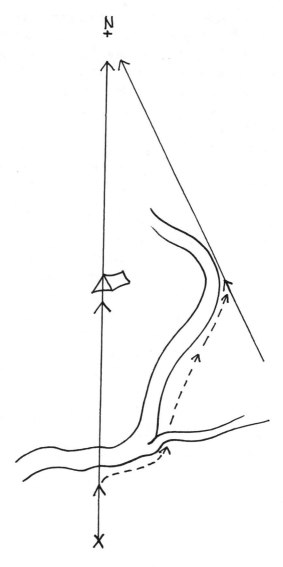

Bearing from route and bearing from lateral drift position

Depending on your view of the surrounding land, this is more or less precise. If you are in a wash that is filled with dense cover, you will need to take into account the terrain of your backtrail, noting how many washes you walked through.

You should be able to identify the wash you are in and approximate where in the wash you are based on other indicators, such as bends, how much you climbed, or descended, and what, if any, landmarks you saw on your way in. If you have a good view, you can orient your map to true north and locate hilltops or mountaintops that are visible on both the map and landscape. Take a bearing on them, and draw a pencil line on the map that corresponds to that bearing. After doing this with one peak, you have identified a line on which you are located. To determine where on the line you are, you must repeat the process with another landmark that is preferably not close to the first one. Where the two lines intersect is your current location. To really pinpoint your location, find a third landmark and draw a line. Much of the time it will not intersect the first two lines in the spot where they cross. The result is a small triangle called the triangle of error. It is within this triangle that you currently stand.

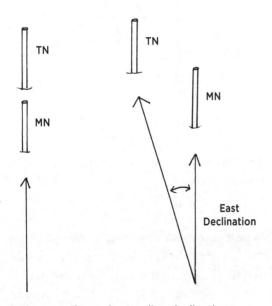

Stake setup for understanding declination

As you gain experience reading the land and remembering the type of terrain you have passed over, you will not need to spend much time verifying your position nor with the frequency mentioned here. Additionally, as you better learn to read maps, you'll find it easier to hold a three-dimensional picture of the terrain in your mind, which will also reduce the frequency with which you need to check the map.

DECLINATION

By far the most difficult aspect of map and compass work for the novice to understand is declination or variation, but it cannot be ignored; thus, the following must be understood. There are two North Poles—the terrestrial North Pole and the magnetic North pole. The Earth rotates on its axis, one end of which is the terrestrial North Pole and the other the terrestrial South Pole. Unfortunately, magnetic north is not in the same place; as of 2008, it was about 365 nautical miles (442 statute miles/711 kilometers) from true north. According to the Geological Survey of Canada, magnetic north is moving at a rate of up to forty kilometers per year. At issue is that maps are oriented to true north while compasses point to magnetic north.

To make the concept of declination more clearly understood, drive two stakes into the ground four or five feet apart. For clarity, mark one "MN" for magnetic north and the other "TN" for true north. Leave a good foot or more protruding above the ground, and stand back twenty feet so that both stakes are lined up, with the MN stake closer to you. This view illustrates zero declination or the *agonic line* (because both the MN and the TN stakes are in line with you, the compass will point to both). Begin walking slowly in a circle around the two stakes and they will, of course, no longer be aligned with each other in relation to you. A gap will appear between them and will grow as you walk. The difference in angle between one and the other represents the declination. A westerly declination "pulls" the compass needle to the west of TN by x°, or the local declination. An easterly declination pulls the needle east of TN also by the local declination.

This is the most daunting aspect of orienteering to the novice, so I will explain, step-by-step, how to plan routes using a map and compass, a map alone, and a compass alone.

In order to use a compass and map to good effect, you must factor in declination and adjust your compass and map accordingly.

Orienting the Map and Factoring in Declination

If you are using a map and compass together, the following steps can smooth the navigational aspects of following a fixed route.

1. Plan your route and draw it on the map.
2. Orient your map to MN: turn the bezel until the N and the direction-of-travel arrow are lined up. Place the edge of the base plate along one side of the map (lined up with the margin line), with the direction-of-travel arrow pointing to the top of the map. Rotate the map with the compass on it until *Red Fred Is in the Shed*. Your map is now oriented to MN. Unless you happen to be sitting on the agonic line, the orientation of the map will not jive with the surrounding landscape,

because the map is drawn to true north and you've just aligned it with magnetic north.

3. If, for example, your declination is 18° east, that means that the compass needle is pulled 18° to the east of TN and you need to cancel out the 18° by subtracting it from your bearing and rotating the map 18° to the west. If your declination is 12° west, this needs to be canceled out by adding it to your bearing and rotating the map and compass to the east by 12°. Some people find it easier to remember to add the number of degrees of a westerly declination and subtract the number of degrees of an easterly declination, but only when taking the direction from the compass and applying it to a map.

4. Place the edge of the base plate along the first leg of your route, with the direction arrow pointing in your desired direction of travel.

5. Rotate the bezel until the needle is housed in the orienting or north arrow (i.e., put *Red Fred in the Shed*).

6. Look at your direction-of-travel arrow and the corresponding line in the bezel for your uncorrected heading. At this point, your heading is off by the declination for your area.

7. Add or subtract the local declination (found at the bottom of the map) from your uncorrected heading. Remember, *East Is Least* (subtract), *West Is Best* (add). For an easterly declination, subtract the declination from the uncorrected heading. If your declination is westerly, add that number to your uncorrected heading. Example: if my declination is 14° west and

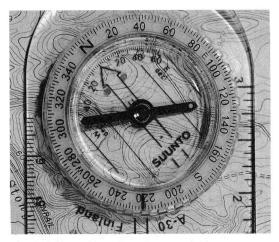

Red Fred out of the shed

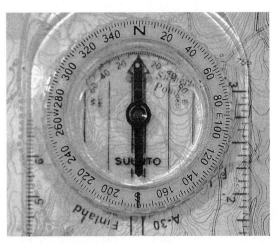

Red Fred in the shed

my uncorrected heading is 140°, adding the two gives me 154°, my corrected heading. (*East Is Least, West Is Best* applies only when you are getting your direction from the map and applying it to the compass. The rule is reversed when you are applying your compass bearing to the map.)

8. If your compass is equipped with a fixed declination scale, then step 5 above can be

altered in the following way to eliminate step 7 altogether: Instead of turning the bezel to put *Red Fred in the Shed*, merely turn the bezel until the needle is pointing at +14°, or whatever your local declination is on the fixed declination scale. Proceed to step 6 and you will see your *corrected* heading.

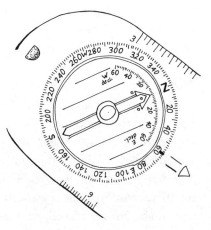

Compass oriented to magnetic north

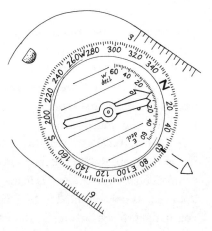

Compass oriented to true north using the built-in declination scale

Modifying the Map for Declination

If figuring declination in the field is just too much to remember, you can simplify the process by altering the map to read in magnetic degrees prior to your trip. This simply involves drawing a series of parallel lines across your map at the local angle of declination. When you are doing this, make sure to work on a smooth, flat surface with no magnetic metal in the area—this includes the straightedge or hardware in the work surface.

1. Lay out and **orient your map**.
2. Follow steps 1 through 3 on page 71.

3. Consult the declination scale at the bottom margin of the map, and either grab your protractor and straightedge or a base-plate compass and straightedge. From this point, you can follow either the protractor method or the straightedge method.

Protractor method

For the **protractor method**, you will need to draw a latitude line connecting latitude marks on the edge of your map (make sure that they are the same).

Map with magnetic north lines drawn in

Modifying the Map for Declination (*continued*)

1. Place a mark on the latitude line near where you will be hiking.
2. Place your protractor on the mark, and then make another mark that corresponds to the local declination.
3. With your straightedge, connect the dots. I like to extend the lines over the whole map if conditions allow.
4. You can continue by using the protractor or by simply running a line down the other side of the straightedge and then shifting it over, lining it up with the previous line and drawing again.

Straightedge Method

1. Adjust your **compass** so that the orienting arrow is pointing to the direction-of-travel arrow, and place it on the map.

2. Rotate the whole compass until *Red Fred Is in the Shed*. Your compass now points to MN.
3. Place a straightedge along the edge of the base plate (be sure to hold it firmly), and draw your MN line.
4. Continue either by using the compass as a protractor or by running parallel lines on either side of the straightedge as in step 3.
5. Once the map is oriented with the magnetic north lines to MN, any bearing taken does not need to be corrected for declination.

FOLLOWING A BEARING

If you have never used a compass to follow a specific heading, it may seem like a fairly easy task, but when you consider the often circuitous route through trailless areas, it becomes clear that such a task is more challenging than a stroll in the park. Trees, boulders, bodies of water, cactus patches, dense growth, cliffs, and other objects prevent you from moving in a straight line. Even the path of modern highways is affected by the topography and geology of a given area. The idea of walking due north, for example, by keeping the compass needle pointing to the same degree line on the bezel, becomes preposterous at best. Perhaps the first hundred feet of your course are flat.

Then you may need to walk around a boulder, so you move to the left and resume your course on the other side. If the boulder or other obstacle is small and you are not traveling far, this may not be too much of a problem. If the obstacle is a river and you need to travel more than a few feet up- or downriver to find a safe crossing point, your chance of resuming your course on the opposite bank in a straight line with your trail from the beginning is very small indeed. After a number of these obstacles, large or small, you will have wandered more to one side than the other. Depending on the original distance to your destination and the size of your target, you may walk past it and not even know it. This is called lateral drift and is shown on page 69.

It is possible to line up objects in the distance in order to regain a heading after you have circumnavigated an obstacle. Refer back to the illustration on page 61. The same can be done with a compass, but this method is far easier to do. It must be noted that this compass technique is used even in easily walked terrain, not just for dealing with obstacles. If the obstacle is a lake, a bearing is taken and a corresponding landmark on the opposite side is found. If possible, a bearing is taken on your backtrail and a landmark is noted, thus allowing confirmation that the original bearing has been regained once the other side of the lake has been reached. If the object in your path is a mountain, a bearing is taken and a landmark

located; once the landmark is reached, the process is repeated.

Returning to Start Point

To travel out from a known point, it is important to first note any landmarks that will help you identify your camp location. These should be large enough to note from some distance. Sometimes a large tree or rock outcropping can provide the marker; other times it will be the proximity to an easily recognizable hill or mountaintop. You may describe the location somewhat like this: "When in camp, the pointy peak is just to the right of the mesa, and the butte looks like it's resting on top of the little mesa."

When I leave a new camp, I use two techniques for remembering the way to and from camp more than any others. The first is that I look up. I look at the tree branches and the surrounding hills or mountains and note prominent or odd and intriguing shapes. This method helps, because these features can be seen even at night when features of the ground or trail are either not visible or are distorted by the beam of a flashlight. The second tool that I utilize is that of observing my backtrail and noting my back bearing. I do not simply take a casual glance over my shoulder; I stop and turn and really look at where I am coming from and what it will look like when I return. It is always so heartening when you recognize, with surety, a landmark telling you that you are on the right path and that you are not as lost as you had assumed. Part of assessing your backtrail is to see if your camp markers are prominent enough to serve their purpose. Some terrain is tricky in that, from camp, close landmarks look prominent but from a half mile or more away they are lost in the landscape—still visible, but not

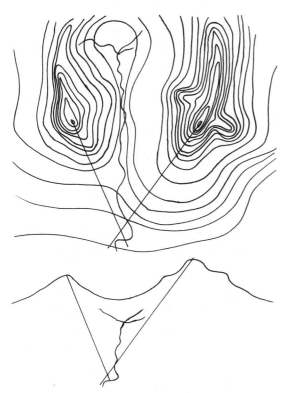

Triangulating with bird's-eye view and ground view

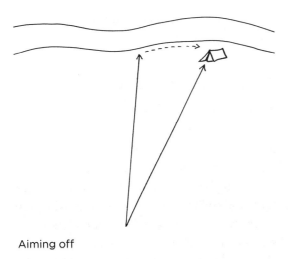

Aiming off

prominent. In such cases, it is wise to find larger landmarks beyond your camp. Note their direction so that, upon your return, when they are both at the same compass points, you should be able to see your smaller landmarks that will take you right to your camp.

If you are camped near a river, by a prominent line of cliffs, at the foot of mountains, near a railroad, or by some other fairly straight landmark, you can, upon your return, "aim off"—that is, intentionally aim 5° off of where your camp is. This means that even with lateral drift you will still be to the side of your camp when you reach the straight landmark and will therefore know which way to go.

There are other methods that utilize the compass, but they are more mechanical and, in my view, are less reliable unless the terrain allows you to count the paces or your pace is steady enough to allow the timing of each leg. In such cases, it is possible to head out from your camp on, say, a due-north heading. Paces are kept as even as possible and are counted. After a given number of paces, the heading could be adjusted by 90° and

the same number of paces counted off and so on until you return to the starting point.

PLANNING A ROUTE

When you are planning a route for a trip over new ground, you must account for physical ability, terrain, weather, and the like and, if possible, glean information from all sources like books, the Internet, or—best of all—people who are familiar with the area. For the example below, let's look for the easiest route. Assuming that all of the information you have on the area is your topo map, planning a trip might proceed as follows.

1. Select your starting and ending points.
2. Now that you know where you want to go and from whence you wish to begin, you need to select a route that for many may be the easiest and shortest (not always one and the same). Others may wish to visit a few other points of interest (POI) that are more or less out of the way. If you are including such points, they, along with your start and finish points, need to be marked on the map.
3. While looking at the terrain, you need to connect the dots and assess the route that these connected dots have you walking.
4. Adjust the route if necessary. The line between your start and the first POI may have you scaling a seventy-foot cliff rather than skirting it. I usually adjust my travel lines to be more or less straight. Each straight section is called a leg.
5. Orient your map to TN, and on a piece of paper put down a number for each leg.

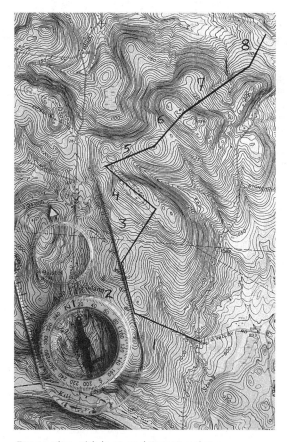

Route plan with legs and target points

Start at the top of the page and descend. Take the bearing for each leg. This is accomplished by placing the edge of the compass's base plate along the route with the direction-of-travel arrow pointing in the desired direction of travel.

6. Rotate the bezel until *Red Fred Is in the Shed*, and read the degrees where the direction-of-travel arrow intersects the bezel.

7. Adjust for declination, remembering that you are applying your bearing to the map from the compass. (For west declination, subtract degrees of declination; for east declination, add degrees.)

8. Write the corrected bearing next to the leg number, and measure the distance using the appropriate scale on the side of the base-plate compass. (The distance will be approximate, as most terrain will not allow you to move as the crow flies.)

9. At the end of the leg, jot down a few notes on landmarks that will help you confirm your position (as done on the following page). Taking the bearing on a few peaks or other landmarks that you believe will be visible from there can be handy if you are in any kind of rush while you're on the trail, because with the bearings already written down, you will only need to confirm them with the compass.

10. Follow the above steps for each leg.

I imagine that I am sending the instructions out with a novice, making sure to write them simply and clearly so that when I am exhausted, wet, or otherwise operating with decreased mental acuity, I can still follow and understand them and get where I need to go.

The final step in planning your trip is to tell a reliable friend or two where you will be going and when you expect to return. I suggest a little more detail than "See ya man, going to Everest, be back next Sunday." If you really want a bombproof emergency plan, make copies of your route plan and direction sheet, including your earliest and latest estimated completion times as well as what your friend should do in the event that you do not show by the scheduled time. Leave those with your friend or loved one and stick to your plan. If circumstances require a trip alteration that will delay your return, LET THEM KNOW ASAP!

Leg	Bearing	Approx. distance	Landmarks
1	314°	0.6 miles	arrive in saddle with peaks at 30° and 210°
2	10°	0.4	passing west of small peak on saddle, hit first peak at 10°
3	56°	0.5	follow 56° to ridge/saddle
4	332°	0.5	follow ridge NNW until "The Knob" is visible through saddle @ at 130°
5	90°	0.4	follow heading of 90° upslope to peak
6	62°	0.3	drop down, then climb up to plateau
7	80°	0.6	drop to drainage, traverse slope until peaks at 32° and 102° are seen
8	55°	0.3	hit road and head easterly until it intersects Hide Road
9			
10			

Route plan and direction sheet

CHAPTER 6
MEDICAL EMERGENCIES

In a survival situation, your body is your greatest tool. Much depends upon your physical capacity to find or create shelter, obtain water, gather wood for a fire and keep one going, and possibly travel on foot to safety. I don't have to tell you to try to stay healthy and to be careful to avoid accidents, but sickness and accidents occur even to the careful.

Thankfully, mortality rates are much lower now than in the nineteenth century, when medical science was relatively undeveloped and good medical knowledge was not widespread. The nature of microbial infections was not understood, and death from "minor" cuts was not at all uncommon.

Once, while butchering a deer, I failed to properly support the hanging carcass. It slipped against my knife hand and drove the knife through the wrist of my free hand. I cleaned the wound, went to the hospital, and had them treat it. Within a day, it started to hurt badly, but the tendon and hand specialist thought that I was just a whiner and sent me home. A day later, I was admitted to the hospital with a raging infection that took four days to reduce with antibiotics. In the wild, that moment of carelessness would have killed me.

But injuries need not be so grievous to be dangerous. A friend and I were on an excursion, prowling the hills barefoot as usual, when he got a very shallow slice on his foot. It did not cause him much pain and so he ignored it. A few days later, he was limping but hanging tough, and when I finally looked at it I saw clear, red lines running up his leg from the wound. We immediately aborted our trip, got out, and got medical help. It would not have mattered how tough he was in the wild, or anywhere for that matter; without attention, this wound would have killed him!

Do not mess around with injuries! Apply first aid immediately. Then, if you have any doubt about the injury's severity, seek outside help if at all possible.

FIRST AID

It is not uncommon for injury or illness to occur while you are in the backcountry. Because all members of a party must depend on one another for the health and safety of the group, it is your obligation to alert the other members if you have injured yourself or are feeling ill. In this way, the group can help assess the situation immediately and not midway up a multipitch climb when you simply cannot go on. A good acronym to remember is **S.T.O.P.**

S. Stop and calm down. Don't move (unless your life depends on immediate action). Assess your injuries and realize that you are in a survival situation. Even if you think it will all work out, maintain a survival mindset until you are really in the clear.

T. Think, do not act, until you have thought through the next few actions. Make conscious decisions that will not turn around and bite you.

O. Observe your surroundings and make a full assessment not only of your body, but of your location and your assets, which include others in your party and any materials that can aid you not only now but until help arrives.

P. Plan out your next course of action—not only what you will do, but how. What resources will it take, and what will it leave you with?

When you have a plan, a known course of action, your efficiency will improve, progress will be made toward your goal, and your morale will get a boost. There are situations that can go from helpless to hopeless. That is when you need to dig deep and use your mental toughness to work your way through a problem. When a decision is made, don't waffle—act. All too often, people become overwhelmed by a situation that they find too far outside their norm. They make decisions, start to go with them, and then second-guess themselves and take a different tack. This wastes energy and

resources, kills moral, and greases the slope to despair and tragedy. Keep your head on your shoulders and use it!

First-Aid Kits

Having the tools to deal with a medical emergency or preventing a minor medical incident from becoming a medical emergency is key and is not too difficult. Remember that having a first-aid kit does not mean that being careless is OK. When I worked for the park service as a hog hunter, we had an individual on the trail crew who wore Kevlar chainsaw chaps when using a chainsaw. This particular individual's chaps were shredded, because his impression was that the purpose of the chaps was to stop the chain from hitting flesh; therefore, that's what he used the chaps for. Other members of the crew had unblemished (if dirty) chaps and used them only as a second line of defense *after* using common sense.

Below is a list of foundation items for a first-aid kit to be included in a survival kit. They do not cover every possible contingency, so add items that you think you would need; keep space and weight in mind, too.

- Band-Aids, assorted: Get the cloth ones, because they stick better, last longer, and are more breathable.
- Sterile pads: Two-inch-by-two-inch pads are great for small wounds that initially bleed more than a Band-Aid can handle.
- Nonadhesive sterile dressing: for those larger wounds and burns.
- Antiseptic towelettes.
- Moleskin: When you start to get hot spots on your feet—those irritating red spots alerting

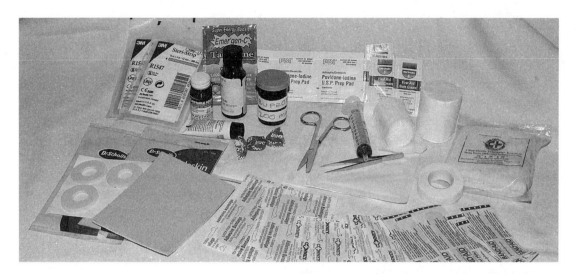

First-aid kit laid out and packed

you to points of friction and the future site of a blister—put this on so that you can still walk tomorrow.

- Foam bunion doughnuts: If you weren't quick enough with the moleskin, these foam doughnuts placed over a blister can make it possible to keep moving if you have to.

- Small, sharp scissors: Handy for removing *avulsed,* dead skin that can keep catching dirt and resealing over the wound. (An avulsion is a cut wound resulting in a flap of skin or flesh that becomes partially separated from the flesh beneath it.)

- Steri-strips or butterfly Band-Aids: Steri-strips are great in lieu of stitches for holding cleaned wounds together. (Make sure that the wound is clean before you seal it up.)

- Gauze roll: for wrapping burns and holding on sterile pads.

- Cloth sling: for use as a sling to support an arm and/or a shoulder. It can also be rolled or

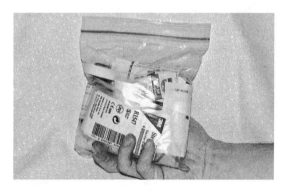

folded into a strip about four inches wide and wrapped bandage-style around a dressed wound. In addition, it can multitask as a debris filter for water prior to iodine treatment (pour water through it as you would a strainer to remove larger bits of debris) and as a head covering.

- Neosporin/triple antibiotic ointment: apply to cuts.

- Plastic syringe: For forcefully irrigating cuts with clean water, find one with a flexible tip. This is handy but not imperative to have.

- Ibuprofen: provides relief from allergies.
- Waterproof sports tape: for holding dressings in place and adding joint support.
- Iodine drops, 2 percent: Five drops per quart of clear water; let the solution stand for thirty minutes before drinking. Dirty-looking water should be filtered through a cloth or, if you have more than one container, left to settle. Then you can pour the clear water off into your drinking container prior to treatment. If the water still looks unappealing, add up to ten drops and let it stand for an hour before consuming. Cold-weather use of iodine requires a longer sit time, according to both the Wilderness Medical Society and the National Safety Council. Five drops per quart at 40°F require a three-hour sit time, while ten drops have it ready in one hour. To prevent getting ill by ingesting untreated water from the lip of your water container, simply leave the lid partially unscrewed and upend the bottle, allowing treated water to dribble out and clean the mouth as it does so.
- Hard candy: A little sugar can help morale and give a quick burst of energy when needed.

HEAT-RELATED PROBLEMS

In hot environments, overheating is not hard to do, especially in areas of high humidity where cooling due to the evaporation of sweat off the skin is slowed because of the moisture already in the air. In dry, desert climates, I have had moisture pulled from my skin before I ever began sweating. This left salt crusted in my facial hair and eyebrows; I got no relief because the moisture

in my body was evaporating before it was able to wet my skin and then cool it as it evaporated. Working or engaging in physical activity at such times taxes your body as it attempts to dispel excessive heat. If you continue the activity, your core body temperature may rise and cause one or more of the four following illnesses as you become **hyperthermic (overheated):**

- Heat syncope
- Heat cramps
- Heat exhaustion
- Heatstroke

Heat Syncope

Heat syncope is a minor heat illness brought on by inactivity when you are in a hot climate. It is also brought on if you rise quickly from a sedentary break. As you sit in the heat, your vascular activity increases as your body tries to keep cool. The lack of muscle movement hinders the efforts of the heart to move blood, causing it to collect in the lower extremities. This means that less blood is being pumped out of the heart and less is going to the brain. As a result, fainting can occur.

To treat heat syncope: Lay the victim down and keep him or her shaded while resting. The person should improve quickly. If the victim fell, he or she needs to be assessed for other injuries.

Heat Cramps

Heavy activity in hot climates can bring on heat cramps, especially when you are sweating and not replenishing your electrolytes. Cramps occur in the most active muscles.

To treat heat cramps: Cramps should be massaged and stretched in opposition to their cramping or contractions. A teaspoon of salt per quart of water will help the victim as well as prevent heat cramps from occurring.

Heat Exhaustion

Heat exhaustion should be suspected when a member of your party exhibits some of the following: muscular cramps, vomiting, excessive sweating, thirst, low fever, nausea, loss of appetite, and a drop in blood pressure upon standing.

To treat heat exhaustion: Move the victim to a cooler location if possible while keeping him or her lying down. Do not allow the victim to walk unassisted if he or she is "muscling through" their discomfort. A fall would likely exacerbate the situation and add potentially life-threatening injuries to the equation. Loosen restrictive clothing and remove heavy garments. If the victim is able to drink or swallow, give the person room-temperature water with *one-half* teaspoon of salt stirred or shaken in. This should have the victim well on his or her way to feeling much better. If the victim does not improve, exhibits an altered mental state, and shows an elevated temperature beyond a low fever, the person needs prompt medical attention. Get the victim out or get the search and rescue (SAR) team in!

Heatstroke

Heatstroke typically occurs due to excessive activity in a hot environment. Some other factors are wearing too much clothing, not acclimatizing to higher temperatures than those to which you are accustomed, and your body not having the ability to dispel heat for a variety of medical reasons.

Symptoms include: skin is hot to the touch; a temperature taken orally is often above 104°F;

and the mental state is altered, ranging from being dizzy and having a headache to being unresponsive and having facial flushing, although the skin may be pale. If left untreated, the victim will likely exhibit signs of increasing damage: he or she may become delirious, have seizures, vomit, or discharge bloody stool and/or diarrhea.

To treat heatstroke: Heatstroke is deadly, and a heatstroke victim must be treated quickly and continually until he or she is in the care of professionals.

1. Get the victim out of the sun or heat.
2. Cool the victim down with any of the following means: remove clothing; place ice, if possible, in the armpits and crotch; wet down the victim by sponging him or her with water, using a cloth; fan the victim if no breeze is blowing.
3. Continue to assess the victim; check the victim's temperature. Discontinue cooling when 99.6°F is reached, but resume cooling if the temperature of the victim begins to rise again.
4. Check and record the pulse and respirations.
5. Elevate the feet eight to twelve inches to help if shock occurs.
6. Get the victim to advanced medical help as soon as possible!

COLD-RELATED INJURIES

Cold is one of the more dangerous challenges we face in our day-to-day survival. Cold causes our blood to be shunted away from our extremities and held in our core. The initial result is a lack in dexterity, general clumsiness, and numbing of the more exposed parts of the body. In some conditions, frostbite can cause permanent damage in a very short period of time, while in milder conditions, it can sap your energy and directly impact your ability to perform simple tasks. A lack of sleep further taxes your body's resources.

Hypothermia

According to the National Ski Patrol, hypothermia is when the core temperature of a person drops below 95°F. In cold environments, keeping your body to that sacred number, 98.6°F, is paramount to your survival, and it's all too easy for that number to drop if you're not careful.

Prolonged exposure to cold with inadequate protection (clothing and shelter), damp clothing, and/or direct contact with cold materials (including submersion in water and dealing with wind) can all bring on hypothermia in short order.

As the body temperature drops to 95°F, involuntary shivering begins as the body attempts to generate heat. A loss of dexterity and experiencing general clumsiness, as well as stumbling and having an inability to think or speak clearly, also are clear indicators of hypothermia. The ability to touch the tip of your thumb to your pinky fingertip of the same hand becomes an impossible task, illustrating how this condition can quickly spiral into a deadly situation. If you can't move your fingers effectively, how can you put on more clothing, get wet gear off, erect a shelter, or start a fire? If help does not arrive or the situation does not improve, then shivering will stop as your body temperature drops below 90°F. It is at this point that you will need external heat to warm yourself up. Your breathing and heart rate slow as you slip into an unresponsive condition. When your temperature drops below 80°F, death is soon to follow. Depending on the situation, this can all happen in less than an hour.

Hypothermia can be divided into two categories: mild, 98.6 to 90°F, and severe, below 90°F. Another defining quality that differentiates one type from another is the duration that the victim has been exposed to the cold. In acute hypothermia victims, exposure is an hour or less, whereas chronic hypothermia victims are exposed to the cold for extended periods. A cold-water submersion would classify as an acute case, whereas a chronic case would likely be found on a ski slope amongst inadequately dressed skiers.

To treat hypothermia:

1. Stop further heat loss. This can be accomplished by removing wet clothing and donning dry clothing. If no dry clothing is available, get out of the wind and weather, and get in a sleeping bag or a pile of leaves.

2. Rewarm yourself. Do this by any means possible—body-to-body contact (get in a leaf pile or sleeping bag with them), hot packs (not great, as they provide little heat, but even so, do not place them directly on your skin), fire, hot liquids, water containers filled with hot water, or heated stones. Heated objects should never be placed directly against the skin, because the skin is more sensitive to heat on a hypothermia victim. Such objects should be tested first by touching them to the wrist, as you would test the heat of bottled milk for a baby. In the case of heated rocks, be careful. Water should not sizzle when it is dripped on the rock, but should spread and evaporate slowly. These objects will

do the most good when you place them in the armpits and along the sides of the neck and groin.

3. Warm liquids serve two purposes: They heat from the inside (valuable even though little heat is actually transferred), and they provide liquids to victims who are often dehydrated as well as hypothermic.

4. Handle the victim gently. According to Warren Bowman and the National Ski Patrol (*Outdoor Emergency Care*, 1998), ventricular fibrillation—a condition in which the lower chambers of the heart flutter instead of beat due to disordered electrical activity, thus causing the heart to fail as a pump by moving little or no blood through the body—is the most common cause of death in hypothermia cases. This can be brought on by sudden jarring of the patient who has a core temperature below 90°F.

Frostbite

The freezing of a body part from exposure usually occurs on the nose, cheek, ears, fingertips, and tips of the toes. Frostnip is the precursor to frostbite, and although a few ice crystals may be present on the skin, the area underneath is still soft so that only the upper or superficial layers of skin freeze. Frostnip does not even result in blistering.

In true frostbite, there are two categories— superficial, involving the layers of the skin, and deep, involving not only the skin but the underlying tissue, tendons, muscle, and bone. The affected body part is hard, inflexible, and yellowish in color; it stops hurting or tingling when it reaches this point. When thawing occurs, the affected area may be grayish purple in color, painful tingling may occur, and clear or yellowy, liquid-filled blisters may form. In deep frostbite, the blisters are often smaller and filled with a reddish purple fluid; in less severe cases, no blisters form on the dark purple, puffy skin, which is common in the most severe cases.

To treat frostnip: Heat the affected area by directly placing it against another part of the body; for example, a frostnipped finger can be placed in the mouth or armpit.

To treat frostbite: Do not allow the affected part to refreeze if it has thawed by the time it is noticed. If you have a sheltered area and can ensure proper protection for the affected area, it can be rapidly thawed in a water bath. This is tricky, however, because the temperature of the water needs to be within a few degrees of 104°F until the affected area is thawed. This is a painful process and, if possible, should be left for the professionals. If you are not equipped to work on a rapid thaw and you are only a few hours from help, leaving the frozen area alone may be the best option. Do not rub the affected area with snow, pop blisters, or try to rewarm the part by the fire.

PHYSICAL INJURIES

When it comes to dealing with severe injuries like broken bones, severe sprains, and concussions, there is not a great deal that an *untrained* person can do other than seek medical attention from trained professionals. It is not uncommon for untrained "rescuers" to exacerbate an injury while attempting to help. If a member of your group, or you, suffers a concussion, for example, what action could you take? Without a hospital (including a CAT scan in your back pocket), your only choice is to seek help. If you want to be able to handle severe injuries, the time to learn how is now, not with a book while you are kneeling next to an unconscious victim at the base of a cliff, or while you are cradling a freshly broken arm. A number of organizations offer courses in wilderness first aid (WFA), wilderness first responder (WFR), and wilderness emergency medical technician (WEMT). While these courses may not prepare you for all emergencies, you will be vastly more able to deal with most injuries that may crop up. Included here are injuries that are fairly typical for backcountry hikes and camping trips. These injuries can range from minor to severe, but keep in mind that even the smallest splinter can cause infection if it is not dealt with properly. Infection can be deadly.

Open Wounds

Caring for open wounds in today's society is fairly simple, but step into the wild places without the comfort of even the most rudimentary first-aid kit and a splinter could be the end of you. A first-aid kit is an invaluable first line of defense. First, a few definitions:

- *Lacerations* are slices in the skin that have a rough edge.
- An *incision* is a similar wound but has clean edges.
- *Punctures* typically have small openings but can penetrate quite far into the flesh.
- *Avulsions* are wounds in which a flap of skin or flesh is partially separated from the flesh beneath it.

To treat open wounds:

1. If possible, have the skin around the wound disinfected with iodine, alcohol, or warm, soapy water.
2. Except for punctures, open the wound, and irrigate it with sterile water. Remove any foreign material.
3. Triple antibiotic ointment is applied to the wound, which is then covered with a sterile dressing.

This is simple enough if it is as described above—a nonbleeding wound with a patient, patient. If there is profuse bleeding, then direct pressure with a sterile dressing is called for with the wound elevated above the heart, if possible. In my experience, it is a good idea, if you are tending someone other than yourself, to have the victim apply the pressure. This frees you up to prepare sterile water and bandages and arrange for help.

When I have been unable to get medical attention for a few days or more after suffering an injury, I made sure that the top of the wound stayed open so as to allow any weeping or pus to flow out of the wound and not get trapped inside by a healed-over opening. I deal with shallow, infected wounds by chewing the young leaves of broadleaf plantain to a pulp (very bitter) and applying it as a poultice to the wound. Left there for a few hours, it does wonders.

Splinters

Splinters can be an annoyance or a more serious problem depending on how deep and how large they are and what's on them. One danger is that a splinter can introduce foreign material, in addition to itself, deep into the flesh. Deep, infected wounds are tricky, because often the entry heals closed and leaves a festering mess inside that can quickly become very dangerous. The approaches I use if the splinter is too deep to grab with tweezers or fingernails are to let it sit for a few days and then soak the area in water, warm if possible, and then reopen the entry site. I will then squeeze from two sides, and the little bit of pus that has appeared will often eject the splinter partially or all the way as it is forced out. If you consider your choices, they are, quite simply, to either leave the splinter in or remove it. Either way, seek medical treatment at the earliest possible time.

Burns

Burns can be a common occurrence for people who are not accustomed to using fire for their daily living needs. When you are tired and/or cold, errors in judgment and clumsiness increase and can result in an injury. During one of the episodes of the *Survivor* television show, one of the contestants was blowing on the campfire, and, through a combination of hyperventilation and smoke inhalation, he lost consciousness and fell into the fire. He was only out for seconds, but when he came to, his hands were burned and flesh could be seen hanging off of them. He was transported by medevac and did not return.

There are three classifications for burns.

- **First-degree burns** are superficial, causing redness and some puffiness, like sunburn, and there are no blisters.
- **Second-degree burns**, or partial-thickness burns, affect the skin down into the inner

layer of skin. Blisters are present, and pain can be moderate to severe.
- **Third-degree or full-thickness burns** are the most serious, as they extend from the surface down through the skin and into the underlying flesh and fat. The skin is discolored and has a grilled appearance to it.

The greater the surface area of a burn, the more severe it is. Third-degree burns do not hurt as much as lesser burns because the nerve endings have also been burned. However, the surrounding areas may be intensely painful due to first- and second-degree burns.

Most burns encountered around camp life are minor, such as stepping on coals with bare feet, grabbing something hot and blistering your fingertips, and singeing your eyebrows and hair. For situations involving more serious burns, such as those covering the hands or what might be sustained in a shelter fire, you or someone in your party need to get advanced medical help. Smaller burns can be dealt with in the following manner.

To treat burns:

1. Stop the burn and pour water on the burn.
2. Cover the burn with cloth and pour water over it frequently, or submerge it in water. The faster it gets cool and the longer it stays cool, the better off the victim will be.

Keep the burn clean and do not pop blisters or apply any oily ointment. Aloe vera gel or juice from the plant are great on first- and second-degree burns and provide immediate relief, but it needs to be reapplied often.

The best relief in my experience has been submersion in cold water. Not only does this relieve pain, it can also reduce the overall outcome. I once grabbed a piece of clayware just out of firing, having confused it with a previously fired piece. My skin hissed and I set the clayware down promptly. I could see where it had contacted my hand and fingers and knew that it wasn't good, but after soaking my hand in 60°F, flowing water for half an hour, the pain stopped and came back only briefly after I took my hand out of the water. The blisters that had started to form went down, and a day later there was no sign of any injury, either visually or to my touch.

PART II

BEYOND SURVIVAL

PRIMITIVE SKILLS FOR WILDERNESS LIVING

CHAPTER 7

SHELTERS FOR THE LONG TERM

The shelters covered here are not practical for short-term survival, because they require more work, time, and/or materials than the expedient shelters discussed in Chapter 2, but they can also be drier, warmer, more spacious, more convenient, and more pleasant overall. If you plan an extended stay in the wilderness, the extra effort may be well worthwhile.

PIT SHELTERS

Just as digging into the snow is sometimes the best option in finding shelter, occasionally digging into the soil or sand is the best way to find protection from the elements. Typically, an earth-type shelter requires too much work to meet the needs of a short-term situation. The point to remember is that you never know when a short-term delay turns into an extended survival situation. I would rather leave a perfect shelter unslept in because of an early rescue than have no shelter to sleep in due to the lack of an expected rescue.

As with all shelters, the key is a good location. In this case, that means plenty of wood and grasses for the roof, the insulation and the bedding, and diggable soil. In areas of sandy ground

or other loose or easily dug substrates, a pit shelter can be fairly easily constructed with a little more effort than some other shelters require. Sand is by far the best substrate in which to make these shelters provided it is not too loose and dry. It provides easy digging and good drainage, which means less issue with rot, and it is easy to camouflage. I once made a pit shelter in an area with too much clay that initially posed no problems other than the impractical amount of energy required to dig it. After a good rain, however, it turned into a sensory deprivation tank—it was dark, quiet, and full of water! Other spots had so many large stones that I dug as far as I was able and then made up the difference with log "walls" on the surface, around the pit—harder to hide, but definitely manageable.

Building a Pit Shelter

Locate a safe area as described in Chapter 2. Unless you have a replenishable food and water source, avoid exerting too much energy in building this shelter. If you really need it make sure that the ground is easy to excavate with a digging stick or other improvised item. To reiterate safety issues, critters may find their way into your pit and like it there. Scorpions are easy to miss and can make sleeping difficult. Other good locations are found in coastal areas with plenty of sandy substrate and next to no risk of flooding.

Mark out the shelter plan by marking your shoulder width, plus two hand lengths, and the length of at least your body, plus two heads. The depth should be about that of your inseam. Digging without a shovel in any substrate is tough, so start by loosening the area in which you will be excavating with a digging stick (see Chapter 16), and then remove the loosened material by scraping with a flat stone or piece of wood. I use my hands, but be leery of this, because if you wound yourself, it can be dangerous once infection sets in. Pile the diggings along either side of the pit about eighteen inches away to prevent them from inadvertently getting kicked back into the hole. This material will be used later to cover the roof.

There are a few entrance options. The most practical is a ramp entrance that leaves from the shelter at the head, perpendicular to the pit. This doorway minimizes the amount of dirt that will enter your bedding with each entry and exit. Another option is to not have any ramp, and to make the end of the entry pit farthest from your head deeper than the shelter. This will ensure that any rainwater will not flow into your sleeping area.

Lie down in your pit and see how (un)comfortable it is, and make adjustments.

Once the pit is dug, the hole needs to be excavated at least six inches wider all the way around to a depth of six inches. This is the shelf that will support the roof pieces and the dirt that will cover and insulate the shelter; therefore, it needs to be wide enough to support a lot of weight. In other words, if the shelf is only two inches wide, the weight of the sticks and roof may cause the wall below the shelf to buckle and crumble. Sometimes

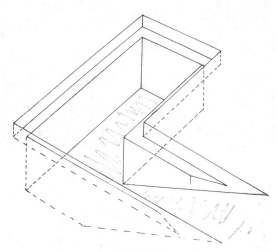

Cross section of pit shelter

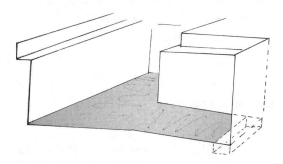

Entry pit with water well

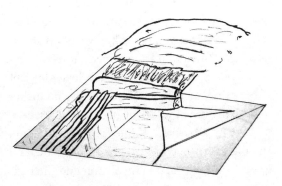

Pit showing shelf and partial roof

I have skipped the shelf altogether, but it took a lot of sand to really seal the place up. The choice is yours.

Gather loads of grasses, inner bark, leaves, or other insulation materials and lots of sticks and logs for the roof. The wood for the roof, if you plan to leave the shelter up for any length of time, should be hardwood like Osage orange, locust, or oak. Other woods work well, too, although I stay away from American hornbeam, ironwood, and any birches, because they rot very quickly when they are kept moist by soil. (I saw an earth shelter built using ironwood; a year later, it was a heap of dirt and rotten wood.) Sand drains far better than soil and thus will not hold moisture next to the wood for as long of a time, which helps the wood last longer. If you have a choice, however, go with the harder stuff.

Place the sticks across the pit, making sure that they have plenty of length on both support shelves. The entry ramp can be covered, but leave enough space to allow easy entry to and exit from the shelter. Cover the stick roof with grass and then with the excavated material. Lastly, pack in the bedding and insulation, leaving a large bundle to pull in, after your feet-first entry, as a door plug.

Sometimes combining the pit shelter with a wikiup or other shelter type works well. A dug-in base with a debris or thatch roof will help keep a shelter cooler than the ambient temperature in hot weather and warmer than the ambient temperature in cold weather due to the insulating qualities of the soil.

Keeping It Hidden

The following options are best for shelters that you wish to remain secret. If this is your inten-tion, you need to think carefully about the loca-tion; i.e., does the surrounding landscape direct passersby away from or toward your shelter?

When you are excavating the pit, it is a good idea to temporarily remove the natural ground litter (leaves, sticks, grasses, small plants) from the area where you will deposit the diggings unless you have a tarp. This will prevent freshly dug dirt from being clearly visible on top of the ground cover.

Make the support shelf lower to accommodate the following door: When you are covering the pit with logs, leave a section with no covering to one side of the middle of the pit. Make sure that it is just large enough for you to enter the pit feet first before proceeding. Add sticks, log-cabin style, around the opening (first perpendicular to the rest of the roof logs, then parallel to them). As you build up to grade, make the entry so that it looks similar to a funnel or like it would hold an inverted pyramid. Continue the building process as above with the grass and the dirt. For the door, you will need a basket that sits in the opening without falling into the shelter. The basket should be lined with grass, filled with sand, and sprin-kled with the local ground cover. Leave two han-dles accessible that are well attached to the basket. The rest of the shelter and any disturbed ground can also be covered with the leaves and other materials you scraped together prior to begin-ning. A rain will always help the scene blend in better.

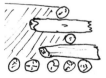 

Cross section of a conical door hole

Basket plug

Another door option is to make a disk by bending green branches into a hoop and lashing them with cordage or twisting them around themselves. Waterproofing can be attained with grasses, bark, leaves, clay, or a combination of any of the above.

Upkeep

Maintaining your shelter is important, especially if you want it to last for repeat use. I remove bedding and insulation when I plan on being away for more than a few weeks. This prevents mold and makes drying it out with a small fire much easier upon my return. The logs used in the construction of the roof are important, especially in soils that can hold water, because rot can require them to be replaced inside a year. The door cover, if you are using a basket-type entry, should be removed and replaced with sturdy sticks, as the baskets tend to thin out and drop into the shelter as a result of gravity and moisture.

When you are reopening a pit shelter after an extended absence, be cautious—many a small, pointy critter will be right at home in your home away from home. If you have poisonous reptiles, arachnids, ants, or anything else that likes cool, dark places in your area, you may have to evict them carefully. I often make a fire outside the shelter. Then, when I have some good coals, I'll throw a heap inside on the earthen floor and cover them with leaf litter or other organic material to get lots of smoke. Creating an opening at the foot of the shelter can help get smoke and heat to really saturate the inside. This also deodorizes, preheats, and dries the interior. Do not do this just before stuffing the pit with insulation, for obvious reasons.

THATCHED HUTS

Thatching has fascinated me for some time. How can it be that natural materials still in their raw state can be such an effective covering for buildings that many a modern island or coastal business or dwelling sports a thatched roof? Sure, some of them have a "proper" roof beneath with the thatch just for looks, but many do not. After watching a team of thatchers work on a roof in southern Mexico my attitude toward it as a survival tool cooled. I felt that thatching sounded great until I understood the amount of cordage or string that was needed. So, if you have a few thousand feet of spare cordage, by all means, go thatch a hut! Joking aside, thatching can provide a great shelter and a fine area in which to work. After much thought and mucking about with thatching, I came up with an idea that reduced the amount of cordage required by about 75 percent or more. I later learned that, as is the case with many "inventions" regarding primitive skills, the idea was not only old, but documented and photographed. I call it the split and pinch method.

Thatched huts are practical when an extended stay is expected and you have plenty of building materials on hand for the structure. However, you also must be in an area that will support you in all of your other needs as well. Three methods of attaching the thatch to the frame are covered below.

The Frame

Many considerations must be addressed prior to your grabbing the first stick. Figure out the general design and how you intend to utilize the space.

The two designs with which I am most familiar are the longhouse style (vertical walls, curved roof) and the dome style. My first round thatched hut (better for windy areas) was large enough to house a few people but was so tall that I wasted considerable amounts of materials and heat to have air above my head inside. The advantage to all that air space was in the storage department. Plus, I used the hut with an interior fire for two years before I burned it to the ground. Another roof option—more labor intensive but far more sound—is to put a peaked, A-frame roof on the structure. This provides a better pitch for shedding water.

Use your body as a way to measure out sleeping areas for all people who will use the hut, and figure in work space, some of which can serve double duty as both sleeping and work areas. Most people can sleep in a space that is two feet by six feet, and it is the sleeping space that needs the most protection from the elements. If you are building round huts for a number of people, it seems best to build one for sleeping quarters and another for a work space. In this way, there is no need for a tall and spacious structure and, if you

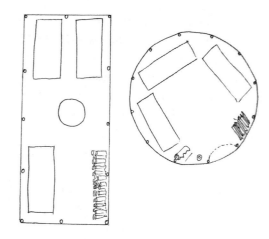

Bird's-eye view of two frames

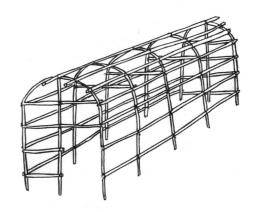

View of the longhouse frame

View of the dome-style frame

do burn it down, at least you'll still have a place to sleep! (For more on round huts, see "Desert Shelters" in Chapter 2).

Native peoples used fire inside thatched huts, but this can be tricky—if not outright dangerous—given the flammable nature of thatching. I suggest that an outside fire area be used away from the shelter. If you must have an inside fireplace, be sure to have ample room around it, and make a smoke hole in the roof above it. *Parge* the inside of the thatching near the smoke-hole opening (i.e., cover it with a fire-resistant coating by smearing on a wet clay or a mixture of clay and grass mixed in a 75:25 ratio). Keeping the fire to a small size is wise, too.

With longhouses and thatch huts, a space can be left in the gable ends. This allows the smoke to rise to the ceiling and be carried away by a cross draft; it also avoids compromising the integrity of the roof. However, it makes warming the interior next to impossible unless the openings are kept small.

Whatever your floor plan, mark out on the ground the shape of the structure and where the posts will go. Mark the corners of the shelter, and make a mark where the walls will be every three to four feet for uprights.

Harvest all the saplings you will need for crosspieces and posts. Poles can be fresh cut or seasoned (green wood is more flexible). Either way, they should be of a hardy, rot-resistant wood like cedar, Osage orange, or locust. Oak stands up quite well, as does ash. Avoid using birches, ironwood, hornbeam, and softer woods. These may be hard when they are upright, but they turn into sponges in the ground and rot with alarming speed. For the longhouse style, use thicker material—two to four inches for posts and about one to two inches for the crossbars (measurements are

from the base of the saplings to be used). For the dome style, use thinner stock—two inches for the posts and one inch for the crossbars. If you want your shelter to stand up to snow, you will need to use thicker materials, provide cross bracing in the more horizontal surfaces, and potentially add more interior support for the winter.

One method to anchor the uprights is to pound a three-foot hardwood stake halfway into the ground at each corner and each wall-post mark. Work the stake around until it is possible to remove it from the ground, or continue working the stake until the post will fit in the resulting hole.

Another method is to pound three-foot stakes halfway into the ground at each post site and leave them there, then lash saplings, thick end down, to each protruding stake. This way often seems easier if you have modern cutting tools, although I prefer the first method.

After you have anchored the uprights by either method, bend the opposing saplings toward each other, overlapping them until you obtain the desired height in the hut. Lash them together or wrap them around one another to hold them in place. At this point, thinking about symmetry will just irritate you, so don't waste your time trying to make it look perfect. That will come later . . . maybe.

In *Practicing Primitive* (2004), Steven M. Watts describes how he prefabricated the arches by laying the saplings for a given arch on the ground, thin end to thin end, with the ends overlapping by three feet or more. (Marks or pegs can be stuck in the ground to ensure that all arches are the same length.) Then he lashed them together, dropped one end into its hole, and bent the arch until the opposite end could be placed in its hole.

Next, attach crosspieces between the uprights. Place the first one at ground level and additional ones at least every three feet. Actual spacing will depend on the length of your thatching material, which I'll discuss soon. Cordage is the best way to attach the crosspieces. (See Chapter 15 to learn how to make cordage.) If cordage is in short supply, there are other methods.

For the vertical portion of the walls, "Y" sticks can be pounded into the ground alongside the uprights and the crosspieces rested in them. Another option is, if you have access to long saplings or your uprights are close together, to weave the crosspieces through the uprights as if you were making a basket. It sure makes for an ugly duckling that will, unfortunately, never be beautiful. If the shelter begins to sag under the weight of the crosspieces, the saplings you used for uprights were far too slight and must be replaced or reinforced with a vertical post inside. A Y-shaped stick is ideal.

Thatching

Once the crosspieces are in place and the uprights are reinforced (if necessary), the structure is ready for its skin. Here are three thatching techniques. Each one has advantages and disadvantages.

BUNDLE THATCH. Probably the most common way to thatch a structure is to prepare bundles of the thatching materials by tying the thin ends of the grass, straw, or whatever is to be used together. Beginning at the second lowest crosspiece and working horizontally these bundles are tied tightly next to each other all the way around the structure before you move up to the next crosspiece. The second row as well as each subsequent row must overlap the preceding row by a good six to eight inches, if not by more, to ensure good weatherproofing. While the technique requires much cordage, it is widely used and has been for some time.

Detail of skeleton and framing

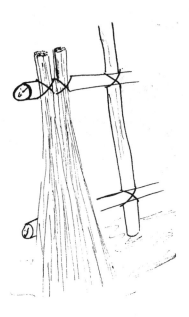

Thatching attached to the crosspiece

PINCH THATCH. This method works especially well for flat-walled structures or those that have very little horizontal curve. Longhouse-styled structures can also use this on the roof, although a thick layer is required to prevent leakage. This is a good option for peaked, A-frame roofs. This provides a better pitch for shedding water.

Use either very straight saplings or split them lengthwise and keep the halves paired. Place one-half, split side up, on the ground, and put on your thatching material (I prefer cattail because of its abundance) perpendicular to it and evenly, with the thick end extending eight inches beyond the sapling.

Place the second half of the sapling on top of the thatching over the first half, and bind it every two feet or so. If some of the thatching seems loose, simply tug it downward until its increased diameter causes it to snug up. If you are using green materials, shrinkage will occur as they dry; the larger ends, however, will help keep the materials in place. Even so, be sure to cinch the cordage very tightly. These "thatch mats" can then be attached to the shelter in the same manner in which siding or shingles are put on a house. Start low and work your way up. Make sure to overlap each row. With cattails used upside down, it is a good idea to overlap them well beyond the six to eight inches recommended due to their irregular length and rather wispy tops. When I measure the overlap, I measure only the thatch that extends below the previously placed crosspiece. This ensures that the integrity of the walls is not compromised by snugging down the thatch. If the mats are too thin or the pitch too slight, their ability to shed water is diminished.

BEND THATCH. This method is well suited to round or domed shelters. It requires a minimal amount of cordage but a great quantity of thatching material if a waterproof shelter is the goal.

Cattails or tules (a type of bullrush) are draped over a crosspiece (the crosspiece must be less than half the length of the cattail or tule off the ground). The half of the cattail falling on the inside of the shelter is run on the outside of all crosspieces below the one on which it rests. This keeps it from hanging into the interior of the shelter. It does not seem to make any real difference whether the tops of the cattail fall inside or outside, because they both end up making up the wall. Once all of the thatch is in place, thin, flexible saplings or branches need to be wrapped in hoops around the shelter just above the ends of the thatch. This prevents the wind from whipping it around. If a smoke hole is left in the top, an inner hoop may need to be lashed on the inside of the roof surrounding the opening.

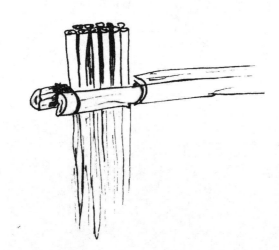

Cattail thatch pinched between sapling pieces

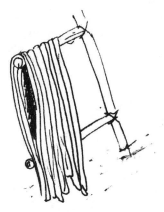

Cross section of thatch application

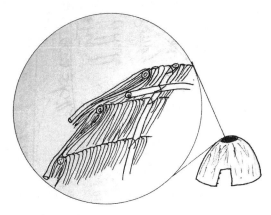

Inner hoop holding up the thatch

More Thatch Hut Tips

- Doors should be kept small to reduce draftiness and heat loss. Be creative—add awnings, make mats on which to sit and sleep, and make the amenities you want to have so that you can enjoy your stay.
- When you find a leak, don't get mad—figure it out. Break it down. Where is the water coming from? Where is it entering from the outside? What needs to happen to stop it?
- The steeper the shelter, the better it will prevent rainwater from entering. If you live in a particularly rainy area, you may find that a tipi-style frame works better than a dome.
- People usually build their hut too large; the amount of space that a person actually needs is pretty small. Sleeping and work areas make up the bulk of your spatial needs. If you intend on staying for a few months or longer, remember that you can always extend the length of the shelter, add awnings, or build other shelters (smaller or bigger).

CHAPTER 8

FIRE-MAKING TOOLS

Primitive fire-making methods, while fun and effective, are skills that can largely be passed over for the short-term survival situation. A cigarette lighter is small, light, and cheap, is easily stowed in any pocket, and is quicker and more reliable (as long as the fuel holds out) at producing a flame with which to ignite tinder. (See Chapter 4 for basic information about fire building.) For longer-term situations, however, the ability to make your fire from the surrounding materials is liberating and a great skill to have. Yes, a fire can be tended and the coals protected, but when that drenching rain comes and shuts your fire down, it is nice to know that you can coax fire from the wood in your area. This chapter covers four fire-making tools: the bow drill, hand drill, fire saw, and fire plow, in addition to the "long match"—a method for preserving and carrying fire. The pump drill, covered under "Hand Tools" in Chapter 16, is another tool that can be used to start fires, as well as for drilling holes.

BOW DRILL

I have been told that trees are made of stored sunshine. I believe that natural fire making is a way of asking the sunshine to release itself, and only asking in a humble way will draw the desired results. The bow drill is one such method. Here I can provide you with the technical directions for this fire-making ceremony; the humility must come from you.

The apparatus is made up of five components: the fireboard, the spindle, the cordage, the bow, and the handhold. With the fireboard placed on the ground, the spindle wound once in the cordage, and the ends placed in the sockets of the fireboard and the handhold, the bow is moved back and forth parallel to the ground. The bow strokes rotate the spindle in the sockets via the cordage. Simultaneously, downward pressure is applied on the handhold, creating friction on both ends of the spindle. Conifer pitch or needles placed in the handhold socket minimize friction at the top, which also results in a greater amount of heat-generating friction in the fireboard socket. As the spindle moves within the fireboard socket, small particles of wood wear off and fill the notch with fine powder (fire powder). This fine powder is dark brown or black in color and, due to its intense heat, gloms together and forms a coal. The coal is then removed from the notch and placed in a tinder bundle. The bundle is blown into a flame and put into a prebuilt tipi fire.

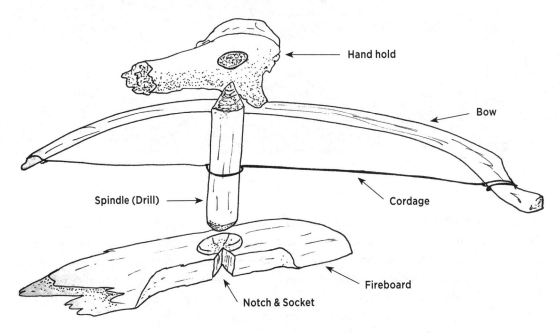

The bow drill

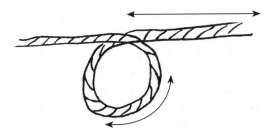

Spindle rotation

Making the Components

It is possible to make a bow-and-drill fire with any nonresinous wood. Working with the harder hardwoods such as oak, locust, ironwood, and others is a fun challenge but not desirable in a survival situation for the following reasons: First, such hardwoods take more time and energy to fashion into a bow-and-drill set. Second, the endurance required to make a coal with these hardwoods will use up your valuable energy. And third, making cordage that can withstand such continuous use required for an oak bow-and-drill fire is difficult. Woods such as white cedar, juniper cedar, cottonwood, aspen, sycamore, maple, birch, and basswood work beautifully for the bow and drill; though some of these are classified as *hard*woods, they are from the softer end of the hardwood spectrum.

Each tree, however, is different, and the hardness of wood may vary from branch to branch. An aspen growing with one side to a cliff and one side in the open will give you very hard wood on the cliff side and much softer wood on the exposed side. I strongly recommend experimenting. When you are harvesting bow-and-drill wood, it is best to find a dead branch that is still in the tree. A branch on the ground can feel dry, yet be moist inside due to absorption of moisture from the ground. A branch in a tree is surrounded by air, and the wind helps to evaporate moisture quickly even after a good rain.

For instructions on making the bow string, see Chapter 15. All of the other components are described below.

The bow should be about waist height and have a very slight curve. I prefer a bow with some flexibility, although this is not imperative. Keep the bow light, as a heavy bow will require more energy to move back and forth. The diameter should be between a nickel and a quarter in size. One end should fit comfortably in your dominant hand. Notch the bow ends to help hold the string in place.

I prefer spindles that are nine inches in length and the diameter of a quarter, although in damp weather I'll use a wider spindle to create greater friction between the fireboard and the spindle. This helps dry the wood and thus the fibers that fall into the notch. The spindle can be taken from a dead branch with the desired diameter or split from a log and carved into a round shape. Both ends should be tapered bluntly. The spindle should be of the same wood as the fireboard or of a similar hardness.

The length of the fireboard is less important than its width. I typically use a piece that is nine inches by three or four inches. The thickness of the board should be about one inch but no more.

As with the spindle, the wood can be split from a log or taken from a dead tree branch. A fireboard made from a dead branch will likely be narrower than three inches in diameter and should be split lengthwise to create a flat bottom. If you're using rocks to make your apparatus, you will need to crush the branch with a larger stone and use the sharp edge of a rock to abrade your notch when you are ready.

A handhold made of pine often does not need to be lubricated, because it has a residual pitch still in the wood. In areas where there are no conifers, a bone or stone handhold works well, although it may take more preparation if you can't locate one with a pocket for the spindle end. The key aspects of a handhold are that the socket is deep enough to hold the spindle well, yet not so deep as to create more friction when the spindle sides contact the socket wall. The handhold should be comfortable in your left hand if you are right-handed (the opposite if you are left-handed), and the hole for the spindle should be directly below the center of your palm. Make sure that it is large enough so that you can hold it without touching the spindle. If it's too small, your fingers may touch the spindle and suffer burns.

To mark the socket location in your handhold and fireboard, lay the spindle on top of the fireboard, flush with either long edge. Roll the spindle toward the center of the fireboard a quarter inch and stand it up on its point. Twist the spindle

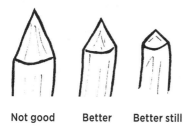

Not good   Better   Better still

Spindle tips

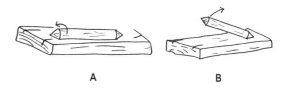

A   B

Marking the socket location

back and forth, creating a small dent in the fireboard. With the handhold end of the spindle, create a small dent in the middle of the handhold, as described above.

Tie cordage to both ends of the bow, being careful not to make it tight. Exactly how much slack is required will depend upon the diameter of the spindle. Place one end of the bow under your right armpit, with the rest of the bow out in front of you. With the spindle in your right hand, place it across the cordage (step A in the accompanying figure). Swoop under and around the cordage with the end of the spindle (step B), and with both hands, force the spindle to a perpendicular position with the cordage (step C). Hold the cordage and spindle firmly, because the spindle is held under tension and could fly out. Note: if the cordage is too tight (you can't complete step C) or too loose after completing step C, then adjust the cordage and try again.

Place the fireboard on the ground, with the small hole that you started on the right end. With the ball of your left foot resting on the fireboard to the left of the hole, drop down to your right knee and place the spindle tip into the hole in the fireboard. While you continue to hold the spindle

to keep it from being flung out by the cordage, place the handhold on the top so that the point of the spindle rests in the handhold starter hole. At this point, you should be resting your chest on your left knee. Your left wrist should be brought against your shin while you exert downward pressure on the handhold. Grasp the end of the bow in your right hand, and begin moving it back and forth so that the spindle rotates. In all likelihood, the spindle will pop out with annoying frequency and the cordage will ride up and down the spindle and come off. This is due to a lack of form and occurs when the spindle is not kept perpendicular to the cordage or the handhold. I really "lock my hand in" by pulling the wrist joint back against my shin so that both my hand and arm are stable. This keeps the spindle perpendicular to the fireboard and handhold. The cordage can be kept in the center of the spindle by giving even, level bow strokes.

A trick for helping with this is on the backstroke, when your bow hand is passing your knee. Try to drive the back end of the bow into the ground a foot or so behind your knee, paying attention to the effect this has on your bow wrist. Do the opposite on the forestroke. By using full

A   B   C

Stringing the spindle

Bow drill position

bow strokes (i.e., all of the string, not six-inch strokes), and by adding more or less downward pressure in the handhold, you will produce enough friction to cause the sockets to smoke. As you play with the speed of the strokes, more or less smoke will be generated. This burning-in process is generally done until the sockets have the same diameter as the spindle.

The handhold socket is now ready for some lubricant. Conifer needles work beautifully, as does the sap, and, as mentioned previously, a handhold made of pine may contain enough resin so as not to need any additional lubricant. Oils from animal fats also work.

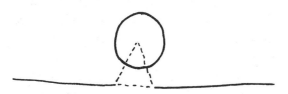

The notch in the fireboard

Put a few pine needles in the socket, and forcefully twist the spindle end in the socket, smashing and smearing the needles around. After you have lubricated the handhold, mark your spindle so that you can tell which end is up. If the lubricated end is used in the fireboard, getting a fire may prove to be rather difficult.

To carve your notch in the fireboard, look at the burned-in socket and imagine that it is a whole pie. Your notch should be no greater than one-eighth of the pie. It is important that it be wedge shaped and clean on the sides. It should go into but not include the center of the socket.

Using the Bow Drill

Now you are ready to create a coal. Tinder (see Chapter 4) can be placed either under the fireboard and notch or set aside, and a wood chip or leaf can be placed under the notch to catch the coal. Begin with smooth, even strokes, and watch

Moving the fireboard

the dust build up in the notch. The goal is to have fine dark brown or black dust. Light brown or white dust means that you have not used enough speed. Coarse brown dust is asking for less hand-hold pressure, and no dust at all and loud squeaking indicate fire hardening and require an increase in both speed and pressure.

When the notch is full and a lot of smoke has been coming from the fireboard, add ten good strokes to "pack" the coal. These packing strokes ensure that the coal has enough material to feed on as it grows. Stop your bow strokes, and gently remove the spindle from the fireboard. A wisp of smoke should be rising from the dust in the wedge. Place a twig or the back of your knife blade gently on the dust and hold it there. Roll the fireboard away from the dust, leaving the coal in the open. If the smoke is weak, leave it alone for a minute or so; the coal may grow.

Gently deposit the coal into your prepared tinder bundle, and fold the tinder over it. I like to let the coal heat up the tinder a little before I give a few long, soft breaths into the bundle. Holding the tinder up to the sky is a good idea. Not only is it a great way to give thanks, but also it prevents the coal from burning a hole out the back of your

bundle and dropping to the ground. It also keeps the smoke out of your face. When the smoke builds into a good billowing cloud, you can put it in your tipi fire and blow it into flame then, or you can do so in your hand and quickly transfer it to the fire. Once the bundle is in place, you may need to give it a few breaths to really get it going.

So, good luck, and work through the frustrations. Sometimes it is a good idea to take a break and set the bow and drill aside for a few days before going at it again.

HAND DRILL

The hand drill is a comparatively simple fire-making tool, at least in theory. Like the bow-and-drill method, it uses the same components, but they are of different dimensions. And, rather than using a bow and a handhold, your hands are used to both rotate the spindle and apply downward pressure.

A spindle has one end placed in a notched, round indentation or socket near the edge of a fireboard. The spindle is then rotated by moving one hand forward while moving the other one back and simultaneously applying downward pressure. Typically, your hands will shortly end up at the base of the spindle and must quickly be returned to the top for another run unless *floating* has been mastered (a technique I will get into later). This procedure is continued until plenty of smoke emanates from the socket and fire powder (black powder worn off of the fireboard and spindle due to friction) has filled the notch to capacity and beyond. From here, it is a matter of transferring the coal to the tinder, as described in the "Bow Drill" section of this chapter.

I remember when my friends and I discovered the hand drill. The excitement was strong and the desire to outdo one another stronger. I also remember very consciously deciding to shelve the thing when I saw the full palm and finger blisters my friends were sporting. No thank you. I figured, watch them, let them figure it out, and when they got it nailed, swoop in and copy the technique that works! Six months later, after watching, practicing in my head, moving my hands together in a somewhat circular manner, and keeping my fingerprints, I got a fire with rather little effort. The lesson here is that technique, not calluses or brute strength, is the key.

Components

For the spindle, find a straight, dry, pithy stalk or softwood stick from pencil thickness to that of a nickel and from about four to eighteen inches in length. Thinner and longer sizes tend to be easier for beginners. Experiment with soft woods and pithy plants in your area, such as:

- Goldenrod
- Burdock

- Willow
- Cattail
- Cedar
- Yucca
- Mullein

Fireboards should be made from softwood like poplar or cedar and can be made quite easily from a dry, dead branch crushed between two stones or otherwise split. To make the socket in the fireboard, stand the spindle on end near an edge and score the circumference. Then, simply split out enough of the socket to create a lip that is sufficient enough to keep the spindle in the socket (one-sixteenth inch). The socket is notched such that if it were a pie, a slice of about one-eighth would be removed. The notch is carved or abraded from the edge of the fireboard to, but not including, the center of the socket.

Making Fire

With the tip of the spindle in the socket place your hands palm to palm, sandwiching the spindle between them. The action of moving your right hand forward while moving your left hand backward, then reversing the motion, rotates the spindle. Doing that hand action while also applying downward pressure is what provides adequate friction to generate a coal. Unfortunately, this process also causes your hands to work their way down the spindle to the fireboard. At this point, you must quickly move your hands to the top of the spindle again without allowing the spindle to come out of the socket or remain still too long and cause significant cooling. Quite a trick for the beginner. A spindle of eighteen inches or so is preferable for folks who are just getting the hang of it.

Floating is a technique in which downward pressure can be applied without moving your hands down the spindle. In fact, with practice, downward pressure can be applied while you move your hands *up* the spindle.

Imagine that the spindle rises through the center of an inverted rainbow or arc. When you move one hand forward and the other backward, make sure that both hands follow the line of the arc as they move in opposite directions. This allows downward pressure to be applied while the hands retain their location on, or ride up, the rotating spindle.

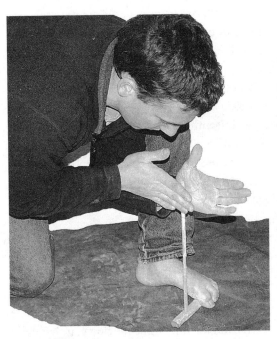
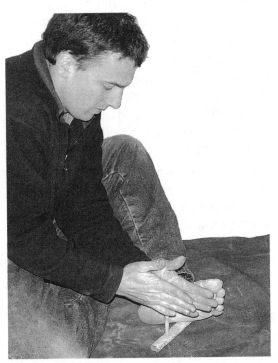

Hand drill posture

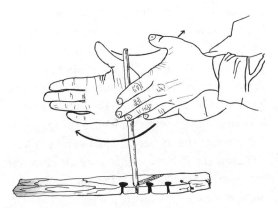
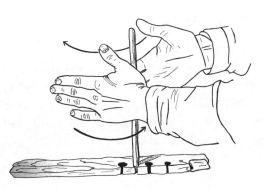

Hand drill showing floating

Hand Drill Tips

- I begin by floating until I get good smoke and have plenty of dust in the notch, because floating is less labor intensive. Then a few quick bursts down the spindle will usually generate a coal.
- The dryness of the materials has, in my experience, proven to be paramount . . . dry, dry, dry!
- Just because one mullein stalk works easily one time does not mean that all mullein stalks will be easy. Experiment with different woods, or even with different sticks of the same wood, to find what works.

FIRE SAW

While hiking in the Fijian jungle with four native guides, we stopped for lunch. One fellow jumped in the creek and pulled out a number of prawns. Two others headed off into the bush and soon returned with some kind of fruit and a couple of lengths of bamboo. The fourth man built a fire next to a cliff, expertly lighting it with a Bic. The bamboo sections were loaded up with the prawns in one and the roots in the other, water was added, and leaves were stuffed into the openings as stoppers. The cooking "pots" were then leaned against the cliff over the fire and the contents were soon steamed to perfection.

After eating, the recollection of a reference on the fire saw seeped into my mind and I walked off into the jungle in search of bamboo. In short order, I had a thirty-inch piece of dead bamboo. Bringing it back to our lunch area, I split it down the middle and, with the edge of my knife, scraped a small pile of shavings from the split edge. I placed them in the underside (formerly the inside) of one piece. Putting it flat on the ground, rounded edge up, I placed my left foot on one end and made a small hole in the top surface near the middle and directly over the bundle of shavings. With the other half held like a saw, I began sawing back and forth over the hole. I added pressure with my weak hand on the forward end of the saw piece and, within a few strokes, had smoke fairly billowing out from the point of contact. Within about twenty-five strokes I stopped, turned over

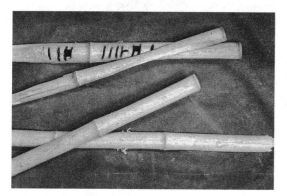

Fire saw components

the fireboard piece, and blew down its length. A flame was quick in erupting from the smoking tinder bundle.

The natives were floored. They inspected the setup, had me demonstrate again, and tried it a few times themselves. Back in the village, word quickly spread, and soon many of the inhabitants had turned out to see me perform my fire magic.

Well, that was when I began calling primitive fire-making skills *ego busters*. With the whole village watching, all I could do was get smoke. Since that day, I have worked on the fire saw and learned a few things about technique and manufacture of the tool.

By sliding a piece of bamboo (the saw) at speed over a small hole in a second piece (called the fireboard) while applying downward pressure, friction is generated, resulting in heat and the wearing off of material in dust from both pieces. This superheated dust falls through the hole onto the tinder, where it gloms together. If enough dust is generated, it will form a coal that can be blown into flame with the aid of tinder.

There are two methods to make a fire saw. We'll start with the simplest way I have found to coax a coal from bamboo.

Moving Saw Method

1. Start with a piece of standing dead bamboo (bamboo that was harvested after it had died, not harvested green and then dried), about two feet in length.
2. Split it in half lengthwise.
3. With the edge of your cutting tool, make a palm full of tinder shavings by scraping a sharp edge along the split portion of the bamboo.
4. Wedge the tinder in the middle of one piece of bamboo (the fireboard) on the inside and place it on the ground, with the tinder and split portions facing down.
5. Directly above the tinder, bore a hole into the bamboo. It does not need to go all the way through, because it is just there to give the saw a guide; however, to save energy later, it is advisable to make the hole all the way through to the tinder or to even cut a groove that is perpendicular to the length of the fireboard.
6. Grip the second half of the split bamboo (the saw) in your strong hand like you would a sword (right for righties, left for lefties), and place your weak hand on the forward end.
7. Place one split edge in or on the hole or groove that is perpendicular to the fireboard, and saw back and forth while applying downward pressure. Strokes

Fire saw position 1

should measure about eight to twelve inches. Don't worry about the cant of the saw piece in relation to the groove, as friction will quickly wear both to a perfect fit. I have seen people chase their tails carving their set and trying to get everything to fit just so, and after three strokes, none of it matters anyway. For your first time, I recommend sawing until you can't saw anymore while you are still producing plenty of smoke.

8. Put down the saw, roll the fireboard over, and when you see a wisp of smoke, gently blow down the length of the bamboo. Smoke should increase until a flame rises up.

9. Now simply put the tip of the fireboard in your prebuilt fire and push the flaming tinder bundle in with the saw.

In good conditions, this whole procedure should take less than four minutes, start to finish.

Tips for the Moving Saw Method

- Place the fireboard on a raised surface or mound to reduce the risk of bashing your knuckles.
- Drive stakes into the ground, two on each side of the fireboard, to help hold it in place.
- Use full, smooth strokes; i.e., use the maximum amount of the saw's edge as possible instead of using short, jerky strokes.
- If the ground is moist, protect the tinder with a dry leaf or stone.

Moving Fireboard Method

1. Follow steps 1 through 5 of the moving saw method, above.

2. Kneel, and brace the saw on a slant from your torso to the ground. It is advisable to place some sort of padding between your body and the bamboo, as the one is quite sharp (read Punji stake) and the other quite soft.

3. Grip the fireboard in both hands so that you can place both thumbs on the tinder, and place the groove or hole against the edge of the saw piece so that it can be slid up and down the saw.

Fire saw position 2

4. Move the fireboard vigorously up and down the saw, adding pressure and speed until plenty of smoke is generated. Continue until you tire or can no longer produce smoke.

5. Proceed to step 8 of the moving saw method, above.

FIRE PLOW

If you've ever rubbed your hands together vigorously, then you have felt the result of the friction generated between the two. The fire plow merely substitutes your hands for a more combustible material, although the energy expenditure is somewhat more significant in order to get a coal.

Traditionally a fireboard or hearth that is four to five feet long (shorter hearths work, too) is placed on the ground, and a ten-inch plow (a stick with a chisel-like tip) is rubbed vigorously back and forth in a six-inch shallow groove on said hearth. Material is worn off both the plow and the hearth as speed and pressure increase. This dust is deposited at one end of the groove, where a continuous flow of new, hot dust is added. The heat soon gets to the point where it ignites, not to a flame, but to a coal that is then added to a tinder bundle.

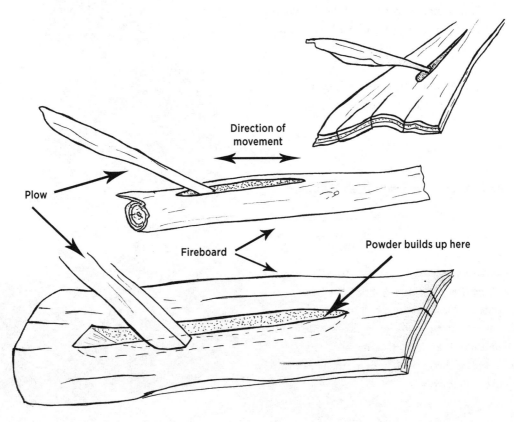

Fire plow components

To build a fire plow, harvest a straight piece of dry (or green and let it season), soft wood like Atlantic white cedar, poplar, sotol, or some wood that has been dead for some time and is getting punky, but not so soft that it just tears apart. It has been my experience that trunk wood from the unsheltered side of trees works best, although getting such a piece is a bit tricky. Second best is an unsheltered branch. The reason for this preference (only if you are not in sotol country) is that unsheltered wood grows faster and is softer than sheltered wood, and it has tighter growth rings.

The plow is a ten-inch piece of wood (I prefer the same species) that has a beveled, flat, or wedge-shaped tip about one-fourth-inch wide. A five- to nine-inch line is scraped longitudinally in the hearth with a blade, a rock, a stick, or the plow itself. The set is ready to use. The following directions apply for right-handed users; lefties should reverse the directions:

1. Sit astride the hearth and grip the plow with your left hand so that the chisel end (the tip) protrudes a couple of inches below your pinky.
2. Place your right hand in the same fashion above your left hand.
3. Slide the plow back and forth in the groove so that the whole tip is in contact with the groove. Initially, the groove and plow tip will not match up well, but after a few strokes, this will improve beyond what anyone could easily carve.

Fire plow posture

4. As you increase pressure and speed, you will notice dust building up at the far end of the groove. Not going too far with your strokes requires practice; the goal is to stop just at the pile's edge. If you go too far, you will break up the potential coal. If you don't go far enough, the hot dust generated will not add anything to the dust pile.

Fire Plow Tips

- As you plow, you wear away wood from the groove, and if you always stop the plow at the same point, you will quickly form a wall. If you miscalculate one stroke and hit the wall with the plow, you can lose your coal as the hearth is jarred or the plow jumps the wall and scatters the dust.
- Fatigue is also an issue, although the well-practiced practitioner can get a coal in less than twenty seconds. It still requires a real energy commitment and burst of determination.
- Just as with the bow and drill, analyze your work. Look at the dust you are generating. Is it small and dark? Good, keep going. Is it light in color and small? Add speed. Is it light and large? Reduce pressure and increase your speed.
- Fire hardening is an issue here, as it is with other techniques. The glossy surface of the groove can be scraped away with a knife or stone or burned through. (I suggest scraping, as it requires less energy than burning through. If you choose to burn through it, put a few grains of sand in the groove to help sand it out.)

5. Continue rubbing the plow back and forth, and as smoke builds, shift the plow so that the leading edge is all that is in contact with the groove. This increases the heat generated by the tip, as pressure is not spread out over the whole base of the tip.

6. When you see smoke rising from the dust pile, transfer the coal to a leaf or piece of bark. If the coal is small or the dust pile is looking unsteady, gently blow on it to help spread the coal prior to moving it to your tinder bundle.

LONG MATCH

Carrying fire from one camp to another is somewhat of an art form. I don't find it to be of particular value in a survival situation, because the effort involved in learning how to master the making and tending of a long match (coal carrier) is tantamount to what it takes to learn a fire-making technique. However, while you need to acquire *specific* skills for making fire, you can blunder through the long match with only a *general* idea of how it's done, although you will have varying and unpredictable results. I can imagine that there may be a situation in which a primitive fire-making technique is not known, matches or other modern fire-making devices are in short supply, and the long match could be of value.

In the long match, a less flammable or non-flammable outer shell holds a tinder bundle and a coal within it and limits the amount of air available to the coal. If the coal receives just enough oxygen to keep burning, it will slowly spread through the tinder, until, when needed, it is opened up and blown into flame to light another fire. My preferred long match looks like a giant, poorly made, hand-rolled cigarette and consists of a long core of refined tinder surrounded by a layer of rougher tinder, like lightly buffed bark or dried grasses (running lengthwise). This is then rolled or bound in raw or unrefined tinder, like bark tied with cattail.

First, collect tinder that is similar to the papery inner bark of dead trees, such as those in the poplar family, and/or dry grasses, cedar bark, basswood bark, cattail down, dead century plant, or yucca stalks. Do not refine or buff (rub it briskly between your hands so as to fray it) all of it; leave some in larger pieces so that it will take more time to burn. The outside can be made of sturdier material like bark or a container of wood, shell, clay, or the like.

Use green bark strips, cattail leaves, or other pliable material to tightly lash the bundle of fine tinder, which is surrounded by rougher tinder. The goal is to control the air that gets to the coal; too much air and the tinder burns up too fast, but with too little air, the coal goes out. When you get it just right, the coal will last for many hours. It can be a bit of a fine art, building and maintaining the long match. It requires that you pay attention to detail like the tightness of the tinder, the flow of air into the bundle, the materials that you use, and the moisture content of the materials. Practice is the best way to gain proficiency with this skill.

As you get ready to set off, drop a coal in the top of the bundle. Once the coal has caught the new material, a piece of bark, a flattened bit of clay, or some other object can be used as a damper, i.e., a tool for reducing the amount of oxygen available to the coal via the open ends. The process is not always quite as straightforward as that, though. If the bundle is too loose, you will likely

Long match

end up carrying a full-fledged fire in short order. Conversely, if the bundle is too tight, you are in danger of smothering it, although with the right tinder, it is harder to do than you might think. The bundle may require some movement to feed air to the coal; often, just carrying it in your hand and waving it gently around is enough.

Occasionally, you may have to tamp it down with a blunt stick or move unburned material over the top of the coal. This serves two purposes: it provides fuel and adds insulation; thus, it has the same effect as closing the damper on a woodstove.

Shells, clay, and wood products can act as the outer carrier or case. A case that is easily opened and closed can have material added as other material burns down, avoiding the need to stop to light a new fire and have to start the process all over before continuing.

A word of caution: Many areas have strict fire regulations. Please be considerate of them, and if you want to test out just how long your long match will burn, do it in a safe place and don't leave it unattended.

CHAPTER 9

FOOD AND DRINK

A balanced diet is composed of foods that supply enough nutrients to the body for the production of energy and heat, as well as for the growth, healing, and maintenance of cells. According to the United States Department of Agriculture (USDA), a balanced diet should include the following:

- 2–4 servings per day of fruits for vitamins A and C
- 3–5 servings per day of vegetables for fiber, vitamins A and C, and minerals
- 2–3 servings per day of meat, poultry, and fish protein for B vitamins, iron, and zinc
- 2–3 servings per day of dairy products for protein, minerals, and vitamins

Many foods that we take for granted in our everyday lives, however, do not grow locally in the wild and, if they do, may not be in season. Fruits, vegetables, and meat are available, yet milk products are not an option; therefore, these proteins, minerals, and vitamins must be acquired from other sources. Liver is a good source of iron, zinc, and vitamin A. Vitamin D, according to the National Institutes of Health, can be acquired by exposing your skin to ultraviolet rays, because they trigger vitamin D synthesis in the skin.

Carbohydrates are also important in your diet. Sustained activity or a low intake of carbohydrates can cut endurance by half in as little as one day.

Water is also vital, and even in cold, wet weather, when you may not feel thirsty, you are losing water and need to replenish it on a regular basis. According to the National Ski Patrol, a sedentary person loses 2,300 milliliters (more than half a gallon) of water daily as follows: 1,400 ml (about a third of a gallon) in urine, 800 ml (a little more than three cups) through respiration and evaporation from the skin, and 100 ml (less than half a cup) through defecation. In hot weather, water loss jumps to 3,300 ml (three-quarters of a gallon), and with sustained physical effort, it can be up to 6,600 ml (one and one-half gallons) per day.

The best keys to your hydration are the color and smell of your urine. It should be clear and odorless. If it is dark and pungent, you need to increase your water intake, not through guzzling one-half gallon at a time but through regularly taking smaller drinks.

EATING IN THE WILD

In society, we are used to sitting down to a "full" meal, whereas in the wild, snacking on available tidbits is par for the course. In summer, when food is abundant, snacking on berries, roots, and leaves reduces the craving for a meal that will leave you feeling stuffed. Often, the "meal" will be some seasoned meat in between snacks.

It is important, in times of abundance, to collect and preserve as much food as possible for three reasons. First, in the event you are injured, ill, or unsuccessful in hunting, having a supply of food can save your life. Second, the winter may be harsh and long, making the harvesting of any root crop impossible. Plants don't have much to offer during this time. Third, sometimes a thaw in the winter will rot meat, or a leak will destroy some of your preserved dry foods. Having extra supplies can see you through challenging times.

The following are a few tips for a wilderness diet, drawn from personal experience in which health was (apparently) maintained. However, because I am not a dietitian, I recommend that you seek professional guidance in developing your own wild diet.

- Eating some form of carbohydrate daily, whether it be burdock root, wild carrot, leek, Jerusalem artichoke, hog peanut, grass seed, cattail, and, of course, acorn flour, helps keep up your energy.
- Fiber from greens is also worth the effort of harvest. Lamb's-quarters and ladies' thumb are great additions to any stew or salad; they'll help keep your bowels moving, too. Burdock can be found in disturbed soil, field edges, and stream banks and beds. As a biennial, the energy of the first year goes into the root, which can be eaten raw, boiled, or fried. Young leaves can be cooked in changes of water. For a discussion of milkweed, another good choice, refer to "Vegetables" under "Meal Preparation and Cooking" later in this chapter.
- In the fall, any nuts—acorns, hickories, walnuts, butternuts, walnuts, and beechnuts—are great sources of proteins and oils. (Acorns need to be processed prior to use. See the sidebar "Acorns" for directions.)
- During the spring and summer, strawberries, raspberries, blackberries, gooseberries, blueberries, elderberries, serviceberries, grapes, and a host of other fruits are available to provide plenty of vitamins and minerals.
- Consuming meat three times a week is a great source of protein. Meat also provides more energy than plant matter, especially in the colder months when pemmican becomes more of a staple. Access to fish is good, but also make a point of eating red meat at least twice a week to augment a fish diet.
- Meat can also be easily preserved, as discussed under "Preserving Food" in this chapter. Geese, ducks, turkeys, grouse, pheasants, and doves are all fine additions to any diet. Venison, woodchucks, squirrels, and rabbits are good, tasty sources of red meat, and snapping turtles, fish, snakes, and their eggs add variety to the menu if you're not too squeamish.
- Tea should be a regular thirst quencher. Pine needle and hemlock (from the tree, not from poison hemlock or water hemlock) teas are great sources of vitamin C, an absolute must to prevent scurvy. Mints, young birch leaves, and the inner bark of black birch, pine, and sassafras are all quite tasty.

Acorns

Of the many sources of food in the wild, acorns are a real boon to those willing to process them. Oaks can be divided into two basic varieties: red (or black) oaks and white oaks. They differ in a number of ways important to acorn harvest.

- **Red Oaks,** like the scarlet oaks, begin to bear fruit at about twenty years old but don't reach their full potential until about fifty years old. Acorns take two years to mature and contain high amounts of tannins, giving the acorns a bitter taste. They generally produce a good crop every three to five years. One tree may produce a good crop while the tree next to it may be having a poor year.
- **White Oaks** can produce acorns every year, some with so little tannins that they can be eaten raw. According to the USDA Forest Service, even though white oaks can produce high numbers of acorns, good years are sporadic, occurring once every four to ten years. Sometimes a few years will pass with no crop at all. Even in good years not every tree will produce a heavy crop of acorns, so when a healthy crop is available, it should be taken advantage of. It should be noted that white oak acorns germinate quickly upon falling to the ground, thus diminishing their nutritional value.

Acorns should be harvested in the fall when they are dropping naturally. Competition for acorns can be stiff, but on a good year you should have no problem collecting more than you can deal with. If you are not against extra protein in the form of acorn weevils, you should never have any problem acquiring plenty of acorns. When found on the ground with the cap still attached, acorns are almost certain to contain weevils, as are acorns with a brown spot or a hole in them.

Preparation of acorns is needed not only to remove the tannins, but also to ensure that you don't lose your harvest to mold. Acorns should first be shelled (they are easily cracked when thumped with a stick), and then the tannins can be leached out in one of two ways:

- **Cold leaching:** The shelled acorns are left in a bag or basket in flowing water until they can be eaten raw with little or no bitterness. This can take a few days; much depends on the flow of the water and the porosity of the bag. Shelled acorns are also subject to theft by critters, so beware.
- **Hot leaching:** Acorns, crushed or whole, are boiled in changes of water until the water remains clear or only lightly colored. According to Karen Sherwood of Earthwalk Northwest, the acorns must be immersed in *already* boiling water and each successive change should be boiling prior to adding the acorns, or the tannins will be removed yet the bitterness will stay. The tea-brown water should not be thrown out. It is an antiviral and antiseptic, making it a good wash for dermatitis and, according to Dan Fisher, an effective laundry detergent, though it will lightly stain white clothes.

continued

continued

Once the tannins have been leached out the acorns need to be roasted and pulverized to a fine powder. Store in a cool, dry area.

Acorn flour lacks wheat's cohesiveness and produces a crumbly product unless cut 50/50–75/25 with another flour. Other additives are cattail pollen, bulrush, or other ground seeds, ground beechnut, walnut, and hickory nuts (nuts that need no treatment other than shelling). For porridge, a mixture of the any of the above, in any ratio, can be made by adding hot water and stirring well.

FLAVORED DRINKS

While a natural diet may increase your appreciation for fresh, untreated water, there are times when a little flavor can enhance a drink and provide a well-received treat for the taste buds. When your diet does not involve flooding your pallet with powerful flavors, chances are you will begin to notice more subtle tastes that you would otherwise miss. I often eat violets as a test to see how sensitive my pallet is. If the violet is sweet, then I am not overseasoning my food; on the other hand, if the taste of that little purple flower is bland, it's time to lay off the spices a bit. Thus it is that a little additive goes a long way in changing the flavor of a drink. Any food with flavor can be added to water, hot or cold, to make tea.

Harvesting Plants for Tea

The best time to use a plant for tea is fresh upon harvesting it. If you wish to preserve the plant for use at a later date, then it needs to be dried as soon as possible after harvesting. Many harvested plants never get used due to mold, because they are set aside upon the return to camp—all the verve of the herb seeker gone after walking, searching, and collecting. Treat the herbs as you would a dead animal. I would no more leave a bunch of mint plants out in the sun than I would a deer carcass after a hunt.

- For leafy herbs on the stalk like mint, collect them, tie them in bundles, and hang the bundles upside down in a cool, dry place. Do not dry the plants too quickly. The upper area of any shelter is usually sufficient, or, in dry climates, herbs can be hung from a line between two trees in the shade.
- For loose leaves like spring birch leaves, place them on a cloth, rock, or other dry surface. I have done this in direct sunlight and in shade with no apparent difference between the two.
- For roots, like that of the sassafras, simply keep them in a cool, dry place, or, to speed up the drying process, split the root lengthwise.
- Bark, such as that of the black or golden birch, can be stripped from the sapling or branch and left in a cool, dry place and then kept in a breathable bag in the top of your shelter.
- Fruit, like prickly pear (called "tuna"), can be sliced and dried on hot rocks in the sun after singeing off the spines. The dried disks can be left as is or pounded into smaller pieces and stored in a bag until ready for use.

Making Tea

Hot tea is made by adding boiling water to herbs that are already in a container; cover them and let them steep (stand) for about twenty minutes. The quantity of herbs used is up for debate. Some recommend using a 1:15 or 1:20 herb-to-water ratio. If a large quantity of tea is to be consumed, I have made stronger batches and simply added more water as needed. The first batch is made fast and strong, and it's all downhill from there. A cautionary note: Many herbs have medicinal qualities and compounds that can be harmful if too much is taken at any one time. See the Appendix for recommended books on edible and medicinal plants.

For cold tea, add the herbs to the water and let the solution stand overnight.

- **Sassafras** has been used for many years as a seasoning. In teas, it has long been credited with staving off illness. The bark, roots, and leaves are full of flavor and can add to that of any other tea. The root must be boiled in water to really pull out the flavor. The young leaves can be dried, ground into powder, and added to soups.
- To prepare **pine needle tea**, harvest the needles and dice them. A one-inch-diameter bundle makes about two cups. Put the needles into hot water, and simmer them until the water takes on a golden color.
- Harvest leaves from **birch** trees when they first come out in the spring. Dry them by placing them briefly in the sun or by hanging a whole branch upside down in a cool, dry place. To make tea, boil water and add the leaves. Let

them steep for about five minutes before drinking.
- **Mint**—either individual leaves or the whole plant—can be harvested and prepared in the same way.
- To prepare a tasty **bark tea**, use the inner bark from pine and black birch trees. Strip the bark from a live sapling or branch, and add either fresh or dried bark to boiling water. Let it steep for five minutes and then drink it. Both inner barks, when dry, can be pounded into flour in an emergency.

MEAL PREPARATION AND COOKING

When I was a boy and learning about wild edibles, I would fry everything I got my hands on. Traipsing about the woods with my .22, I'd shoot grouse and fry it; dig up roots and fry them; grab a squirrel and yes, fry that, too. Eventually, my mother caught me at it—something about feathers under the stove—and introduced me to some of the finer points of meal preparation. I took it to heart and took these ideas to the woods. Below are a number of ways in which food can be prepared. Bon appétit.

Vegetables

It is one thing to know that a plant is edible and another to know how best to prepare it. The edible plants in North America number in the thousands, and with many good books on the subject I have chosen ten widely available plants for their ease of use, accessibility, and nutritional value.

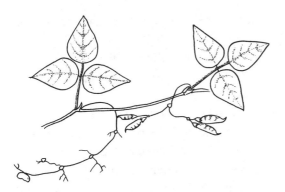

Hog peanut

Jerusalem artichoke

HOG PEANUT. The twining vines of the hog pea-nut, an annual, can be found in moist woods and rich soil. Its alternate leafs are divided into three light green, ovate leaflets, among which the white- or lilac-colored flowers can be found between July and September. Beneath the detritus of the forest floor, threadlike creepers produce petalless blos-soms that are similar in shape to a shelled peanut or bean.

Use: Harvest the hog peanut in late fall through early spring. The "peanuts" can be soaked for a few hours or overnight in water, the shell removed, and the meat boiled for about ten min-utes as an additive to any soup or porridge. If the peanuts are not soaked, the shell is harder to remove and the peanuts require more time to cook.

JERUSALEM ARTICHOKE. This rough, hairy peren-nial spreads through its roots rather than pro-ducing seeds. The mature stalk commonly stands in excess of six feet and can reach as much as ten feet. Several yellow flower heads adorn each plant. Leaves on the upper portion of the stalk are alternated, while those below are usually opposite. Large, potatolike tubers are found in among the roots. The Jerusalem artichoke is found in waste grounds or disturbed soil, in damp field edges, and along streams where sun-light is available.

Use: This perennial can be cooked like a potato or be eaten raw, dried and ground as a flour additive, or be used as a hot cereal or stew thickener.

STINGING NETTLE. This leafy herb stands, when erect, at two to six feet in height. Its square stem is nonbranching and covered with little stinging hairs. The ovate leaves are toothed and clearly veined; the underside is also covered with sting-ing hairs. It is commonly found in moist, rich soil, in field edges, and on stream banks.

Use: Young shoots can be boiled or steamed for three or four minutes and eaten like spinach.

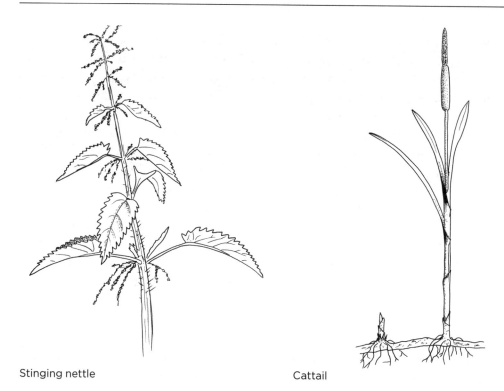

Stinging nettle

Cattail

Leaves or whole, young plants can be used to make tea (drink the water in which you cook nettles). The roots can be gathered from fall through spring and are tasty cooked like potatoes. Note: Each tiny hair on this plant has a bit of formic acid at its base. When it is introduced to your body through contact with the hair, it causes an itchy, stinging rash that some find unpleasant. If nothing else, it stimulates blood flow.

CATTAIL. The swordlike leaves of the cattail are rather stiff and erect. At the top of a nonbranching, stiff stem, clusters of tiny flowers form the familiar cylindrical female head above which the male or pollen head rises. The pollen head is gold in color when it is full of pollen but quickly turns brown and rather ragged, leaving only the spikelike top of the stem.

Use: The cattail plant is one worth becoming acquainted with, as it can provide some sort of food year-round. In the spring, the young shoots are easily broken off of the roots (some roots can be pulled to the surface with a stout stick, while others may require you to wade in). They are then peeled and can be eaten raw, steamed, or added to a soup. Young stalks less than thirty inches in length can be steamed and eaten. In the late spring, the young flower heads can be boiled or steamed and eaten. The flower heads can be tricky to spot when they are still young enough to eat, because they are still in the sheath created by the leaves; therefore, you must carefully look and feel through the cattails. If you miss the flower heads, wait until early summer for the pollen spikes that will rise golden above the flower head. The pollen can be gathered by placing a bag over the head, bending it over, and shaking it vigorously. On a windless day, an open container with high sides can also do the job. Much can be gathered in a short time in this way. Dry the pollen thoroughly before you store it or you will lose it to mold or rot. Pollen can be used as a flour additive or stew thickener. In the late summer, as the roots prepare to spread, the tips produce pointy sprouts that can be peeled and eaten raw or boiled. From fall through early spring, the roots can be pulled up, washed, and skinned. The remaining root can be squeezed, kneaded, and generally manhandled in a container of cold water. You will see clouds of white spread out into the water as the starch is released, and in short order the water will become slick and viscous as the starch concentration increases. Once the water becomes syrupy, I suggest that you start a new container, because the ability of the water to remove starch seems to decrease as it becomes supersaturated. Remove the fibers left from the roots as you proceed. I simply run my fingers through the solution, although if you happen to have a wire mesh strainer in your pocket, by all means use it! The starch will slowly settle to the bottom of the container, making it possible to pour off the water and leaving the starch on the bottom. Dry the starch on a flat rock near the fire by spreading it out. Once it is dry, it can be stored indefinitely as long as it is kept dry. The cattail starch can be used as flour or yet another stew thickener.

PRICKLY PEAR. The prickly pear is made up of jointed pads with large, easy-to-spot spines surrounded by finer tufts of hairlike fibers. The yellow flowers in bloom during spring to midsummer can be found along the edges of the upper pads. The fruits, available from midsummer to late summer and into the fall, are purple to red and

also have the large spines as well as many smaller hairs. This hardy cactus can be found in much of the United States both as an ornamental as well as in the wild. It is much more prolific in the desert Southwest.

Use: The fruit is delicious raw or cooked. The small hairs should be wiped off with a cloth or, better yet, singed off in a flame. Skinning, wiping, brushing with vegetation, and scorching are the methods I've used to deal with the small hairs. Scorching is by far the best method, but it's not always possible due to fire danger, etc. While the small hairs are not terrible, they will stick in hands and mouth alike and, when pushed, will cause minor pain until your body breaks them down. In the hands, this can take a few days; in the mouth, expect them to dissolve in about twenty-four hours. The fruit can then be cut in half and the inside turned out and eaten, much as

Prickly pear

you would eat half of a grapefruit. The seeds can be eaten, but they may cause intestinal discomfort. If you plan on eating many fruits, remove the seeds and eat only the pulp. Pulp can be spread out and dried for later use. The seeds can be dried and ground; the flour will not cause the discomfort that the raw seeds do. The pads require the same treatment, followed by skinning and roasting them whole or cutting them into strips and steaming them. While hunger is the best seasoning (next to butter and garlic), I do not find myself craving the pads as I do the fruits.

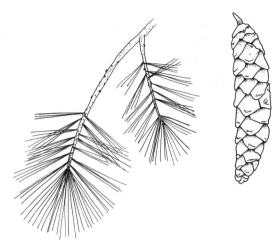

Pine

PINE. Easily identified, this evergreen has long needles, either single or in bundles of two to five. The needle bundles, in cross section, make a circle, and the individual needles make up their respective fractions of that circle (with five needle pines, each needle is a fifth of the circle). Pinecones vary from one type of pine to another. The white pine often reaches heights of 150 feet and has long, slim cones with open scales. The piñon pine is a low, shrubby pine with egg-shaped cones and closed scales.

Use: There are many listed uses for pine, some well founded and others a little more far-fetched or requiring a near-starving condition to merit any attempt at ingestion. The needles of pines are high in vitamin C, a necessary component of any diet. For tea, dice a handful of young needles found at the branch tips, and simmer them for anywhere from five to twenty minutes; then let the solution steep for fifteen minutes or more (overnight if you wish). While this tea is good, too much is not good for you. Have a cup or two every day or two if you have no other sources of vitamin C. The inner bark is often said to make a pasta substitute. I am not sure where these people get their pasta or how they cook it, but pine inner bark is nothing like pasta. While the inner bark does contain starches and sugars, among other nutrients, it does not taste good, and even when it is boiled, it is tough in the mouth as well as in the gut. If you simply must eat it, I recommend chewing it, swallowing the juices, and spitting out the rest. The pinecones contain seeds between the scales. They are edible, are high in protein and oils, and have varying tastes. All are edible, although some can be tough to remove from between the scales. In such cases, dry the cone by a fire or in the sun and the scales will open, allowing easier access to the nuts. It should be noted that the nuts of some pines are quite small and their collection can be rather tedious.

STRAWBERRY. This plant is small and low to the ground, standing up to six inches in height. Leaf stalks are long and have three large-toothed leaflets at the top. The flowers (one-half to one inch across) are white, five petaled, and symmetrical; they appear on a separate stalk in midspring with the fruit appearing about three or four weeks

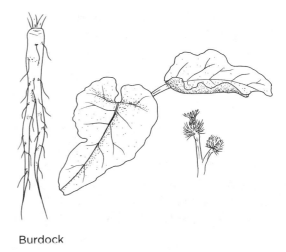

Burdock

Strawberry

later. Strawberries can be found in open meadows, along forest edges, and in other areas that are exposed to the sun.

Use: The berries can be eaten raw or mushed on a flat rock, then be left to dry either in the sun or by the fire and stored dry for future use. The leaves can be harvested and used for tea that is rich in vitamin C.

Note: Strawberries are easy to overlook, as they can grow in grasses, but once you see a plant, finding others is easy. That being said, gathering strawberries can be easy and slow but very rewarding.

BURDOCK. This plant is a large, heart-shaped, rough-leafed biennial; its leaves can be longer than two feet and wider than one foot, in its second year of growth. The undersides of the basal leaves are covered with wooly fuzz, and the branching stalk can exceed six feet in height. Many thistlelike, green burrs or (flowers) with lavender centers can be found at the branch ends.

The first-year plant forms a rosette of large (up to one foot), heart-shaped leaves with no stalk. The lower stems are often somewhat purplish and fade to green as they get closer to the leaf. Burdock is found in waste ground, along riverbeds, in fields, and in meadows.

Use: The first-year taproot is long and generally slender, light brown, and tasty raw, boiled, or steamed. The use of a digging stick eases the harvest of these roots. Note: the roots of second-year plants are quite large but very woody and, in my experience, not worth harvesting.

The young leaves and stems can be steamed or boiled; older leaves tend to be very bitter and require boiling in at least two changes of water.

LAMB'S-QUARTERS. This is an herbaceous, widely branching, erect plant that has a slightly grooved stem with reddish shading near the base of the leaf stem. The underside of the diamond-shaped leaves has a powdered white appearance, while the tops are a soft green. The flowers appear in dense clusters on spikes and are small and round.

Lamb's-quarters

Bullrushes

They become tinged with red as they mature and eventually turn more brown in the fall.

Use: The young plants and new leaves on older plants can be eaten raw or boiled with older leaves for ten to fifteen minutes. The flowers can be eaten raw or boiled, or you can let them mature and harvest them in the fall. Winnowing is a good idea unless you crave fiber. The ground seeds can be used as a flour additive or, better yet, as porridge. The hulls, if left on, will give the porridge a consistency that takes either hunger or some getting used to. They are not bad for you, but those who have a discerning palate may be challenged.

BULLRUSHES. This plant has a smooth stem and is round or triangular, pithy, and dark to light green in color. It stands from two to nine feet in height. Leaves are absent, although the sheath tips can extend away from the stem as much as eight inches. Flowers are found at the end of the stems in clusters of brown spikelets that are one-half to one inch in length. Roots are horizontal, scaly, and stout.

Use: Lower stalks and young shoots make a juicy trailside, thirst-quenching snack. From the fall through the spring, the root stock can be harvested, crushed, and dried, and the fibers can be removed. The remaining dry-root material can be ground for flour or cooked with water as a porridge. Bullrushes have many seeds, and the husk must be separated from the actual seeds. If you are hungry or picky, you may not want to separate out the seeds. I have eaten quantities of seeds in porridge, both winnowed (seed hulls removed) and unprocessed. The latter was definitely better, but either way works.

All plants should be positively identified before you consume them. Use a field guide, or ask an herbalist to be sure that you are collecting safe plants.

Other uses for wild plant items include the following:

- Wild carrot or Queen Anne's lace can be eaten raw, added to soup or salad, or roasted.
- Burdock root can be prepared like wild carrot.
- Bullrush seeds can be cooked in water as porridge. Add honey and/or berries if any are attainable. Begin by rock-boiling water (see below); add the seeds and stir.
- Wild garlic, leeks, chives, garlic mustard, hog peanuts, and Jerusalem artichokes can be added to meals as flavor enhancers, nibbled raw as a snack, or cooked.
- Milkweed pods can be harvested before they open and rock-boiled. Put enough water in two containers so that each can easily accommodate the rocks, and allow the pods to submerge. Rock-boil one container, and then add the pods. As the water turns murky, add hot rocks to a second container. Only when this is boiling, move the pods to the clean, hot water. Then, dump the contents of the first container and refill it with clean water. Add rocks and boil yet again. Add pods to this third change of hot water, and after three minutes, remove them and eat them. Note: Do not remove the pods from hot water and place them in cold water, as this can inhibit the leaching out

of the sap. Hastily cooked pods will lead to nausea.

Meats

For fresh meat, the easiest and juiciest way to prepare it is merely to toss a chunk into the fire. The outside will burn and seal in the moisture, allowing the meat to steam in its own juices. After it has cooked for a bit (the larger the piece, the longer the cooking time; you need to experiment), pull it out with some tongs (see Chapter 16) and break it open. It should be pink, not red. If it is still red, toss it back for a bit. The downside to this method is that some meat is lost when the outside burns.

Woodchuck is best eaten freshly roasted because its fat and flesh are marbled. This means that the fat does not just sit in one layer next to the hide; instead, it can be found throughout the meat, like in bacon. In woodchuck jerky, greasy spots can be clearly seen, and the threat of the fat becoming rancid and giving the meat a bad taste is a real one. Because the fat melts at a lower temperature than venison fat, this animal is great for roasting.

Geese, ducks, turkey, and grouse are all fantastic roasting birds. The fat dribbles down the roasting stick into the fire, creating awesome smells and a juicy meal to die for. If you don't like liver as a rule, try roasted goose liver; it can't be topped.

Venison fat melts at a very high temperature and therefore does not provide the natural basting action of other meats like goose or pork. Therefore, if you are making kabobs or other roasts, cook them to medium rare so that some of the juices are retained. Venison makes good, long-lasting jerky (see "Drying Meat" under "Preserving Food," later in this chapter).

Snapping turtles should *not* be cooked in their own shell. You will only burn the meat. Instead, cut the meat out and roast or jerk it. Roasting with herbs or jerking suit this meat well. Prepare it as you would prepare venison.

Fish

With a sharp rock or knife, cut from the rectum along the belly to just below the gills. Remove the guts and rinse out the cavity.

Trout up to about eleven inches can be stuffed with herbs or herb paste and steamed. (Garlic mustard leaves, mustard seeds, chives, and leeks are a few herbs that can be ground into a paste either together or separately.) Lacerations on the outside of the fish can also be smeared with seasoning before you wrap the fish in wild grape leaves. Place the fish in the ashes *near* the coals. White ash, not actual coals, should cover the entire fish. If you don't want to turn the fish to cook both sides, then coals can be raked in a circle around the ash-covered fish; this will ensure even cooking. An eight-inch trout should take about four to six minutes to cook (overcooking is better than undercooking). Carefully remove the trout. The grape leaves should be dry on the outside and stuck together. Blow off any loose ash and remove the leaves. If the back fin pulls out with ease, the fish is cooked, steamed in its own juices and those of the herbs.

Wrapping a fish in clay also works well, and you can use raw, unpurified clay. Learning how long to leave the fish in the clay, or how long to put the clay in the fire, is the trick, but there is one break you get using this method: the fish is sealed in, and it would take a number of hours for it to dry out.

Large trout (greater than eleven inches) are better roasted with a stick jammed through the mouth and stuck deep into the tail. Start with the back (spine) down, as this is the thickest part. Then cook either side and finish with a quick heat underneath.

Cooking trout on sticks to perfection requires some practice. If you cook the fish too long on one side, it will spin on the cooking stick and may end up in the fire. If you think that a side is done, try to remove a fin. If it pulls out cleanly with the internal bone still attached, that side is done.

Once the trout is roasted, place it on a slab of bark, remove the fins and head (eat the cheeks), and gently separate the two sides of the fish by cutting the skin along the spine and pulling the head of the spine up and away from the lower side. Fingers or a stick may be required to help separate the fillet from the ribs and spine. This should give you one boneless fillet. Now, simply pull the spine away from the remaining side. Garlic mustard leaves are then used in lieu of a utensil. Not only does this give you the illusion that your hands will not get greasy—it also adds a fantastic flavor to the trout.

PIT COOKING

The pit cooking method has a number of variations, yet the one described here is my favorite. It is great for cooking large game or big meals. I often cook a few geese or turkeys, as well as some fish and corn, in one cooking.

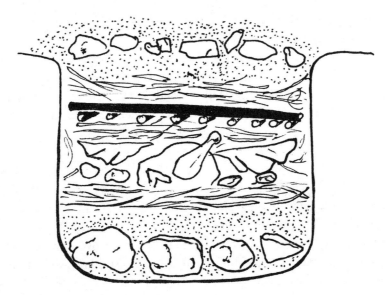

Pit cooking setup

Hot rocks on the bottom of the pit heat the soil and grasses above, creating steam, which then surrounds the food and cooks it evenly. The rocks above also generate heat, ensuring that the tops of the bigger food items get cooked as well. The soil prevents the grasses from burning and dropping the food directly on the hot rocks. The basket makes it easier to remove the middle layer of soil without getting your food dirty.

Preparing the Pit

The pit should be two feet deep or more and wide enough to accommodate everything you plan on cooking in a single layer without any items touching each other. Keep the soil in a pile close by, and pull out any rocks that are larger than grapefruit size.

1. Collect rocks the size of cantaloupes, enough to cover the bottom of the pit two

and a half times. Keep in mind that you will need to move these rocks when they are red hot; therefore, only heat rocks that you have the means to move.

2. Harvest enough long grasses for two four-inch layers in the pit.

3. Create a safe place for a large fire near the pit (ten to fifteen feet away), and gather plenty of wood to keep the fire going for a minimum of two hours.

4. Harvest burdock or other large leaves for covering the meat.

5. Find a forked stick, or two long, stout sticks, to transfer hot rocks to the pit.

6. (Optional) Collect some saplings that are one to two inches in diameter, and lash them together to make a grid or basket that will just fit inside the pit.

7. Start a tipi fire, add the rocks to it, and put more wood on top of the rocks before you move well away. I often use rocks directly

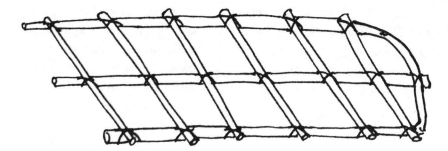

Pit grid

from streams and have never yet had one explode, and I hope I never do. But to be safe, I move off to where I can still keep an eye on the fire to make sure that it does not spread yet be out of harm's way if a rock does explode. (The beauty of the tipi fire is the fact that it does not need to be tinkered with.) After an hour, you can safely approach the fire again.

Packing and Unpacking the Pit

After about two hours, the rocks should be red hot and ready to be moved into the pit.

Moving hot rocks is dangerous. One method is to carry them with a forked stick, and another is to drag them on a piece of bark. Either way, pay attention and watch out for hot pieces of broken rock between the fire and the pit, and wear shoes.

Put one layer of hot rocks in the pit. It is OK if coals or ash get in there, too.

1. Cover the rocks with about three or four inches of soil.
2. Add a four-inch layer of green grass.
3. Place all items to be cooked on the grasses, being careful that none are touching, as this can hinder the cooking process. The

larger the item, the bigger the margin around it needs to be.
4. Cover items with burdock or other large leaves and then with about two inches of grass.
5. Place the basket (optional) on top of the grass, and add an additional few inches of grass inside the basket.
6. Add another four-inch layer of soil.
7. Add another layer of rocks.
8. Finally, add another layer of soil.

Be careful not to pack or compress any of the layers in the pit, because this results in poor transmission of heat and convection of steam.

A fifteen-pound bird takes about two and a half hours to cook, but it does not hurt to let it cook longer. Due to all of the steam, this is one bird that won't dry out. When it's time to open the pit:

1. Carefully remove the soil and hot rocks.
2. If you used a grid or basket, remove it along with any remaining soil. If you didn't use a grid or basket, carefully remove as much soil as possible by hand.
3. The grasses are, with luck, very green due to their recent steaming. If not, the food

needs to be cooked longer. Remove the hot grasses carefully, exposing the burdock-covered food.

4. Remove the food from the pit with the leaves still on, and place it on whatever your eating surface may be.

ROCK BOILING

Rock boiling is a technique whereby rocks heated in a fire are used to cook or purify liquids such as soup or water. You will need the following items:

- Waterproof container, such as one made from stone or bark (see Chapter 17)
- Eight egg-sized stones (per half gallon of liquid)
- A pair of tongs (see Chapter 16)
- A good fire

The steps to rock boiling are as follows:

1. Collect your rocks. If they have been gathered in a water-rich area, such as a creek bed or lakeshore, heat them slowly and/or keep out of the fire area to avoid injury due to exploding rocks. Some rocks have small cracks, invisible to the human eye, that, over time, allow water to enter. When these rocks are heated, the water in the stone turns to steam and leaves through the crack by which it entered or expands faster than the crack can accommodate and breaks the rock. Often, the rock simply falls apart, because there is not enough room within the stone to allow pressure to build up. However, sometimes there is

room and the pressure builds to such a level that the rock explodes with potentially deadly force. Quartz rocks are known for exploding because of the many cavities found within them where steam pressure can build.

2. Place the rocks in a hardwood fire, leaving a few inches between each rock to allow for better heating.

3. Fill the container one-half full of water or soup, and wait for the rocks to heat; it will take about forty-five minutes for the rocks to become glowing hot.

4. Remove the rocks from the fire with tongs, and carefully blow the ash from both. Slowly lower the rocks into the liquid, and keep adding rocks until a boil is achieved. One-half gallon of water requires three to five egg-sized rocks and about thirty seconds to achieve a boil. To maintain a boil, periodically remove stones and add additional hot rocks.

STORING FOOD

Any number of animals, from ants to grizzly bears, may try to take advantage of your food-gathering efforts. One way to protect your stores is to toss a line over a high branch, tie a food satchel to it, and haul it aloft. As long as the satchel is high enough without being too close to the branch above it, or to the tree trunk, it should be out of reach of most critters.

Another way to keep food safe is by keeping it in a storage pit. Dry areas are best for long-term storage, but any soil type will work for short-term storage.

Storage pit and lid

One type of pit can be made by digging a hole in the ground about two feet deep, two feet wide, and as long as necessary. Four inches from the top of the hole, widen the pit all the way around by four inches to create a "shelf." Line the pit up to the bottom of the shelf with stone, and pack the seams with a raw clay or a mud and grass mixture. Make a small fire inside to drive out any moisture.

For the lid, cut sapling trunks that are the width of the hole plus eight inches for the shelf on each side. Lash the trunks together until you have a lid that can be rested on the shelf over the hole.

For handles, a piece of sapling with two branches growing out of it can be lashed to two opposing corners of the lid. Paste over the lid with the grass and mud mixture in a few one-inch-

thick coats. Let it dry between each coat to avoid cracking. Cover the last coat with leaves while the mixture is still wet, as this aids in camouflaging the cache and adds a little rain protection.

Dried grasses or leaves should be placed in the pit and the food nested within. Adding dried aromatic plants to the pit, like sweet fern or mint, can help mask any lingering food scents. Once food is inside the bin, the top can be laid in place and sealed with more clay or mud for an extended absence, or it can be covered with more leaves if the food will be used every day. Pieces of bark with leaves piled on top can be placed over the lid as added protection against the weather.

PRESERVING FOOD

Hunting and food gathering are necessary components of wilderness living but should not consume all of your time. As seasons change, various edibles come and go. With this in mind, you should gather food beyond your immediate needs when opportunities present themselves and preserve it for future use.

Berries

In much of North America, many fruits can be found from June through the early frosts of the fall. Some of them are raspberries, blackberries, huckleberries, elderberries, mulberries, apples, pears, prickly pears, blueberries, persimmons, and many others. Most can be harvested in a straightforward way, sliced or mashed out flat, and dried for later use. Others require a more specialized harvest and preparation.

Prickly pears, for example, offer up their pads the best when they are young in the spring. Their fruit comes in August and September, with some still available in October. Their spines and small, hairlike stickers deter the overzealous harvester and provide sharp reminders to be careful. I regularly have run-ins with the hairy stickers while eagerly trying to shove the delicious fruit down my throat. The stickers are not terrible. They are irksome at first, but in the mouth, they offer little pricks for about twenty-four hours or less. In your hands, they last for a few days. Harvest the pads and fruit by impaling them with a sharp stick and pulling or cutting them free of the plant. Then pass them through the flames of a fire to burn off the spines and stickers. Once the pads are free of deterrents, they can be sliced and dried.

Saguaro and mesquite also offer tasty foods, although work is required to obtain the nutrients. I have used saguaro ribs to knock the fruit off of the plants, after which I cut them open and scooped out the red insides—some of which I ate while I dried the rest. The many little seeds can be dried and eaten or ground into a paste or flourlike substance and added to cereals. Mesquite requires yet more work. You can harvest the pods directly from the tree and then lay them out to dry; this is followed by shelling and pounding or grinding the pods into flour.

In order to capitalize on the abundance of crops in your area, it is wise to prepare ahead of time. For succulent fruits like berries, I have gotten rock slabs and pecked grooves in some of them to channel the juice of the mashed fruit to a container below. I also wound cordage around other rocks in the place of grooves to prevent the fruit mush from sliding down. With the cordage and a hot fire, the juice quickly thickened and dried with the mush, adding to the amount of fin-

ished product. I smeared the crushed berries into a jamlike consistency on drying rocks, then spread the berry paste evenly over the rocks. I then propped up the rocks at a steep angle facing a bed of coals in the fire pit.

It is important that you not cook or burn the mush, only dry it. A good gauge is to watch the drippings; if they start smoking, pull the rock back carefully. Keep monitoring the berry mush until the steam coming off of it is greatly reduced. Then set the rock aside to cool. It will take some trial and error until you get it just right. For apples and other more cohesive fruit that can stay intact through slicing, the racks described below for drying meat work well.

If you leave the mashed berries near the heat for a shorter period of time, you will end up with sticky fruit leather, whereas a longer exposure will result in fruit chips (easily reconstituted with water). The chips will last indefinitely *if* they are kept dry—a tall order in humid conditions. A good idea is to store them in a well-dried-out, pine bark box in the rafters of your shelter or in a protected location where the heat of your fire will regularly dry the air around them.

Drying Meat

The meat that we eat nowadays is so full of spices, preservatives, and foreign flavors that few people can really differentiate between venison and beef. This is not to suggest that all meat prepared in the wild must be eaten with no spices, but merely that the true flavor should not be drowned out, only enhanced. Contrary to popular belief, all meat does not taste like chicken, and each has its own unique qualities and flavors.

Without the aid of cold weather to preserve meat, utilizing an entire deer carcass before it begins to rot requires a great many mouths, a large appetite, or another way of preserving it, such as drying. Survival has traditionally been a group effort, with each person specializing in a few skill areas. This made for easier utilization of a large animal carcass and therefore was not as daunting of a task as it was for an individual.

Drying the meat of an entire deer carcass is not difficult, but it is time consuming, and in warm weather you must tend the meat and fire continually. The first time I dried the meat of a deer, it took two and a half days. My weather-forecasting skills (or lack thereof) detected rain only once it started falling; thus, a big, sustained fire was needed to keep the meat from spoiling.

There are a few important points to keep in mind when drying meat.

- The goal is to *dry* the meat in a number of hours, not cook it. Cooked meat will spoil, and bad meat will make you sick.
- Flies must be kept away from the meat, and the meat must be kept clean prior to drying. It is a good idea to have a fire next to your work area to help keep flies away. A fresh piece of meat dropped on the ground will have all manner of things stuck to it, both visible and microscopic. I use the animal's hide as a work surface for the meat as I prepare it for the rack.
- Wide crossbars on the rack will prevent speedy drying of the meat that is in contact with the wood and will require the need for regular shifting to expose its entirety to warm, dry air.

Drying racks are simple affairs. Build one even before you begin to hunt. Large animals may require more than one rack.

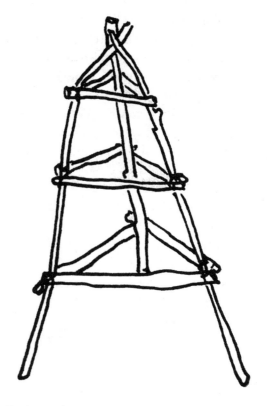

Drying rack

Larger constructions have a main skeleton of heavier sticks for support (one to two inches in diameter) and thinner cross sticks on which to hang the meat. Smaller racks can be built entirely out of thin sticks (one-half inch in diameter). Make your rack freestanding and sturdy enough to be moved when it is loaded with meat.

Let's assume that the animal has already been skinned and gutted and is either hanging from a tree or lying on the green hide (see "Carcass Care" in Chapter 13). In addition to your drying rack and a fire, you'll need a cutting board. A piece of pine bark, inner side up, works well. (See "Bark Containers" under "Cooking Containers" in Chapter 17 for details on working with bark.)

1. Meat is muscle and is divided into easily definable pieces that are separated by a thin membrane. Remove the fat and separate the muscle groups in the hindquarters.

2. Work your way up the carcass toward the head. Some parts, like the ribs, may be put directly on the fire for immediate consumption.

3. Set aside a choice bit like the tenderloins or a piece of the back strap; the rest is for jerky.

4. Looking at the meat, you will notice that it has a "grain" formed of parallel muscle strands. Tough jerky is cut along the grain (the same direction as the muscle fiber), and soft jerky is cut across the grain. I like it either way. The meat is sliced into one-eighth-inch-thick pieces and as long and wide as is manageable.

5. If you've harvested some spices, now is a good time to rub them into the meat. Garlic mustard, wild leeks, wild garlic, chives, and other mustards are some of my favorites. Look in a field guide to find out what is in season, and make sure that you are 100 percent positive of the plant's identity and edibility.

6. Place the pieces of meat on the rack close together but not touching.

The grain on meat

Once the drying process starts, you need to keep at it until the meat is dry. For small quantities of meat, I'll place the rack on the leeward side of the fire so that the breeze blows warm, dry air over it. If it is windy, you can create a windbreak with stacked wood, hide, cloth, or stone, or, better yet, you can find a more sheltered area in which to work. At no time should the meat be hot to the touch. You should be able to place your hand anywhere over the rack and keep it there indefinitely, but you should also be able to feel the constant warmth of the fire. When it is done, the jerky should be dry enough to crack when you bend it, but it shouldn't be brittle. Nor should it be greasy or shiny. Shininess often indicates fat in the meat, which must be removed in order to prevent the meat from becoming rancid.

Pemmican

Pemmican is a mixture of rendered fat, jerky, and dried berries. Because fat is flammable, a great way to render it in a primitive situation is to rock-boil water and add chunks of venison fat to it. It takes a lot of hot rocks, but the end results are great. Another method that works well is to use your pecked berry-drying rock on which to place chunks of fat to heat, then you simply let the fat run off. This is finicky work, as you don't want the fat to burn, just melt. And, unlike pork fat, venison fat has a high melting point; woodchuck, waterfowl, and other animal fats have lower melting points. The trade-off is that pemmican from venison fat will not melt and leak as easily when it warms up. I have had a hunk of venison pemmican with dried raspberries in my hunting jacket pocket for more than a year now and nibble on it now and then; it tastes the same as the day I made it.

When the fat chunks have been greatly reduced or have disappeared altogether, any chunks floating on top should be removed, along with any impurities that you can see. Let the water cool. When the fat is cool, it will congeal and float, and you can lift it off the water. You can grind up jerky and dried fruit between two stones or pulverize them with a stick, then add them to the fat.

As long as it is kept dry, pemmican will last indefinitely. I have had some get wet, and the waterproofing that the fat provides does a good job. The berries and meat exposed to water will get nasty, though, so do try to keep the pemmican dry.

CHAPTER 10

FISHING

Wading upstream in a long, shallow pool, I continue to probe under the banks with my hands. The water is like ice, and it doesn't help that I'm in the shadow of the streamside trees, sheltered from the warm touch of the sun. At one point, I force my goose-bump-covered body beneath the surface to reach farther back under the bank. Aha! The unmistakable, smooth side of a fish brushes my fingertips and moves even farther back beneath the bank. I am no longer cold—the fish has my attention—and I consciously calm the excitement within me; it is as if the water embraces me.

Lying in a shallow pool, my nose, one eye, and a quarter of my mouth are all that are exposed to air. My fingers, swaying like grass in the current, slowly move upstream, searching. There! A trout, and a big one, too! I've found the alpha trout of this pool, hiding about three feet back under the bank. I can't see it, but I can taste it. I dance my fingers gently along its lower side, envisioning how the fish is sitting in its hiding place.

I'm going to need two hands! My right hand locates the gills, thumb gently caressing one side and middle finger stroking the other, while my left hand cups underneath, about six inches from the trout's tail. I am relaxed and do not rush.

Then, I jam my thumb and middle finger together through the gills, and at the same time, I clamp the tail. I've got the fish! Slowly, I emerge from beneath the bank and marvel at this magnificent trout measuring eighteen inches in length. If it were not for my hunger, I would surely return this beautiful creature to its waters.

As it was, he cooked up quite nicely. I am still grateful.

WHAT METHOD?

The flow and characteristics of the water are what dictate whether you should hunt with a spear or with your hands. In pools that have little or no cover for fish, a spear is preferable, whereas in moving water and in pools that have cover (overhanging banks, big rocks, clumps of grass, root systems), hand fishing may work the best. Trying to dislodge your spear from a tangle of roots while trout are nibbling your toes is a humbling experience not easily forgotten. In still water, especially with lots of plant life on or near the surface, a hook and line can yield the best results. (See the section on hook-and-line fishing later in this chapter.)

I really enjoy both hand fishing and spearfishing in pools, where the varying challenges are consistently rewarding. Pools without vegetation or hiding spots tend to house skittish trout. Without vegetation, fish do not become accustomed to being touched, and without hiding spots, they will swim laps around you. It's almost impossible to hunt with hands in these situations, and a spear is the right approach. Or, you can create hiding spots, then use your hands. Stack rocks to form niches, or add logs and brush where the fish will feel safe. Then, check these spots in about a week.

HAND FISHING

Over the years, I have found only literary tidbits on hand fishing. Some writers tell about slowly mesmerizing the fish by stroking its belly. Others suggest placing your hands below a trout and quickly flipping it onto shore. One source even suggests using your hands to make a false cave entrance to lure the trout. Once the fish is in your hands, you're supposed to simply grab the trout. Maybe these techniques really work, but I still haven't caught a trout using them. What follows are some of the fish-hunting techniques I have used and taught with great success in streams and shallow rivers. The smallest seasonal streams can have a variety of fish in them, especially if their source is a swamp or lake. Some fish, like trout, are easier to catch than others, and I prefer them due to their taste, their lack of pointy spines on which to injure your hand, and the fact that they find nooks and crannies in which to hide thus making them easier to catch. Some streams offer few hiding spots or, for other reasons unknown to me, are home to trout so skittish that catching

them in the manner described below is very hard if not impossible. Other streams are so well suited to this method that it is possible to fill your kreel in minutes.

Finding Fish

I do well hand fishing in shallow streams and rivers that have pools of varying size, depth, and flow. Even ankle-deep streams with intermittent pools can hold massive trout. I recommend moving upstream for two reasons. First, any sediment that you stir up will not cloud your fishing area, and second, trout tend to face into the current—they are hard enough to stalk without moving directly in their field of vision.

As water moves over the riverbed, areas of both swift and still water are created. Even within white-water rapids there are pockets of still water. It is in these pockets, usually underneath or on the downstream side of rocks or other objects, that trout wait for food to swirl in on the current. Many times I have given a quick jab with my hand into an *unlikely* spot, only to have a trout go streaking off. To avoid this, move your hands with the same characteristics of the water in which they are immersed. Just because the surface may be roiling white-water does not mean that the conditions a foot below are the same. Check under and around rocks that might hide a trout. Even at the base of waterfalls, big or small, you will often find calm water; check these areas for trout. Feel with your hands along the edges of rapids, because it is not always apparent where or how far the river has cut into the bank. In long, still, shallow pools, make sure to check under large rocks, under banks, and in sedge clumps, using your hands to "look" for holes leading into cavities that may house trout.

The foundations of bridges are often scoured out, creating perfect trout traps. Floods also create ideal trout-hunting grounds—some better for the hunter, and some better for the trout. The root systems of downed trees, trees along banks, and trees transported by floods create a myriad of hiding spots, some of which may be inaccessible to the hunter. Certain situations require exploring hideouts and catching trout while you are completely submerged, which isn't as tough as it sounds once you get some practice.

In my experience, the biggest trout in a given pool use two hiding spots. They are also the most relaxed of all the fish in the pool, because they are at the top of the pecking order. Thus, the larger the trout, often the easier they are to catch. They are used to smaller fish wriggling up against them in tight quarters. I found a hole in a shale riverbank that led to a small cavern about two feet long and one foot wide. There were so many trout in there that they left no room for the water! So, spook the trout and see the available sizes and where they are hiding.

Be persistent. I remember a pool with a five-foot, submerged rock face. After several frustrating visits to the pool, where the fish just disappeared, I finally found a small hole that led into a cavity. It was jammed with fish and made for easy fishing! Explore every possibility and refuse to become trapped into thinking that you know where trout will and will not be. I am continually surprised.

It is important to learn about the various hazards in your hunting area, such as pollution, snakes, and snapping turtles. I've grabbed many northern snappers by the head underwater with no ill effects, but the alligators and alligator snappers of the South would be another story entirely. In pools that are four feet and deeper, keep a wary eye out for beavers. They do not seem to mind underwater visitors as long as you do not corner them or appear threatening.

Technique

Probably 85 percent of the time, you will not be able to see the trout you are trying to catch. This means that your fingers must become your eyes under the water. When you reach under a riverbank "looking" for trout, keep your fingers limp like seaweed. Let them flow as if with the current, exploring every possible hiding spot. Most trout are used to having bits of grass and other debris touch them as it floats past. They are not, however, used to being goosed.

I once reached under a bank for a trout only to find a twelve-pound snapping turtle; it was quite tasty. I've found snakes that way, too—kind of chewy and tasteless, although their eggs were delicious when poached. Once you've felt a trout, you'll never mistake anything else for one. Be careful and count all of your fingers after each trip.

Let's stick with trout. Once you come in contact with a fish, *stay relaxed*! Slowly and gently feel along its body to locate its head and determine its size. Don't take anything too small, although too small depends upon how hungry you are. Small fry are not bad when toasted, and you can eat them, heads and all.

If the fish is fourteen inches or bigger, use two hands when you are fishing. Cup both hands under the fish, keeping one hand near the little fins just in front of the tail. Use the thumb and middle finger of your other hand to locate the gills. Do not apply pressure yet. But when you do, you must be fast and severe. Drive your thumb and middle finger into each other *through* the gills while gripping the tail with your other hand. If the fish is in a cavity, you can pin the trout against the wall or roof without touching the gills. Do this if you do not have access to the gills or mouth. Once you have grabbed the fish in this manner, it will struggle once and then relax. At this point, you can also relax, but only slightly. Once again, the fish will struggle, after which you can pull it out with minimal fuss. Make sure that you have a good hold on the trout before you remove it from the water.

Some places where trout hide may not allow you access to both gills, in which case you might use one gill and the mouth instead. Be careful, though, because large trout have teeth that can puncture even a callused hand. The pain is really not that bad—just a pinprick—but if you cannot handle that, you don't deserve the trout.

Grabbing the fish through the gills damages it permanently, and if the fish is returned to the water, it will die. If you want to practice catch and release, here is a way to catch fish without causing any immediate harm. Place your hand under the fish as usual, except this time, have the fish lie diagonally across your palm so that its head comes between your middle and index fingers and the tail just touches your wrist. By squeezing your fingers together and simultaneously making a fist, you can effectively immobilize the fish. Be careful not to squeeze hard. Return the fish to the stream gently, holding it in its normal attitude (facing into the current, right side up) until it regains its equilibrium and swims off on its own.

Trout hunting by hand is tremendous fun and very rewarding. It's a great way to see familiar land from a new perspective and provides you with a fantastic meal using simple tools. Remember, though, that you are taking a life. It is important to give thanks and maintain proper respect. Check with your local Department of Fish and Game regarding the legality of this activity in your area, and avoid overfishing areas. We all want to continue fishing trout well into the future.

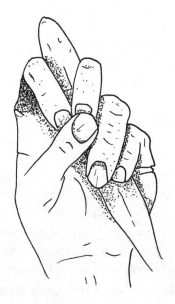

Handgripping a small trout

SPEARFISHING

Spears are simple to make and easy to use. The following design is for pinning, not puncturing, the fish.

1. Find a straight sapling that is eight to twelve feet long and no thicker than one and one-half inches at the base.
2. Sharpen the thick end to a point after cutting off all of the limbs. Leaving the bark on is a good idea, because it aids in camouflaging the spear.

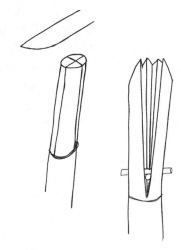

Spear making

3. About nine inches down the shaft from the point, tightly wrap some cordage, wet rawhide, or other string, and tie it off.

4. With a sturdy knife, create a split from the tip to the tied-off string. The string will keep the split from running too far down the shaft; therefore, it must always be left in place.

5. Now, make a second split perpendicular to the first one. This gives you four sections at the tip of your spear. Sharpen each one.

6. Jam a twig into each of the two splits, splaying the tips apart. These twigs can be tied in place or held in by friction. I use the friction method, because it allows for a quick change of twig. If the twigs are too big for the fish I am hunting, I can put smaller ones in, thus reducing the splay of the prongs. Another option is to put a larger twig in one slot and a smaller one in the other, providing you with two size options.

When you spot a fish along the bottom, approach it from behind to avoid spooking it. Bring the spear directly over it (vertical is nice but not imperative) so that two of the four points straddle the "neck" just behind the gills. The other two points of the spear lie farther back. The splay of the points should be such that, when the spear is jabbed downward, the body of the fish forces the points farther apart. After a successful thrust, you can reach down and recover the trout, or, with a sharp, quick twist of the spear, you can break the trout's neck.

Using the spear is rather self-explanatory, although there are some definite no-nos. The tip of the spear must be practically touching the fish if you hope to be successful, so don't strike prematurely from too far away. The most common mistake occurs during the "windup"—there shouldn't be one. When you are in position and ready for the final jab, do not pull the spear away from the fish. The fish is *not* behind you. To avoid this impulse, lean forward until you start to tip, and use that momentum to add force and speed to the thrust. Because the spear tip is already in the water, refraction is not an issue—you can clearly see the spear tip in relation to the fish. (If you are shooting fish with a bow and arrow, however, you will need to aim low to account for refraction. How low depends upon the lateral distance from yourself to the fish; the greater the distance, the lower the aiming point.)

Sharp spears for puncturing fish work well in situations that allow for side shots (see Chapter 12). The side of a fish presents a larger target, and it is far softer than the dorsal (back) area. In addition, a missed strike from the side is less likely to break or dull stone, bone, or wood spear tips.

The spear is adaptable, so use your intelligence and apply it as needed. For example, Mark

Elbroch and I came across a hole in a stream bank a few feet above the water. I crawled in and found a glasslike pool. It was connected to the river below the waterline, diffusing and giving a bluish cast to the light. Suspended in the water hung two beautiful trout. We tried unsuccessfully for awhile to catch one. I used my hands from inside the cave, and Mark used a spear from the outside. We switched back and forth, getting hungrier and colder with each attempt, both wanting to be the one to catch supper and neither wanting to be the one to call it quits. The problem in the cave was that the trout were too skittish and the area too confined. Outside the cave, we only got occasional glimpses of the trout before they moved too far back into the cave for us to see.

In the end, Mark stood in the river outside the cave with the spear tip just inside the cave by way of the underwater entry, while I was lying in the cave, giving him instructions on what direction and how far to move the spear. When he had the spear positioned near the trout, I gave him the word. The water clouded with his lunge, and I couldn't see a thing. Slowly and carefully, I moved my hand through the water, found the spear shaft, and moved down it to the tip. Gravel!?! Mark had jabbed so hard that he'd sunk that trout a couple of inches into the gravel. I managed to dig it up and grab it, and together we shared dinner. The lesson? Be flexible.

HOOK AND LINE

While I was in the Australian outback, I saw many people fish with a hand line. The accuracy of the placement of the baited hook easily matched that of a fisherman using a rod.

Many of us have some experience with fishing with a hook and line. While line fishing is possible with primitive setups, it is tricky to learn and takes a lot of time to make the gear; however, fifty feet of eight-pound test line and a few fishing hooks take up very little space and weigh next to nothing and are thus a good addition to a pack, survival kit, or glove box.

If you are fishing in an area with fish that weigh more than a few pounds, attaching the tail end of the line to a sturdy stick is a good idea. A large fish can easily pull the fishing line out of your hands, causing cuts and the loss of valuable gear. The stick gives you an anchor to help pull in the fish.

Some bodies of water have more fish than others and thus give you a greater chance of success with *any* hook. If you want to improve your ability as a fisherman, regardless of your level of skill, then it is important to ask yourself these questions:

- Why would a fish bite my hook?
- Where is food more abundant?
- Where does nutrient-rich water flow into this lake or that pond?
- When are fish feeding?
- Are conditions for fishing better in the rain or in the sun, in the early morning or the evening?
- What do fish really like to eat?
- Do bass like mice better than frogs?

Asking questions teaches you to be more aware as you seek out the answers. You might notice something that others may not. Perhaps fish really like a particular type of caterpillar that you saw fall into the creek and be devoured by a trout.

Hooks and Bait

The basic principle behind hooking a fish is lodging something attached to a string in the fish's mouth or stomach. Fish as a general rule do not chew their food; therefore, if the object is appealing enough, they will simply swallow it. Consequently, a simple, pointed piece of bone with a string tied to the middle often does the trick.

Gorge and shank

The toe bones of a deer are the right shape for making a conventional hook. A slice out of the center of the bone works well. The edge pieces of the same bone need more work but are stronger. Follow these steps:

Toe bone

1. Draw two parallel score lines around the bone, then score deeply along the lines with a knife or other sharp object.

Toe bone marked for cutting

2. Split the bone along the score lines, and carefully carve or abrade away unneeded bone.

Toe bone showing area removed

3. Do not make an eye for the fishing line. Instead, thin the shaft below the top end, leaving a wider portion or button at the top to keep the line from slipping off.

4. Once the line is tied, dab pine pitch over the knot and sprinkle it with ash.

5. Slide a squirrel femur with both ends removed down the line to the hook. This protects the line from sharp teeth and barbs in the fish's mouth.

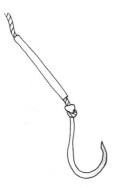

Hook and leader

Another good hook is a wishbone from the breast of a bird with one end broken and abraded to a fine point at about midshaft.

Wishbone

Live bait, while often very effective, can be hard to find and tough for some people to use. Some excellent live baits are frogs hooked through the upper leg, small fish hooked through the mouth, crayfish hooked through the tail, and mice hooked through the hide. Other baits include anything that will draw fish, such as bread, dead worms found in puddles after a rain, and pieces of meat, feathers, or reflective objects such as pieces of shell.

Techniques

There are many different ways to fish, and which one works best depends on the sort of fish you are targeting. Do you jerk the bait on the surface or let it sit on the bottom? Generally, I let live bait stay on or near the surface with little movement from me. Crayfish and minnows tend to do better deeper down, and dead bait seems to work well on top as well as down below. Experiment and see what works for you in your area. Have fun, and remember, fishing is an art.

To set your bait at a specific depth, say, for example, three feet below the surface, tie a rock one foot from the hook and a wooden bobber that is big enough to float the weight of the rock four feet above the stone. If your hook tangles with the rest of the gear, you can tie a stick to the line between the stone and the hook, with the line wrapped around the stick. It holds the rig at depth and keeps the baited hook a given distance from the weight. It also prevents tangling and keeps the entire rig from appearing too big.

Another option is to place your bait a given distance off of the bottom. For this, your bobber should be buoyant enough to float the hook and bait but not so buoyant to float the sinker. If, for example, you want your bait three feet off the bottom, tie a bobber (float) six to twelve inches from the hook; three feet farther along the fishing line, add the weight. The bobber will float up three feet from the weight on the bottom, keeping your baited hook where you want it.

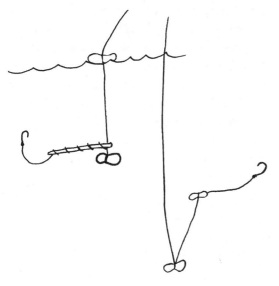

Sinker setup

The following directions for casting assume that you are right-handed. Reverse the procedure if you're a lefty.

1. Coil the cordage loosely on your left hand, leaving about two feet of slack on the end with the hook.
2. With your right hand, spin the baited hook around in a clockwise circle so that your target area is at nine o'clock, the ground is at six o'clock, and the area behind you is at three o'clock.
3. Release on the upswing. The line should uncoil off of your left hand (hold onto the end) and land your hook about fifteen feet out.

The method for pulling in a fish that I've found to work the best is to simply walk backward away from the water and pull the fish onto shore. This is especially important if you are using a primitive hook with no barb. Don't attempt to set the hook or play the fish; just apply constant and steady back pressure. Don't stop your backward pull when the fish is just on the shore; make sure that the fish is well enough away from the water so that no amount of flopping about will land that fish back in the water. A stick or stone can be used to finish off the fish, or you can break its neck by bending the head back until the nose touches the spine.

FISH POISON

I have found and heard plenty of third-party anecdotal information on fish poisons, but nothing concrete, at least not for North America. Much is still to be tested and rediscovered, but the one in which I have enough experience on which to draw is black walnut.

The black walnut has juglone toxin in all parts of the tree, but the strongest concentration is in the hulls of fresh nuts. Every fall, the green, round walnuts, a little smaller than a baseball, fall from the trees. The hulls can be ripped from the shell by hand (although they will stain your skin for about a week), then squeezed by hand underwater in a dammed pool with very little flow. Another method is to make a water-and-hull solution and then pour it all in at the upstream end of the pool. You can see the cloud of dye clearly spread through the pool, and as soon as it contacts fish, they swim as if attempting to get out of the cloud. They will flare their gill covers and come to the surface as they attempt to run more water over their gills for oxygen. In a few minutes, they are easily grabbed by hand or basket. The taste is not altered in any noticeable way, but any prolonged exposure will kill all the fish in the pool; therefore, use this as a last resort.

The hulls can be removed from fresh nuts and dried for later use, but only as a material dye. The juglone breaks down within about a week, rendering it useless for killing fish. After you dose a pool, check it again about six hours later to collect any fish that may have died and were missed. These remaining fish will be covered in a heavy coat of slime that will drip off when they are picked up (like egg white). Wash them off and cook them for a great meal!

Be advised that poisons are indiscriminate killers and should be used only as a last resort. I do know the fish are able to recover in clean water if the exposure was short or the dose mild.

In an attempt to get a handle on it, I dosed a 250-gallon pool with fourteen fresh hulls. There were two trout, seven inches and eleven inches. The effect was immediately noticeable when the toxin came in contact with the fish and made them catchable within about ten minutes. Reopening the flow of clear water into the pool appeared to have a positive effect on the fish, although six hours later all of the minnows and fish were dead. The seven-inch trout was gone and the eleven-inch fish remained, but it was dead and covered in slime. I know from experience that this technique works as a method for obtaining fish, but due to its indiscriminate nature, I will no longer use it except in a survival situation.

CHAPTER 11

TRAPPING

How do you hunt multiple locations while at the same time lounging in camp? Traps are used to hold or kill an animal without direct manipulation by, and therefore often in the absence of, the hunter. Hunting requires time and energy and does not guarantee success, but traps are hunters with great patience. They never tire, cramp, or lose interest. Rather than stalking and waiting, you can use your time and energy for trapping by locating excellent set areas and checking the traps once they are in place. Yet trapping is an art that is honed through trial and error. Making the traps is the simplest aspect of trapping.

Trapping is used primarily when you are staying in one location, because it allows you to become familiar with the area and the game present. It is possible to trap successfully while on the move, but this requires a greater tracking ability in order to identify sites that will be productive within a twelve- to twenty-four-hour window. Staying in one location while trapping is conducive to setting a trapline—a series of traps that are set in a loop or circuit that can be checked twice daily. Trapping on the move is better suited to setting a few traps that are fairly close to camp—this allows for a minimum time investment to set, check, and retrieve the traps.

SET LOCATIONS AND BAITS

Animals have a home range within which they sleep, den, and move to and from feeding areas and day beds. The best place to trap an animal with a *baited set* is on the edge of a feeding area. This way, the animal is already in a feeding mindset and may be curious about a different food.

Incidental, or nonbaited, traps are best set over den entrances and along trails or runs that are used exclusively by your quarry. (On larger trails, other animals will likely walk through your set and destroy it.) If a rabbit is heading to a clover patch, it is not likely to stop on the way for some wilting clover lying on the ground, but it may not notice a noose placed in the trail.

Look at a feeding area to see what foods are plentiful. For example, if the edge of a clover field is the feeding area of a rabbit, you probably won't have much luck using clover as bait. However, red maple buds or a piece of wild apple may bring success. Good bait is often food that an animal would like to eat but that is not readily available. One option is to leave a number of prospective baits close together in the feeding area overnight, then check in the morning to see which ones have been eaten.

TYPES OF TRAPS

Traps can be classified in terms of: (a) where the energy to catch the animal comes from, (b) why the animal goes to the trap, and (c) the killing or holding mechanism.

The energy required to hold or kill an animal comes from one of three sources: the animal's weight or movement, the contraction of a spring stick (sapling or branch), or the falling of a weight or counterweight.

The animal trips the trap either because bait is attached to a trigger or there is incidental contact with a trigger or noose due to placement of the trap.

There are three main types of killing or holding mechanisms:

- Snares use strong cordage and a noose or net to hold or kill the prey.
- Deadfall and live-capture traps use a weight or basket in combination with gravity to crush or capture the animal.
- Pit traps use a concealed hole to hold (or kill by way of stakes in the bottom) game.

Peg Snare

This particular trap is easy to set, and there is no worry of a spring stick accidentally being tripped or taking a set (losing its springiness and gaining a memory of its bent state while the trap is set). This trap is pretty tough on the animal as there is no quick killing mechanism. It is the animal's struggling that causes death due to strangulation.

Type: Nonbaited snare.

Materials: Strong cordage and a peg.

Placement: Trail or run, den openings, water entrances.

Directions:

1. Drive a peg into the ground near the trail or run.
2. Tie cordage to the base of the peg.
3. Make a noose and set it in the trail. If necessary, support it in the open position with a few twigs or grasses. Make the noose a little larger than the animal's head so that, as the animal moves down the trail, its head, but not its shoulders, passes through the noose.

When the noose tightens from the animal's forward movement, the animal panics and strangles itself.

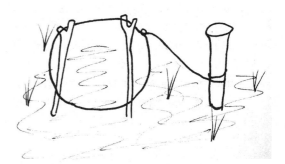

Peg snare

T-Bar Snare

This is a fairly simply trap and one of my favorites, but it does come with a few caveats. First, a bent sapling left too long in the set position will loose its springiness and be ineffective when tripped. Sometimes it may retain enough spring to tighten the noose on the animal's throat but not enough to swiftly lift it and break its neck. Both scenarios work, but the first is to be avoided if possible as the meat will taste particularly gamey, and the animal will have a lengthy battle before it finally succumbs to the noose. Second, this trap can be easily tripped in windy weather.

Type: Baited snare.

Materials: Flexible sapling, two notched sticks, a T-bar (a T-shaped section of a sapling trunk with a branch growing perpendicular to it), a number of twigs, and strong cordage.

Placement: Near feeding areas.

Directions:

1. Harvest two sticks that are about ten inches in length, and sharpen one end of each stick.
2. An inch from the other end of each stick, carve a notch so that when the pointed ends are in the ground, the top of the notch will be horizontal and capable of preventing the squared ends of the T-bar from moving upward.
3. Cut the horizontal part of the T-bar piece to about six inches in length (for squirrels), with the branch at the center.
4. Trim the vertical leg of the T-bar to two inches in length, and sharpen the end to receive the bait.
5. Square both ends so that they correspond to the notches in the pointed sticks.
6. Tie a noose and a length of cordage to the center of the T-bar, and bring everything to the set area.
7. To determine the exact set location, bend a sapling so that the top comes down to within two feet from the ground.

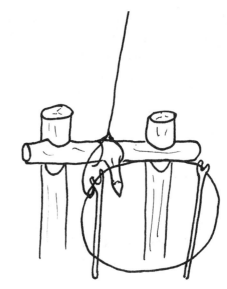

T-bar set

8. Remove a number of the branches to allow the sapling to snap quickly erect. To lend strength and snap to your spring stick, parallel branches or neighboring saplings can be tied to one another so as to work in unison.
9. With the tip of the sapling two feet from the ground, place your T-bar directly under it.
10. Attach the cordage to the sapling, place the bait on the pointed stick, and set the T-bar in the notches.
11. Place the noose around the T-bar, lifting it off the ground with twigs so that the animal must extend its head through the noose to get the bait.

The force used to remove the bait twists and frees the T-bar from the notches, allowing the sapling to snap upward. This tightens the noose and kills the animal.

The T-bar snare can be set with the bait branch horizontal for an approach from above. In this case, place twigs around the trap as a fence to prevent an animal from going under the noose. The bait branch can also point downward for an approach from the front or back (using two nooses).

Keeper Snare

This trap is great when the opportunity presents itself. Don't make the same mistake I made when I spent hours searching for the right spot to take this trap. I was so determined to use it that I missed countless opportunities to set other traps better suited to the location. Good to have in your repertoire, but don't make it the only trap you know.

Type: Nonbaited snare.

Materials: Strong cordage and a rock or a chunk of wood that weighs three or more times the weight of the target species.

Placement: Trails and runs in wooded areas, den openings, water entrances.

Directions:

1. Set a noose on a trail or over a den opening.
2. Run the cordage from the noose up through a Y in a branch and onto another branch above that.
3. Tie a weight to the end of the cordage, and place it on the higher branch in such a way that it will fall with a little tug on the snare line.
4. Lash a one-inch-diameter piece of wood across the Y just beyond the notch, leaving

enough room for the cordage to move without a problem.

When an animal hits the noose, the rock falls off of its perch and plummets toward the ground. The animal is pulled swiftly upward until it hits the bottom of the Y branch and dies. For animals near water, the weight can be perched such that it falls into water deep enough to pull the animal below the surface, drowning it.

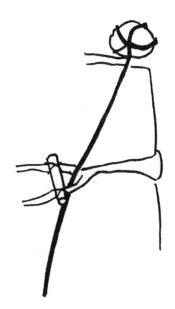

Keeper snare

Figure-Four Deadfall

This trap is one of the most popular primitive traps around. Published in countless journals and books from long ago to the present, it has earned it's place in many hearts for it's simplicity and effectiveness. If you learn only one trap, make it this one!

Type: Baited and nonbaited deadfall.

Materials: Three straight branches, with the size depending on the target species, be it mice, deer, or something in between. In addition, you will need a weight three times that of the target species (to kill the animal), or a box or basket large enough to hold the animal, plus a weight lashed to the top.

Placement: Trail, run, or feeding area.

Components: One upright stick, one diagonal stick, and one trigger stick. The bait or trigger stick and the diagonal stick are similar in length, while the upright stick is longer.

Directions:

1. Square the edge of the upright stick about two and one-half inches up, and make a wedged tip.
2. Notch the diagonal stick three or more inches from one end to correspond with the top of the upright stick; make a wedged point on the other end.
3. Notch the bait or trigger stick to receive the lower end of the diagonal stick; make a corresponding notch on the squared edge of the upright stick.
4. If you are going to use bait, sharpen the end farthest from the diagonal stick. If you are *not* going to use bait, use a branch with a few twigs left attached (so that it will not impede the falling of the weight).
5. To set the trap, place the notch of the diagonal stick on the upright stick. As you put the bait or trigger stick in place, apply pressure on the tip of the diagonal stick, then substitute your hand with either a log or a stone. If the weight tips to either side, drive a guide stake in on either side to allow only upward or downward movement.
6. If the ground is soft, you may need to add a flat rock underneath the trap as a smashing surface.

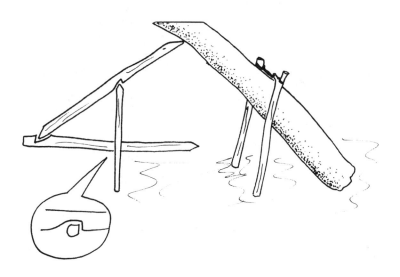

A figure-four

When the bait is taken, the weight falls, crushing the prey. Note that the greater the angle of the weight, the longer it takes to fall. This increases the chance of the animal escaping. If no large rocks are available, you can attach a basket of small stones to a log to add weight.

When you set this trap on a trail, you can substitute a branch with one end left untrimmed for the bait stick. A passing animal that touches any of the branches will cause the weight to fall and kill the animal. If the branch is too sturdy, it may prevent the weight from doing its job.

Snapping-Turtle Trap

This trap doubles as a holding pen for a turtle as no harm is done when the trap is tripped, the turtle's point of egress is merely blocked. Remember, turtles do not need to eat three meals a day and may not visit your trap for a few weeks.

Type: Baited, live capture.

Materials: Cordage; approximately thirty one-and-one-quarter-inch-diameter sapling pieces that are eighteen to thirty inches long with a sharpened end, including two Y sticks; a few dinner-plate-size flat stones; rotten fish or other meat for bait; and one thin, straight trigger stick that is eighteen inches long.

Placement: Lake and swamp shallows, about knee-deep.

Directions:

1. Create a horseshoe shape with the sharpened stakes, with the mouth open to deeper water. The two stakes on either side of the horseshoe's mouth are Y sticks, and they will hold the swinging door.
2. Hammer the sharpened stakes into the bottom of the swamp to ensure that they are firmly embedded.
3. Make the width of the trap about six inches wider than the size of the turtle you want to catch.
4. Have the stakes protrude six inches above the surface, and lash them to one another to prevent splaying due to pressure from the inside.

Turtle trap

5. Line the bottom of the trap with flat stones—the bigger the better—to prevent the turtle from digging its way out.

6. To make the door, place one of the sapling pieces in the notch of both Y sticks so that it spans the mouth; this will be the hinge.

7. Lash sticks to the hinge, four inches apart from one notch or mark to the other.

8. Lash an additional stick across the bottom of the door parallel to the hinge. When the door is placed in the Y sticks, it should be able to swing in a full circle.

9. Tie a stone to the inside of the door; the stone must be heavy enough to prevent the door from floating open.

10. Tie some cordage across the open tops of the Y sticks to hold the hinge in place.

11. Drive a stake into the swamp bottom just in front of the mouth of the horseshoe, and leave enough protruding to prevent the door from swinging outward.

12. To set the trap, swing the door inward until it is parallel with the surface of the water, and prop it open with a thin stick or reed as a trigger.

13. Tie a piece of rotten meat to the back of the horseshoe, and check the trap once a day.

Once the silt has settled from installation of the trap, a snapping turtle, smelling the bait, will swim into the trap. The trigger stick propping open the door will be dislodged as the turtle moves toward the bait. When the door closes, striking the shell, the turtle will move forward toward the bait, allowing the door to close completely. The stake at the entrance prevents the door from swinging open, rocks prevent a digging escape, and the turtle will not be able to climb up and over the walls. You can feed the turtle and keep it alive until you are ready to eat it.

Note: If the horseshoe is not long enough, the door will fall onto the turtle's back without closing completely, and the turtle will escape. Snapping turtles are strong and fast with their mouths; take great care when dealing with them.

CHAPTER 12
HUNTING WEAPONS

There are many weapons and variations of each with which you can hunt, including rabbit sticks, spears, bolas, and bows and arrows. Some require less work to produce and less practice to use than others, but the trade-off is that with less work comes less range. If you pick up a throwing stick, you can hunt immediately but with little range. If you take the time to make an effective hunting bow and the arrows to go with it and spend more time practicing, you can hunt a wide variety of game at greater distances.

RABBIT STICK

The "rabbit stick," quite simply, is a club specifically for throwing. It is the easiest of hunting tools to acquire and can be very effective with a bit of practice. Any solid stick or a weight that can be easily thrown and that measures from your armpit to your wrist will suffice.

This measurement is a general rule. Just take into consideration that the shorter the stick, the faster you can throw it but the more accurate you must be. A larger stick allows for poorer aim but cannot be thrown as fast. Experiment and

weigh the trade-offs to find what works best for you.

The basic rabbit stick is about two inches in diameter and has all of its edges rounded. This helps cut down on sound as the stick flies through the air and gives less warning to your prey. These modifications take little time by using a knife or by abrading the stick on a rough stone. A large, stationary rock works better than a small, movable one.

A whole host of modifications can be made to improve the performance of the rabbit stick. The weighted rabbit stick is much like the basic rabbit stick except that one end is bulbous. When it is

Rabbit sticks

thrown, the stick spins; the bulbous end spins more slowly and acts like a hub, while the handle is like a spoke. The result is that the end of the handle spins more rapidly than other parts of the stick, making it capable of delivering a devastating blow to the target. This weapon is good for short distances in fairly open sections of woods and meadows, as well as in tall grass.

Once you have modified your rabbit stick by carving or abrading it, it is important to camouflage the carve marks to make it harder for the animal to pick up the stick's movement as it approaches. Camouflage of wooden tools can be done by fire hardening, which will also increase the life span of your weapon. The best way to accomplish this, especially in the case of a spear or arrows, is by thrusting them into the sand near, but not in, the fire. If the tool is too close, the wood will burn; if it is too far from the fire, nothing will happen. You want the moisture to be driven out and the wood to be lightly browned. Smooth wood tends to become shiny as a result of this process, so you may want to scuff up such areas to aid in camouflage. In the absence of sand, the wood can be held over the fire or just next to it, but you must closely monitor and rotate it almost constantly or you may char and weaken the weapon.

The Boomerang—a Modified Rabbit Stick

The boomerang, one of my favorite weapons, has a natural curve in it and is carved so that a cross section is elliptical or winglike (one-half of an ellipse). This weapon does not return, as is commonly thought, but flies faster and more silently, as well as farther and flatter, than any other rabbit stick I have ever used. (Most objects move in an

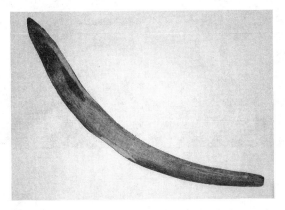
Boomerang

arc when they are thrown, but due to the aerodynamics of the boomerang, the arc is almost nonexistent.) The best terrain for the boomerang is an open field; use the sidearm throw for short or longer distances, as described below.

Throwing the Rabbit Stick

Throws can be made overhand, from a sidearm position, and anywhere in between. A sidearm throw works well with the boomerang in open meadows or other areas where there is enough space between trees to allow for unhindered flight. Overhand throws work well in taller growth or areas in which there is little distance between trees.

The tricky part is preparing to release your weapon. You cannot stalk your quarry and then, when you are in range, rear back and prepare to hurl your weapon—you will give yourself away. Instead, you must slowly position your body and throwing stick into launch position *as* you stalk.

For overhand throws, use your whole body. Don't try to "muscle it" with just your arm. Slowly

Throwing the rabbit stick overhand

Throwing the rabbit stick from a sidearm position

bring your stick and throwing arm back over your shoulder, and bend backward from your waist. Your body, now taut as a bow, is ready to contract, starting with your stomach muscles and ending with your arm and hand snapping forward like the cracking of a whip, hurling the weapon forward at your prey.

Using the sidearm throw is similar in that you use your whole body to launch the stick. However, instead of bending backward, place your stick behind your neck and twist to the right until your left hand and shoulder are pointing at your target (opposite if you're left-handed). Then, in a single motion, whip your body around, releasing the stick as your throwing hand comes to bear on the target. Be wary of nearby trees and low branches.

THRUSTING SPEAR

The thrusting spear is designed to thrust directly into an animal without leaving the hunter's hands. Some animals, like rabbits and other small game, are struck from above; therefore, the spear must be able to withstand the force of being driven severely into the ground.

I prefer a stout sapling about five feet long for the shaft of the thrusting spear. It doesn't need to be straight, and the thin end should be sharpened and fire hardened. I do not recommend using bone spearheads for small game, because you will likely stab through the animal and into the ground, breaking the tip that took such effort to create. For large game, a bone spearhead can be affixed to the shaft, as described below.

THROWING SPEAR

The throwing spear is used for hunting animals at distances up to approximately fifteen feet.

Harvest a straight sapling that is about six feet in length with a diameter less than one and one-half inches. Sharpen the thicker of the two ends and fire harden the tip.

Bone spearheads should be as wide as or wider than the shaft of the spear or arrow on which they are mounted. I use leg bones from deer, elk, or other large animals for spear tips. Smashing the bone leaves many shards of usable size, which can be carved or abraded into the desired shape. Make the tang (the part of the spearhead that is connected to the shaft) as long as or longer than the tip, and flare it at the bottom. Bone can be made only so sharp; it is not a hard enough substance to create a razor-sharp edge. However, serrating the edge increases its ability to cut and takes little time with a good abrading stone.

A shaft ready for hafting

To insert a bone spearhead, wrap strong cordage around the shaft eight inches from the pointed tip. Split the tip down to the cordage. Insert the spearhead tang, and pack around it with pitch and ash (see "Working with Pitch" in Chapter 16). Bind the head tightly with wet rawhide or sinew and let it dry. Once the hide has dried, slather the lashings with pitch and ash. To make a really solid seat for the spearhead, the inside of the split in the upper end of the spear shaft can be carved down to better accommodate the thickness of the tang.

To throw a spear, first find the point in the middle of the shaft where the spear will balance if it is placed across an outstretched finger. Mark the balance point with charcoal, and set the spear in your hand with the mark in the center of your palm. Close your fingers around it, and raise it over your shoulder as if you are preparing to throw. Note where the tip of your index finger touches the spear, and carve a shallow groove all the way around the shaft. Every time you pick up your spear, your fingertip should be in that groove.

The mechanics of throwing properly are worth learning, even if the first few times you throw you feel awkward.

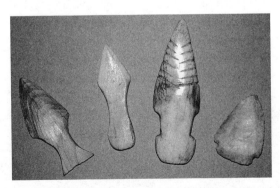

Spear points

1. Start with a target about fifteen feet away and, if you are using a bone spearhead, be sure that your target and the area around it are soft.
2. Face your target with your left arm out in front, pointing at it (opposite stance for lefties).
3. Extend your right arm with the spear straight back; the spearhead should be near your ear.
4. Shift your weight to your right foot as you lean back, and use your left foot as a counterbalance.
5. Keeping your eye on the target, begin moving the spear forward. As your hand moves toward the target, your elbow will move forward, too. During this movement, your elbow should point at the target and pass your shoulder *before* it passes your hand. Run through this step slowly a few times to be sure that you have the motion correct before you attempt a throw.
6. As you release, follow through, with the tip of your index finger and the groove being the last points of contact with the spear. Your throw should end with your finger pointing at the target.

Bolas

BOLAS

The function of bolas is to hold prey long enough to allow the hunter to approach and kill it with a thrusting spear or club. Primary bola game are large birds, such as turkeys and geese, as well as long-legged animals like deer.

Three to seven weights of stone, wood, or leather pouches filled with sand are connected to a loop of cordage by equal lengths (about three feet) of the same material. When thrown, the weights fan out until one or more of the pieces of cordage hits an object, which allows the weights to continue to swing forward and wrap around the wings or legs of your target. This tangles and often temporarily stops any forward motion of the prey.

Contrary to popular belief, bolas are not swung multiple times around your head prior to your releasing them. This would only alert your prey. A more effective way is to start with your right index and middle fingers in the loop at about shoulder height. Meanwhile, your left hand provides tension on the cordage when you lace your fingers through the cordage and rest them on the weights, preventing any tangling. When you are in position to throw, release the bola with your left hand while simultaneously whipping your right hand up and around your head once and following through until your right hand is pointing at your target.

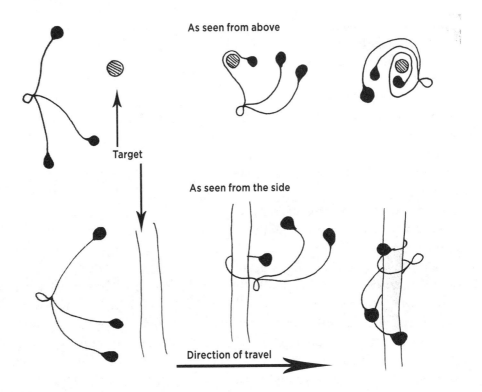

As seen from above

Target

As seen from the side

Direction of travel

Bola throwing sequence

ATLATL

The atlatl (AHT-lah-tuhl) intrigues many people and is definitely addictive once you have one at your disposal. The popularity of this impressive lesson in mechanical advantage is increasing, so much so that a few states now allow the use of the atlatl for taking deer.

An atlatl, in the simplest terms, is typically a rigid to flexible board or branch that is fifteen to thirty inches in length. It has a handle at one end and a projection, hook, or spur to hold and then propel the spearlike projectile or dart, at the other end. The length of the atlatl increases the mechanical advantage of the hunter's forward arm motion. The energy from the atlatl comes first from the hunter's arm and the forward motion of the arm, which (in flexible models) causes the atlatl itself to flex back initially before springing forward. This compresses the dart (again, in flexible models) and therefore bends it somewhat. The dart then snaps back to a straight position and moves quickly toward its target. Overly flexible darts, when springing back from being compressed, go past straight and bend the other way, doing the reverse. This wastes a lot of energy as the dart flops around, and the results may be poorer than with a stiffer dart.

The dart is a rigid to flexible shaft from about four feet to eight feet in length. Fletching is attached to the aft end, on which there is an indentation to receive the projection or hook of the atlatl. A point of stone, bone, or wood is used in the same manner as arrows for taking game.

Making the Atlatl

The atlatl can be from just about any wood with strength to it. I prefer ash, although I've used maple, dogwood, oak, and elder, among others. (The elder seemed brittle compared to the harder woods but worked satisfactorily.) For the finger loops on the handle, I prefer a flexible material like leather, which is lashed to the atlatl with cordage.

Opinions differ as to the purpose of banner stones or counterweights. Some suggest that banner stones make it easier to hold the atlatl in the ready position for longer periods of time. Others suggest that the stones add energy to the dart when it is thrown. I do not use them so will not weigh in on the discussion.

The weapon described here is for close-range (fifty feet or less) hunting of deer-size game.

Some saplings or branches have grown in such a way that their branch placement sets them up to be a great atlatl. Straight-grained woods that are one and one-half inches in diameter are easily split in half, and a branch nub can be quickly converted to a spur. I always try for a flex or spine in my atlatl that compliments the dart or spear. If the atlatl has too little spine, it can break under the pressure of the launch. Optimally, the atlatl bends as the throwing hand moves the handle forward and the inertia of the spear slows down the other end. At a certain point, the spur end begins to catch up with the handle, and the flexed atlatl snaps forward, not only with the arm and wrist action of the thrower but also with the spring action of a just-fired bow. If the atlatl is too stiff, you sacrifice that snap. There are applica-

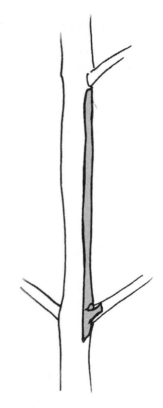

Atlatl preharvest in tree

Atlatl tips

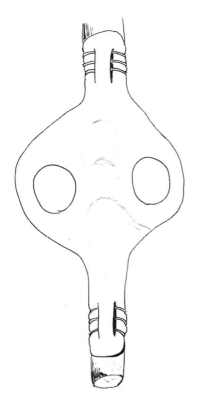

Atlatl handle pattern

Basket-maker tip

With careful carving, all that is left is a flute ending at what is known as a *fluted* or *basket-maker spur*.

Making the Dart

The dart is a projectile commonly made of river cane or bamboo, although I also use carefully selected birch, maple, ash, and pine saplings generally from four to eight feet in length. The dart should be flexible, but if it is too flexible, it will break as it snaps under compression on the launch. If it is too stiff, you will not be terribly impressed with the distance. The fletching can be made of feathers, cloth, or leather, and the tip can made from bone, stone, or wood.

tions for the rigid atlatl, primarily for very close-quarter hunting where the ability to loft the dart a great distance is exchanged for being able to deliver a heavier spear to a target with extreme force. The bulk of my first atlatls were of this type due to my ignorance regarding the mechanics and never attempting a thin-enough dart shaft.

The spur can be fashioned in a number of ways in addition to that mentioned above. A *foreign spur* consists of a piece of material—often stone, bone, or antler—that is attached with a sinew or rawhide lashing. Alternately, the atlatl can be carved flat, and, instead of a spur being attached, a flute or channel is cut into the wood to excavate an area in front of the spur location.

1. The dart or spear is harvested green and as straight as you can possibly find. I look for saplings that, if they are bent, have short, subtle bends, as they are easier to straighten.

2. Remove the bark. This is easiest when the wood is green, but the downside is that there is the potential for splits to develop, because the newly stripped shaft shrinks

unevenly if it dries rapidly. If time allows, leave the bark on for a few weeks prior to skinning the sapling.

3. Straighten the shaft by heating it over a fire, then removing it from the heat and bending it to just beyond the desired position. Hold it there until it is cool and move on to next bend.

4. Bore out a depression on the butt (thin end) to receive the spur tip.

5. Fletch as you would an arrow (see the "Arrows" section, later in this chapter), or simply attach two feathers on opposite sides of the shaft.

6. Fire harden the points, or haft the stone or bone tips as you would for arrows. I recommend lashing the shaft three or so inches aft of the tip, especially if you use wooden points or use the darts for target practice; this will limit the distance the splits can travel.

7. Depending on humidity, you may have to do a quick straightening prior to use, so check your gear before heading out.

Throwing with the Atlatl

Although a handle is not essential, it will allow you to throw much farther. I use a leather strap for the split-finger grip, in which the index finger passes through one loop and the middle finger passes through the other. Gripping the atlatl and dart with your fingertips while both are over your shoulder and parallel to the ground puts you in the ready position.

To begin the throw, drop your elbow. As your hand comes forward, let go of the atlatl, keeping your fingers in the loops only. Due to the flexibility of the loops, the spur end whips around after

Power or split-finger grip

the hand has stopped moving and provides incredible follow-through. If distance is your goal, start with your arm pointing at the ground behind you and the dart pointing up at a sixty-five-degree angle. Run a few steps and launch the dart, but release it early so that it soars up at that same starting angle or a little less. Your results should be impressive. The accuracy of the split-finger grip is due at least in part to the naturally straight follow-through it produces.

Another throwing method is the hammer grip, wherein the atlatl is gripped like a hammer with the thumb through one loop and the index finger in the other. It is not difficult to do, yet the ease with which your follow-through can shift from the middle to one side requires a bit of practice and consciousness when you are throwing. In all honesty, I do not find one throw to be significantly harder than the other; both require practice, and undoubtedly you will develop a preference.

Hammer grip

Throwing the atlatl

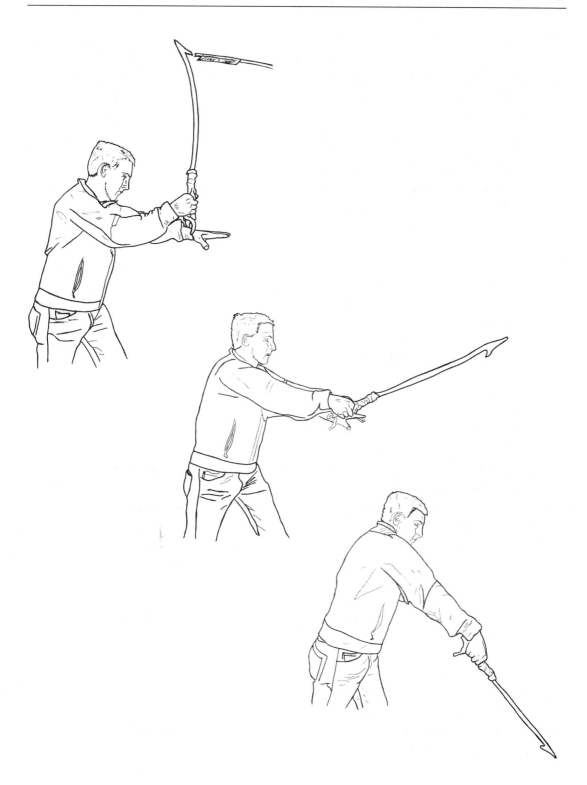

FIELD BOW

A few hours can suffice to make a bow and arrows of serviceable quality, with a few days set aside to allow the bow stave to dry somewhat. But this begs the question, Where does archery and the manufacture of its requisite tools fall in a survival situation? The short answer is that they don't. In the time required to make all of the necessities, learn to shoot and stalk game, and actually take it, the unintentional survivor will either be rescued or no longer be a survivor. For the primitive technologist or long-term wilderness sojourner, however, bows with a range of about fifteen feet can be made in little time and can augment your hunting options. Although it should not be your first choice, once you are able to fill your belly with other means, the bow and arrow is a fine addition.

The field bow requires one fairly straight sapling or branch that is about four and a half feet long and an inch and a half in diameter in the middle. Many a stave that I have harvested straight has taken a back-set or bend within a short time. In such cases, I usually hold the stave so that it curves away from me, creating a naturally recurved bow stave.

Roughing out is simply removing the bulk of the extra wood from the stave, most of which is on the thicker end of (or base of) the limb. Wood is only removed from the belly of the bow (i.e., the side facing the shooter when the bow is drawn), and the handle is left thick enough to provide a good grip.

The bow tips must be nocked to accommodate the bowstring. A rounded groove can be abraded on an angle at either side of the tip, but care must be taken to ensure that the remaining wood between the grooves is sufficient to hold under

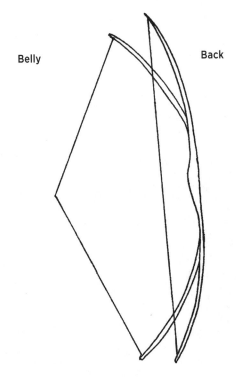

Belly   Back

A bow strung and drawn

full draw. How thin it can actually be depends on the width of the tip, as well as on the thickness and the type of wood used. If your tip is one and one-fourth inches wide by one-fourth inch tall, and you leave three-fourths inch between the grooves, you would be hard-pressed to break the tip of any wood.

Alternately, the tip of the bow can tapered, either sharply enough so that it creates a shoulder for the string to sit on, or more gradually, so that the loop at the end of the string cannot slide down beyond a desired point. This, of course, requires that the loop be small enough to keep it where it is wanted.

Optimally, the limbs of the bow will be matched in strength, and the curve described by

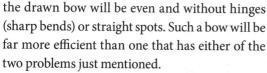

A bow tip without string and a bow tip with string on a strung bow

A hinge with the desired balance curve behind it

A straight spot bracketed by two hinges

the drawn bow will be even and without hinges (sharp bends) or straight spots. Such a bow will be far more efficient than one that has either of the two problems just mentioned.

A hinge occurs at a point that is weaker than the wood on either side. When the bow is drawn, most, if not all, of the flex is concentrated at this point, which quickly becomes overstressed and renders the bow useless. A straight spot is a section where the limb is thicker than the surrounding wood, resulting in a section that fails to bend with the rest of the limb during the draw. Unbent wood lends no power to the arrow, and hinges may develop on either end of a straight spot if the limb is overstressed.

Tillering is the process by which the flex or curve of the limbs is assessed and adjusted to make it smooth and even. With practice, the bowyer will notice hinges and straight spots, and tillering can often correct these problems. Tillering

can also be applied to reduce the overall stiffness or draw weight of a bow stave, making it easier and more comfortable to draw and shoot (although reducing the force behind the arrow in the process). Below are three tillering methods, the first two being practical in the field.

Floor tillering is done one limb at a time by looking down the curve of the lower limb while the tip is pressed against the ground with enough force to cause it to bend.

A tillering stick is a straight section of sapling about thirty inches in length, with either branch

Floor tillering

Tillering stick clean and in use

better view the curve of the bow to look for hinges, straight spots, and evenness of curve between the limbs.

The tillering board is a rather deluxe tool that is impractical in the wilderness, but it can be built and used at home in between wilderness journeys if you plan to use a well-built, primitive-style bow in the wild. A four-by-eight-foot sheet of plywood is painted white, and a precise grid is drawn on it. The size of the grid squares is up to you, although I use ones that are four inches wide and two inches high. A bow rest is placed at one end of the centerline, and a small pulley is placed at the other end of the centerline. The bow-in-progress is loosely strung, and its handhold is placed on the bow rest. A strong string with a small hook on one end is hooked to the center of the bow string, and the other end is run through the pulley. The tillering board is anchored firmly to some solid object. The bowyer can then stand back and pull on the end of the string, drawing the bow. Compare how the opposite tips of the stave line up against the grid, and look at several intermediate places on both limbs as well. Seeing the bow in

nubs or notches in one side. The base of the stick is placed on the center of the handle of the bow, which is strung so loosely that the string is limp. With the bow on the ground, the string is drawn upward until some curve is evident in the bow. The string is then hung on one of the notches or branch nubs, and the bowyer can step back to

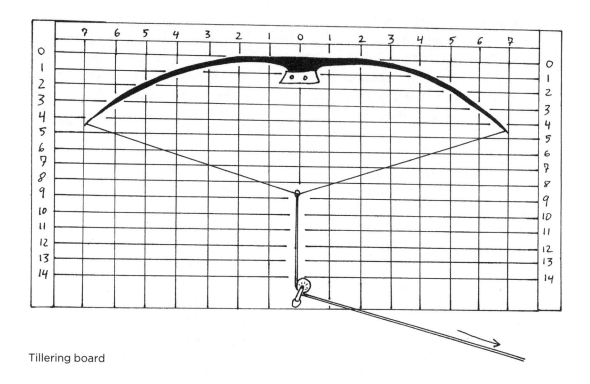

Tillering board

Accommodating a Hinge

When a hinge is developing, wood can be removed from either side to match up the wood's resistance to flexing with that of the hinge. If the hinge has been overbent (overstressed), or the hinge area is too thin, then you can complete the bow, but it may have a six-pound draw weight—not helpful unless you're raiding the Cub Scouts of their marshmallows. I built a beautiful flat bow, sixty-eight inches in length, that developed a hinge on both limbs, each about six inches from the tips. Although I was loath to cut the bow down to fifty-six inches, it was the only way to end up with a nicely functioning bow.

action illustrates how it needs to be tillered. It may draw well for the first ten inches, and then a hinge or straight spot may show up rather abruptly.

The tillering process is completed by removing wood in small quantities, then checking the bow again and repeating the process as necessary. It is not advisable to let the bow sit in a drawn position on the tillering stick or board, as it will likely take a set, or permanent bend.

Here are step-by-step directions for making a bow:

1. A stave is selected and cut.
2. The stave is roughed out, defining the shape the bow will take, and enough wood is removed to allow the limbs to be only

slightly bent. At no time during construction is the bow fully drawn except at the very end!

3. The bow is set aside for about three to five days in a dry location. I have had no problem putting them in the sun, although direct desert sun might cause some excessive checking (cracking as the wood shrinks unevenly when it dries). Remember, a midsummer- or winter-harvested stave will have less moisture in it (sap runs in the spring and the fall, if to a lesser extent), and this can reduce the level of checking.

4. After partial drying, more wood is removed, first from one limb and then from the other. Each limb is frequently floor tillered so that you can assess it and find trouble spots.

5. The tips need to be set up to hold a string. I like to cut or abrade a groove on the sides, below the tip, going from the back of the bow to the belly at a slight angle toward the handle. Do not groove the bow's back (the side facing your target)!

6. Make a string (see Chapter 15).

7. Stretch the string. Tie one end to a tree and the other to a stick, and pull with steady pressure. Or, alternatively, hang a weight from it and leave for a few hours or more.

8. Make a loop on one end of the string if you have not woven one in as you made the string, and then determine where to make the second loop, such that the string will be taut but the bow unflexed when the bow is strung. Gently apply pressure to the string as you draw it back slowly. Watch for problem spots and address them as

they arise. If you have a tillering stick, use it, but do not leave the bow flexed more than necessary to determine areas that still need to be worked. Do not fully draw the bow at first. Some hinges may not be evident until the bow *nears* full draw, as the areas most stressed shift within the limb.

9. Deal with each trouble spot as it appears. Ignoring these areas or hoping that they will go away is foolish, and as their numbers grow, so, too, will their chances of ruining your bow.

10. If step 9 looks to be in order, tighten the string to hold the bow at a resting bend (strung, but not drawn). I usually like a minimum of eight inches from the handle to the string on bows that are sixty inches and greater, and less for shorter bows.

11. Slowly draw the bow to increasing levels of draw. I have caused bows to develop a fine network of spiderweb-like compression cracks all over the belly by fully drawing them too soon. Some field-expedient bows will not be big enough to allow a grown person to draw to his or her personal draw length (the archer may have a twenty-nine-inch draw, yet the bow may have a maximum draw of fourteen inches), so watch the bow and let it tell you when to stop: usually it is the point just before the loud crack. After making a few fine pieces of kindling, you will begin to understand the language of the bow.

Understand that you will break bows. Anyone wanting to make bows is going to lose some; probably a lot at first. If you pay attention to how the bow breaks, you will learn to deal with those problems before they arise or when they are still in their infancy. I broke many a bow due to a lack of patience. I just wanted to be done one way or the other, and I was, with a finely worked piece of kindling. Take care with the final stages and it will pay off.

ARROWS

A great deal of time and energy can be focused on arrows. After all, an archer wants a quiver of arrows that will perform the same way. Making arrows the same in weight, length, and diameter, as well as matching the fletching and points, is quite an undertaking, even with modern tools. The level of perfection required for effective bows and arrows increases with the distance to the target. In other words, making a bow and arrows capable of hitting a target at fifteen feet is far easier than making a bow that can deliver arrows to a target one hundred yards away. Imperfections in the arrow, the bow, and the shooting can grow and become increasingly obvious with distance.

Harvesting

My preferred method for fashioning arrows is to use shoots or other straight-growing wood, rather than splitting out blanks and rounding them out with a cutting edge. Ash, maple, willow, highbush blueberry, arrowwood, birch, pine, river cane, oak, and dogwood are, among others, some of the woods suited to the life of an arrow. Although I have no experience with Sitka spruce, John Massy speaks highly of it in *The Traditional Bowyers Bible*.

Harvest the straightest green shafts you can find. Look around the edges of water and woods, as well as in clearings, which also provide good pickings as new growth stretches for the light. Harvest shafts that are about one-half inch at the thick end and a good six to eight inches longer than the desired finished length. The first shafts I harvested were blueberry, and they were better suited to atlatl darts or throwing spears due to their heft and thickness. A midwinter or midsummer harvest yields shafts with much less sap in them, resulting in less checking. The more you look for shafts, the better you will become at finding those that need little work.

Drying

Loosely bundle ten or more shafts together, and set them in a cool, dry place out of the sun. If time is not an issue, they can be left for a few weeks before you scrape off the bark with a sharp edge, then return them to the bundle for more drying. If time is of the essence, you may need to force dry them—a tricky and often costly endeavor. For a hasty shaft, harvest and debark the shaft all at once. Then cover the cut ends with wet clay, and stand them upright or hang them. After a day or two of dry weather, they are well on their way to being ready for the next step. Many an experienced bowyer is cringing at this point, because this goes against all of the rules in the bowyer's art. Some arrows will develop wide cracks running down their length (shakes) and ought to be discarded, but others will be fine. (I have not studied the performance of using shafts with shakes, but I have used some with narrow cracks as target arrows with no real perceivable difference. More study needs to be done to determine how much more prone such shafts are to breakage or other problems.) I have also debarked shafts, bundled them, and set them in tree branches off the ground for a few days with mixed results. The loss has typically been about 50 percent but has varied about 25 to 75 percent from one batch to another.

Straightening

Depending on the bowyer, straightening is done anytime from directly upon harvest of the shaft to after it has dried. I straighten after a few days of drying and then do a fine tuning before finishing the arrow. Shafts with a significant bend or bow to them, if they must be used, do well with an initial straightening upon harvest and then a final session before the arrow is finished. River cane is well suited to this technique, as the bends occur in the nodes, or joints, of the plant. These dry hard and can make straightening very tough if not altogether impossible.

Heat the whole bent area without scorching it. Bend the shaft so that it bends slightly opposite the original bend (bend it straight and then a little more), and remove it from the heat. Hold it until it is cool. After time, especially in damp environ-

ments, the bow in the arrow will return to some degree and will require another straightening.

An arrow wrench can be made with a piece of wood or bone in two ways. First, and more commonly, is the hole-in-a-stick or bone type. Simply make a hole slightly larger than the diameter of the arrow's largest diameter, round the hole edges to reduce denting, and slide the arrow through the hole to just above or below the bend. The second is the F type of wrench, being no more than a section of sapling in which a capital F can be seen. This is cut and applied by holding the base of the F parallel to the arrow while one of the arms of the F passes above the shaft and the other passes below the shaft. By turning the handle down or up, pressure is applied to the shaft. The wrench

Curved shaft with overlay of corrective bend

Arrow wrench in use

provides more leverage for stubborn bends and helps in forming a fine arrow.

Arrowheads

Although there are many heads, or points, that you can put on your arrows, one of the following three should meet your needs.

- The field point is the most simple of the three and is made merely by carving or abrading the thick end of the shaft into a rounded point. This point should be fire hardened prior to straightening, or you may need to tweak the shaft afterwards. This point is good for smaller game but does not usually cause as much damage as the broad head. If you have a shaft with a pithy core, the point should be off-center, as this allows you to actually make a point with the surrounding wood.
- The blunt is used for stunning small game and may need to be followed up with a speedy, killing blow from a rabbit stick or other weapon. The value of such a point is that it seldom needs replacing (at least in comparison with other points), it can take a beating when you are hunting game on the ground (where hitting rocks is likely), and, as with the others, it works well in the hands of a good archer.

There are two ways of making blunts with which I am familiar. One is to harvest a shaft from a tree like the ash, with the tip being from the joint of two branches. This provides the material from which the blunt can be carved. The other way is to make a separate blunt that is then attached to the shaft, as outlined below.

- The broad-head arrow tip can do more damage than the other two tips mentioned above, because the breadth of the cutting edges lacerates flesh, blood vessels, and organs; it also leaves a larger opening from which blood can drain. These tips are often thought of as beautiful, glittering pieces of finely crafted obsidian, or the more modern, razor-bladed, titanium-tipped arrowhead. I used to lament my lack of skill in the realm of flint knapping and so experimented with other materials for these mythic points of long ago. Bone and wood, both of which are available more often than chert or obsidian, can be carved or abraded into good projectile points. Hard-

 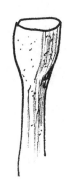  

Three types of points—two blunts, a field point, and a broad head

woods can be fire hardened and polished to a glassy finish with a smooth stone or piece of bone. I add grooves for a serrated edge on both materials. A common error made by the novice is in the size. My first arrowheads were better suited to spears or atlatl darts. Remember, the purpose of the arrowhead or tip is to provide access through the hide and flesh to the vital organs. Given the diameter of an arrow shaft, the width of the broad head does not *need* to be much larger. If you have the means of delivering a larger tip to the target, by all means, go for it, because it will have a greater chance of causing a mortal wound by striking an organ and/or severing a blood vessel. But it will also have a greater chance of hitting bone.

A number of materials are suitable for making points or arrowheads. The gold standard seems to be obsidian, the sharpest natural cutting edge known to man, yet it has its drawbacks: it is not widely distributed over North America; it takes much practice, some specific tools, and guidance in order to produce a good arrowhead; and it does not survive impact well, if at all. Other options include:

- **Wood**. Hardwoods are easily shaped when they are green if a cutting or abrading tool is available. If not, a combination of shattering, crushing, and splitting using found stone wedges should provide you with some usable pieces that can be abraded on a rough stone to the desired design. I prefer a shortened version of the Clovis-type point, because it stands up better to impact than points with notches (notches create break points). Wood tips need to be carefully fire hardened, and adding some

A Clovis point

grooves as a simple serration is not a bad idea either. Burnishing with bone or a smooth stone gives the head a very smooth surface. The downside is that, at this point, I have yet to be convinced of the value of a wooden arrowhead. The inability of the wooden edge to cut through hair and hide (especially in winter) is a major concern. In tests I have conducted, the arrow bounced or broke without penetrating beyond the hide. Such small wounds in a deer or deer-sized animal would do nothing to aid the hunter. For small game, like rabbits and squirrels, an arrow that is sharpened and fire hardened in a simple point

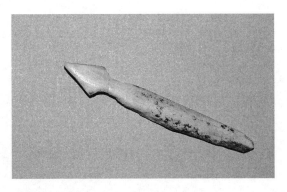

A bone point

is sufficient, and no time needs to be wasted on fancy-looking heads.

- **Bone**. While bone is harder to work than wood, it stands up fairly well to impact provided it is not with stone. The points are not as fragile as wood but take longer to make. I like to add serrations to these, too.
- **Pottery**. My experience with pottery arrow points is somewhat experimental, but my initial impressions are fairly positive. As with wood, the Clovis-type points or a stunted version seem like the most sturdy, and the importance of getting the highest temperature possible in the firing process cannot be understated. (See "Primitive Pottery" in Chapter 17.) The upside is that a mold or form can be made (also from clay), which will allow you to make many identical points. In addition, firing points is far less tricky than firing pots. I ran an experiment by firing two batches of arrowheads. One firing was not very hot, and the points, while sharp, were not hard and were very fragile. The second firing, at a much higher temperature, produced some nice points that penetrated deer to a depth of six inches in the chest and three inches in the thigh. The points broke at some point after entry, but they produced lethal wounds nonetheless.

Prepping the arrow shaft to receive a point is done by abrading or cutting a slot in the thick end of the shaft. This process is easiest when done from either side. It is also a good idea to wrap a bit of sinew below the bottom of the intended slot to prevent splitting the shaft. Tapering the last half inch of the shaft will also ease entry into the target for deeper penetration.

Clay points and a mold

Detail of hafted point showing tapered shaft end

If the arrowhead has a base that is wider than the arrow shaft, sinew lashing is wrapped around the shaft from the top of the head's stem downward to just below the bottom of the stem. This prevents the head from moving. Pitch and ash, or glue, is applied, for both waterproofing and for its adhesive quality.

Three examples of hafting

If the head has no stem, add a groove or two on the lower portion of the cutting edges. Place the point in the slot at the tip of the shaft, and wrap sinew lashings around both the shaft and the grooves in the point.

Fletching

Fletching (also known as flights) is attached to the tail end of the arrow just below the nock to aid in keeping the arrow on target once it is loosed. Feathers, of course, are the most common material. For the short-distance hunting I prefer, the fletching can be very crude, if it is even there at all. I have used pine needles, split turkey feathers, and songbird feathers lashed with sinew on two sides of the shaft. I use the following method to attach fletching.

1. If you are using a turkey tail feather or another large, fairly straight feather, split it with a stone flake or knife. If you only want two fletches or flights, take both from the same side of the same feather. (The natural curve of the feather will encourage the arrow to rotate one way; if you use opposite sides of the same feather, both fletches will counteract each other, resulting in a less stable flight.) They should be about four inches long, although I have seen museum specimens that ranged from three inches to more than seven inches. If you want two smaller songbird feathers, use two that are of similar size and bend.

2. Trim the feathers with a sharp cutting edge so that they are equal in all dimensions. Clean the quill at the top and at the bottom of the flight.

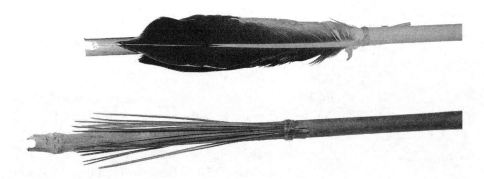

Fletching with needles, songbird feathers, and turkey feathers

3. With a piece of wet sinew, make a wrap around the shaft at least one inch from the nock.

4. Place the thin end of the first flight on the sinew, and continue the wrap. Going over the tip of the flight, add the second flight opposite the first, and continue to wrap a few turns around the shaft. Once the top has been wrapped a few times and tied off, let it dry for an hour or so.

5. With the top sinew dry, you can now pull the flights downward so as to prevent any bowing in them. Then, lash the bottoms as you did the tops. Longer flights may need an additional sinew wrap at their mid-points or some pitch glue underneath the split midrib. I don't shoot enough arrows with glued fletching to be aware of any real advantage or disadvantage. The wet sinew is flat and adheres to itself, requiring no additional glue or knots to secure as long as it is kept dry. Any additional drag it may create is negligible.

The Nock

The nock is the wood with the slot into which the bow string is placed. The incredible amount of force exerted on the wood at the base of the nock slot can split poorly crafted, partially split, thin arrows. The nock can be part of the actual arrow, or it can be a separate piece of harder material that is glued or attached with sinew to the shaft. A commercially produced nock holds the string (you can let go of the arrow once it is on the string and it will remain there). Making such a nock with a knife or primitive tools can be time consuming and tricky. I score the sides of the shaft where I want the nock and then gently bore a hole with my knife tip or stone flake. I then split out the wood from both sides until the nock is clear all the way through. Be careful not to split the shaft all the way through and damage it. More often than not, I'll make very shallow nocks that are incapable of holding the bow string. With this, I have learned that I need a depth of at least one-eighth inch.

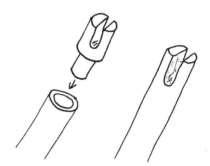

Two types of nocks

Fish Arrows

An extra-long arrow sans fletching serves well for hunting fish or frogs. Contrary to popular belief, it is seldom necessary to have a string tied to your fish arrow when you are hunting fish that are less than about eight pounds. The arrow creates a significant amount of drag and, given that it will never be exactly halfway through the fish, there will be more drag on one side than on the other. This will cause the fish to swim in circles, with one end of the arrow rising up out of the water and providing an easy handle.

CHAPTER 13
HUNTING METHODS

Hunting embodies different things for different people. In the past seventy-five years, however, it has become a luxury for many more people than in earlier times—something done for sport and trophies rather than for subsistence. Many hunters, including myself, would rather hunt for their meat than cough up the money needed to purchase a comparable amount of quality, additive-free meat. Without getting on my soapbox to preach the merits or evils of hunting, I will say that, in wilderness survival, outside of a few tropical climates and especially in the cold seasons, the consumption of meat is necessary in order to maintain health. Vegetarianism is a modern luxury born of rapid, refrigerated transportation. Trying to live off the land, eating locally grown foods, and preserving them without the benefit of pressure canners and freezers are challenges, and if meat is removed from the menu . . . well, try to plan out a year's worth of meals using only in-season or dried local, native flora.

Alright, so the soapbox came out.

Most animals are edible and provide great nourishment. The trick is getting the animal to make the ultimate sacrifice in giving you its body.

Hunters approach this challenge from different perspectives. Some simply think mechanically: the game must eat and drink; therefore, I will wait near a feeding area that I believe it will visit. This approach might work in a few hours, or it could take days or weeks. Spending some time watching your intended quarry will increase your understanding of its habits and thus your chances of locating it at a given time. At some point, most hunters seem to adopt certain philosophies about the taking of game. Some traditional native hunters may fast for a time prior to the hunt or ritually purify themselves (as in a sweat lodge), not only to reduce or eliminate scent but also to cleanse the mind and spirit. I used to make a fire with a bow and drill to lightly smoke myself, my clothes, and my weapons. I have hung my hunting attire in trees through rainstorms, left it submerged in rapids in rivers, washed it without detergent, and eaten only bland foods for days prior to the hunt, among other things.

THE MENTAL GAME

Eventually, I came to realize that the environment dictates to what extremes you must go. In some places, a downwind deer can be shot from ten yards by a hunter puffing away on a cigarette, while in other places, like parts of Montana, Arizona, and other wild areas, a faint hint of something "odd" or a glimpse of "different" movement will send your quarry off in a heartbeat. As for the philosophy, well, you are trying to kill something, and regardless of your religious background, that ingredient in all living things that makes us alive and not an animated corpse is worthy of some level of honor. Learning to be humble in wilderness survival is a lesson you *will* learn if you stay out long enough to provide for yourself in a sustainable way. If you do not opt to follow the rules of the land, you will suffer. Those who "pit themselves against nature" are approaching the situation from a fighting stance, and if they survive long enough, they will be brought to heel. It is when we let go, when we quit fighting and gain a balance with the situation, that survival really becomes less of a struggle.

Once, when I was about eighteen or nineteen, I was heading out to one of my primitive camps for a few weeks of focused practice on fire making and stalking, when I learned some humbling lessons. With my head in the clouds and some "starter" groceries in a paper bag in my hand, I came upon a lone turkey. I first saw her about fifteen feet away and immediately cursed my crinkly bag and lack of a weapon. As I attempted to quietly set the bag down, I scanned the ground for projectiles of any sort and saw an oak branch of rabbit stick size within a step. Alas, when I picked it up, not only did the bird see me, but I realized that the stick was so rotten it would not survive the G forces exerted on it by a kid's merry-go-round, let alone a killing throw. I ran. The turkey was too close to take off (turkeys slow down when they are trying to get airborne in an attempt to get some distance away before taking flight). As

I ran, looking at the bird under my outstretched hand, a thought entered my conscious mind from some small, dark, immature, and disappointingly stupid part of my brain: "What if it pecks me, or worse, scratches me?" I mentally grabbed myself by the throat and squeezed while offering a few choice adjectives to describe my actions, and that was all it took—one millisecond of hesitation and she was gone. I immediately held my breath, attempting to kill the brain cells that had spawned that pathetic thought. How could I have blown such an opportunity? I was fresh out of basic training from the army, I grew up on a farm, and yes, we had chickens! Where was the explanation for this pathetic display of *hunting prowess*? Was I trying to override some not-so-latent ninnyness? After some long and brutal self-analysis, I placed the blame at the feet of my full belly and bag of food. I simply was not hungry enough to take any risk, real or imagined.

Need is a powerful force, and blown opportunities, powerful teachers. The lesson of carrying at least one hunting weapon at all times and maintaining vigilance was not new to me, but these are often the first "edges" you lose once you are out of the woods. An experience such as the one I had with the turkey quickly brought that edge back to the strop. If you pursue game, for food or photo, know that you will be surprised, outwitted, stalked, and left in the dust many times. The key is to look at the situation with the eye of both teacher and student. What is the lesson? What happened and why? Remember the questions and any answers that you come up with the next time you hunt.

Hunting is an essential skill for long-term wilderness survival. It is through hunting that you provide yourself with many of the tools needed to remain in the wild and the sustenance to survive in the shorter term. A short list of the gains made through hunting is as follows:

- Meat and fat provide: immediate and long-term sustenance—fresh, jerked, or made into pemmican.
- Hides give you: leather for clothing and rawhide for lashings, snowshoes, hard protective cases, cordage, glue, bags, and more.
- Sinew is great for: sewing, lashing, backing bows (a technique used to add strength to a bow), and making bow strings, snare lines, and more.
- Bones can be made into tools such as: fishing hooks, arrow points, knives, awls, needles, and buttons, as well as decorative ornaments. Teeth and jawbones can be used for abrading or cutting tools.
- Guts can be used for pouches, water bags, sausage casing, and lashing.

Clearly the value of good hunting skills can make the difference between life and death. The debate for many new hunters is, sit or move? I am an avid roving hunter, because it not only lets me hunt many areas and many types of game, it also lets me see what is happening on the land around my camp. I can collect or note the locations of edible plants, fire-starting materials, and other items that I need or may need down the road. The advantages of still hunting are also noteworthy. As a way to put meat in your belly, it is a tried and true method. With minimal tracking skills, a hunter can determine what areas see a lot of game traffic. You can spend a little time staking out a spot to see if a certain track is aging (i.e., you can determine how long ago the track was made by noting the past weather or the substrate, and seeing how one affected the other). If your skills are not up to the task, staking out a spot will let you know what time of day your quarry frequents the area. Then you have to figure out where to set up and wait.

MOVING AND SEEING

The way in which we as modern people move is more of a controlled fall. It is as if we have a string attached to our chests or foreheads and are being pulled along. This results in two problems. First, we walk with our body at a slant, our head out in front and completely out of balance. Second, we look at the ground and consequently see little of our surroundings.

For a hunter, balance is paramount. You may be called on to stop on a moment's notice and remain motionless, sometimes with only one foot on the ground. And the importance of seeing cannot be overstated. If you wait until game sees you, you will catch very little game.

Stumbling through the woods in an out-of-balance, non-seeing manner is not likely to yield a successful hunt—one of the reasons why many a modern hunter prefers to still-hunt. Going through the following exercises slowly and carefully *will* have a positive impact on your stalking abilities. It is crucial to slow down and raise your head.

Start out by standing squarely on your feet. With your eyes gazing out levelly, stretch both hands out directly in front of yourself, touching each other at eye level. Now, while wiggling your fingers, move your hands simultaneously apart

Bird's-eye view of range of motion for wide-angle exercise

while maintaining both your forward gaze and visual contact of both hands. Bring your hands as far back as possible until you can just catch the movement of your wiggling fingers. You should feel a shift in your vision as you do this exercise.

This wide-angle, or splatter, vision is used so seldom that your impulse will be to quickly shift back to a specific point in view. Keep practicing until you can shift into wide-angle vision without any effort. Athletes in basketball, soccer, and other big team sports use this way of seeing to visually cover a larger portion of the court or field while paying specific attention to a particular player. You will notice that wide-angle or peripheral vision is far more sensitive to movement and light. Pinpoint vision (looking from point to point to make up a whole picture) is time consuming and weak in details pertaining to the overall view.

Taking one glance in wide-angle vision allows you to clearly see the whole picture. For example leaves moved out of place by a passing deer lie differently on the ground than those that have not been disturbed. Wide-angle vision will make the trail stand out, whereas pinpoint vision will not.

Once you are able to easily shift into wide-angle vision, you are ready to move. While balancing on one leg, lift the other foot and slowly move it forward such a distance that you are able to place it flatly on the ground while applying no pressure or weight to it. Remember to bend your knees as you move, and do not lock them during periods of waiting, as this can result in a sudden lurch when you begin stalking again. If you are in wide-angle vision, your feet can, to some extent, become your eyes on the ground. Prior to applying weight onto your forward foot, gently touch the ground with the inside ball of your foot. Slowly roll the foot to the outside so that the entire ball of the foot is in contact with the ground. Then let your heel and toes settle to the ground as well. Be aware of sharp objects or sticks that may break under your weight. If your foot is well placed, slowly shift your weight from the back foot forward to the newly placed foot, and repeat the process. When you are hunting animals, constant, even movement at a rate of one step per minute or less should enable you to move, even when the prey is looking at you. With a lot of slow practice, you can move in a brisk walk and eventually a similar run.

PREPARING YOURSELF

To prepare for a hunt, it is important to become proficient with your weapon of choice and familiar with your hunting areas. While you are walking your hunting grounds, ask the following questions:

- From what direction does the wind normally come?
- What do the prey animals in the area eat? What is the best direction to approach prey from in a given area?
- Will my body be silhouetted against the sky?
- What time of day will the sun aid me by being at my back?
- What type of substrate will I be stalking on or through?

These are standard questions, and you will undoubtedly add to them as you practice stalking prey.

Although it is not always possible, I recommend selecting a specific, individual animal to hunt. Watch it and learn its strengths and weaknesses. When is it alert? Does it wander farther from its hole than others in the area? How can you use its weaknesses to help you put it on the table? Deer, for example, fall into many patterns, and, given the number of deer and car collisions in this area, it is not hard to find a lame deer to hunt if the time is taken to observe the local population.

Once your quarry has been established and the time has been chosen to hunt, you must prepare. What you do spiritually to make peace with the animal that you will hunt and kill is up to you. I physically prepare in the following way. In a remote setting with few to no human dwellings where animals are very sensitive to human scent, I will begin days prior to the hunt. I will eat rather bland food to help reduce body odor. This, combined with a wash in the stream using soapwort or another natural, locally present scent, or nonscented soap, removes my body's odor. Sweat lodges are also a good way to aid in the removal of human scent. My clothes are either left out in the woods away from camp in a rainstorm or washed in the creek and hung to dry. In a pinch, I will stand in the smoke of a wood fire to cover my scent; because fire is natural, smoke does not seem to startle the animals unless it is accompanied by heat and flame. Your rabbit stick or other weapon of choice ought to be carved and handled with clean hands and either smoke stained or rubbed lightly with charcoal to hide any bright white carving marks.

In more populated areas de-scenting can have little to no effect. I have seen hunters still hunting while smoking cigarettes and have deer pass under their stand. So look over the area you are in to determine to what level you must prepare.

In the following discussion, you will hunt using a rabbit stick, and your quarry will be a woodchuck.

It is time to start.

Approach your hunting area carefully. Pay attention to the wind, the sun, and anything else that might give away your location. There will be plenty of times when you will have a dry hunt, with no sighting of your game even after lots of careful preparation. However, when your prey is spotted, watch it for a moment before you begin stalking. Do not look directly at the animal. Watch it only in wide-angle vision, because the animal's sensitivity is acute; the hunt may be over before it starts.

As you stalk, note whether the animal is weary or feeding contentedly. Take note of the direction in which it is moving and why (as in the case with grazers), and try to predict where it may be in twenty minutes. If you make a noise, you may have to remain motionless for a time until it settles and resumes its normal activity.

As you approach, bring your weapon to the ready so that, once you are in range, you have only the release—no cocking back. Once the projectile is released and the animal is hit, move quickly and quietly to it, ready to give a killing blow if necessary. If your initial strike only wounded your prey, you must keep it from escaping to its hole, where it may die a longer and more painful death, leaving you hungry and feeling terrible.

A mortally wounded animal may sprint off, exhibiting no signs of serious injury, only to collapse shortly after reaching cover. If your quarry successfully reaches cover and you believe that you had a solid strike, stay put. Injured animals will often lie in thickets to recover or rest, and you

may startle them into flight and be unable to follow and catch them. After waiting for about twenty to thirty minutes, slowly stalk toward the place where you initially struck the animal and check for visible tracks or a blood trail. Follow the trail as best you can, weapon at the ready, and scan the area. If you get a second shot, make it count.

The best advice I can give is to practice, practice, practice! Injuring an animal is worse than killing it. If it is dead, you can make sure that its body is appreciated and fully utilized. Every time you use a tool that incorporates some of that animal's body, you can't help but give thanks. However, if it is injured, not only does it take an unknown toll on the animal, it also takes a toll on you as you wonder what is to become of it. Good, however, *can* come from a botched hunt in the form of valuable lessons and the vow to never repeat the same mistakes.

Be Double-Prepared

It is wise to carry more than one weapon, because this allows you to immediately make a follow-up strike and ensure that the kill has been made. A stunned animal may appear dead and then, as you approach, get up and hobble off to safety, where it may die from its wounds out of your reach. A case in point: While hunting one day, I stalked a woodchuck and threw my boomerang, bringing the animal down. I approached quickly with my spear at the ready and, with ten feet to go, saw the woodchuck get up and run. A good throw with my spear ensured meat for the evening meal.

Check local hunting regulations for acceptable methods of taking game and the licensing procedure. Practice hard, hunt well, and give thanks.

CAMOUFLAGE

As a supplement to moving carefully, good camouflage will help you to move unseen through the land. Camouflage is intended to break up the outline of a person or object, because it is often the outline that attracts the eye and is recognized by the brain.

Good camouflage has two very distinct parts. The first part is a physical blurring or changing of your outline and the distinctive body patterns that catch the eye, including the symmetry of the face or the series of parallel lines that make up your hands. The second part is the mental aspect—the quieting of the mind and going into wide-angle vision in order to soften or diffuse your intent. Many hunters suggest looking below, beyond, or to either side of your quarry once it is spotted. As children, many of us found out in Hide-and-Go-Seek that intensely thinking, "Don't See Me," or, "I know they are going to find me," draws the attention of the seekers. Animals seem to be far more sensitive in this area than humans.

Of the many types of camouflage that are used by peoples the world over, we will cover two here.

Camouflaged person

Mud Camouflage

Mud camouflage is especially useful when you will either not be moving or you will be moving seldom, as in the case of an ambush for game. Some advantages of mud are its ability to decrease your scent, the non-skinlike texture it gives your body, and the natural dappling it provides as it dries. The disadvantages are the potential for leaving a trail of mud smudges on leaves and the ground as you walk, and its lack of versatility. Gray clay, for example, may be perfect camouflage for a streambed but would stick out clearly in the forest. Mud also cools the body quickly, even on warm days, and a spot in the shade can lead to shivering.

In a moist area or near water, you can make mud by pouring water onto the ground and digging in it with your hands or a stick. The consistency should be such that it sticks easily and does not run or fall off. Once you have an adequate supply, apply it liberally to your entire body, being careful not to get it into your ear canals or eyes. Take the time to see how the mud color compares to that of the area in which you plan on hiding. Remember, mud changes color as it dries.

Before it dries, however, pick up handfuls of dry debris and, with your eyes closed, gently toss them over your whole body. They should stick to the mud and provide a further breaking up of your outline. Glasses can be dipped in mud, and then a line in the center of each lens can be cleaned to allow you to see with little reflective material exposed. Be careful to avoid scratching your lenses.

Now you are ready to get to your hiding spot. Bring an extra handful of mud with which to cover the soles of your feet once you are in position or for touch-up.

Move carefully. Too much movement will result in much of your camouflage flaking off. If you brush against plants, you may give away your passage by leaving a trail of mud on the leaves.

Charcoal and Ash Camouflage

By far the warmer of the two camouflage techniques covered here, charcoal and ash camouflage is also better for times when movement is required. Charcoal is dry and therefore warmer than mud, it does not brush off easily or leave obvious signs of your passage, it can be applied to

Hidden person

blend with almost anything, and it is easily acquired. On the minus side, it is harder to remove and can only be effectively applied to light-colored clothing.

Charcoal from a wood fire can be ground up and applied as a powder or with water added as a paste. White ash, *not charcoal*, when mixed with water into a paste makes lye, an alkali that can cause a rash if it contacts your skin. It can, however, be used dry, and no, it will not harm you if it starts to rain or you wash it off.

Remember—the goal is to break up the outline of your body and the symmetry that easily defines parts of you. As a general rule, you should lighten the hollows and darken the ridges. This does not mean that you should put a black line across your brow and down your nose. Mark your body with charcoal lines running contrary to your body's natural contours. Soften the lines by gently rubbing your hands over them, smudging them. This softens the edges, dulls the sheen on your skin, and gives a dappled effect. Finally, dust and small debris can be sprinkled over your body. This may seem insignificant, as it does not appear to make much difference; however, your body's tiny hairs hold on to some of it and can help blend you with the background.

With mud camouflage, you blend in with a specific background. With charcoal, you blend in with shadows. A few other caveats with mud is that when wet it leaves smear marks on anything you touch; when it dries, it flakes off and leaves more signs for others to follow. Moving within shadow takes practice, because it often requires movement off-trail through thick and potentially noisy debris. You have to learn to trust your camouflage. Anyone can hide behind an object. The goal here is to be invisible while you are in the open.

CARCASS CARE

Your hunt was a success! You are standing over a freshly killed mammal. Now what? Proper care of the carcass is just as important as the hunt. When an animal dies, the bacteria within the gut and intestines continue to live and thrive. The result is ever-expanding gas that will rupture the intestines and foul the meat if the intestines and guts are not removed immediately. Additionally, the removal of the internal organs, intestines, and blood speeds the cooling process and thus helps delay decomposition. The essential step are:

1. Checking to be sure the animal is dead
2. Bleeding the animal
3. Field dressing or gutting the animal
4. Skinning the animal
5. Cutting or butchering the animal
6. Utilizing the bones

Approach the animal carefully and look for signs of life, such as movement from breathing or blinking. You can touch the eye with a stick to see if it blinks; if it does, you need to finish off the animal.

Bleeding the Animal

Cut the throat by driving a knife from the side of the neck just below the lower jaw, through to the other side. Then cut out the front of the neck. This is faster and easier than cutting through the hair, which can dull a knife very quickly. (Hair from a wild pig will dull your knife after only a few inches of cutting. When I worked as a hog hunter for the National Park Service, I was shocked at just how tough the hog's hair is; all cuts beside the initial entry cuts were made from the inside out.)

Blood clots fast when it is not being moved by the heart. If you complete this process quickly, the blood will gush out readily. Placing the animal with its head downhill can aid in bleeding an animal. In the case of smaller animals like squirrels, the meat can be soaked in cold water and the blood allowed to leach out after completing the steps below.

Field Dressing or Gutting

I will use a deer in this example.

Bucks during the rut have active scent glands on the inside of their hind legs—tufts of hair with a smell you can't miss. These strong-smelling glands can be removed if you don't like the smell or are afraid of the meat becoming contaminated through long hanging in such proximity to the glands. Pull on the long hair to draw the hide away from the leg, then slice through the hide behind and toss the glands away. (The udders of does can be easily removed in the same manner.) After dealing with the scent glands or udder, follow the steps below:

1. Position the deer on its back, and cut around the anus (and vagina if the deer is a female) to a depth of three inches.
2. The urinary tract of male mammals travels from the bladder back through the pelvis next to the small intestine. It then loops back along the belly toward the chest. A buck's penis is located on the belly toward the rear. Make a small cut at the upper base of the penis toward the back while holding the penis up and away from the body. This will allow you to separate the penis from the carcass all the way back to just below the anus.

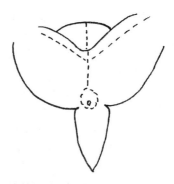

Primary cuts around the anus

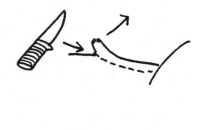

Separating the penis from the belly

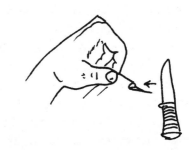

Starting at the sternum

3. Feel down the sternum (breastbone) until you come to the soft spot at the end (the xyphoid process). Pinch a bit of skin, about one-half inch, and pull it up and away from the carcass. Slice through the skin

and thin layer of muscle, being careful to avoid cutting through the stomach. If you see green matter, you have cut too deeply and will have to deal with the stench as well as wash out the cavity later.

4. Once the cut goes all the way through the abdominal wall, slide your index and middle fingers of the non-cutting hand into the abdominal cavity, palm up and facing the rear of the animal. Holding a knife in your right hand, place the blade, cutting edge up, between the two fingers in the abdominal cavity, and slide both the blade and your fingers to cut the abdominal wall down to the pelvis. To further protect against cutting the stomach and intestines, you can lift the abdominal wall with your two fingers guiding the knife. I will often continue the cut to the anus, cutting through the muscle between the legs until I hit bone. This allows the legs to spread to either side and gives easier access for cutting any remaining connective tissue that is still holding the end of the intestines and urinary tract in place.

5. Above the stomach is the diaphragm, a divider made of muscle tissue that separates the abdominal cavity from the tho-racic (chest) cavity. Cut the diaphragm free from the chest wall on both sides, back to the spine.

6. Reach up into the chest cavity toward the neck and feel the windpipe, a hard-ribbed tube. Cut this as high up as possible. Gripping the windpipe, pull it back toward you; the organs (heart and lungs and, in the intestinal cavity, the liver and the kidneys) and diaphragm are attached and will now be exposed. The connections that have not yet been severed along the spine are weak and can usually be torn by pulling forcefully on the windpipe.

7. The heart, liver, and kidneys are great cubed and put in a stew. Harvest the organs you wish to eat, and, if possible, set them in cold water to help the blood leach out.

8. It is now possible to pull the guts out of the abdominal cavity. Grasp the terminal end of the small intestines and urinary tract from inside the abdominal cavity. Pull them through the pelvis and out the incision along with the rest of the guts and organs.

9. Tilt the carcass so that any blood within the cavity can drain out through the pelvis.

Unzipping the gut

Skinning

Some animals part with their hides more easily than others. Deer, for example, can be skinned completely by hand once the primary cuts have been made. Wild hogs and woodchucks, on the other hand, need a blade to help separate the hide from the carcass. These primary cuts should be made just through the hide and not into the flesh. Skinning, when done well, is a bloodless process.

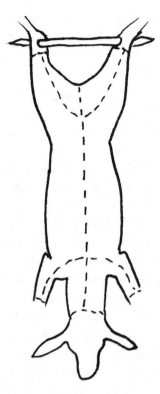

Primary cuts

Here are the primary cuts:

1. Cut all the way around each leg at the second joint above the foot.
2. Make a cut from the anus along the belly to the lower jaw (usually done during field dressing).
3. On the inside of all four limbs, make cuts to connect the ring cuts on the legs to the median cut on the belly and chest.
4. Make one ring cut around the neck and you are finished.

With some animals, deer especially, the hide can be pulled away from the carcass with one hand, and your free hand can knead down between the hide and the carcass. This is preferable to using a knife, because it avoids scoring or otherwise damaging the hide. Bits of connective tissue, such as little tendons connecting the hide to the muscle, allow the animal to shake or shiver portions of its skin to rid itself of flies. These connectors can be broken singly by hand; however, when you are sliding your hand between the carcass and the hide, you may grab a number of them at once. Pulling hard on these thin, bunched connectors can result in a "paper cut."

If you do use a knife or sharp stone as a skinning aid, pull the hide away from the carcass, and gently cut the stretched tissue with the cutting edge angled toward the carcass and not the hide. This way, if you overcut, the damage is done to the flesh and not to the hide.

Butchering

According to the USDA, food kept at 0°F can remain safe indefinitely, and at 40°F, for two to three days. I have let carcasses hang for three weeks at temperatures in the thirties with no bad odor or ill effects. Animals taken in the warm summer months are a different matter and should be butchered as soon as possible, because bacteria multiply rapidly in the "danger zone" (40°F to 140°F).

Hanging the carcass of an animal larger than a fox serves two purposes. First, it makes the skinning and butchering process much easier. The height can be adjusted, and you have access to all parts of the carcass. Second, letting the animal hang lets enzymes within the meat begin to break down the muscle and connective tissue, making it tender and softening the gamey flavor. Hanging is not a necessity but a preference among most hunters. I recommend hanging a carcass for about one week, weather permitting.

A dry crust forms on the exposed meat as moisture evaporates from it. This crust must be trimmed off before you consume the meat. The longer the meat hangs, the thicker the crust and therefore the greater the loss of meat. Leaving the hide on the carcass protects the meat and keeps in the moisture but makes skinning more difficult.

A simple way to get a heavy carcass off of the ground is to make a hole through each hind leg at the point that corresponds to the human heel. On most animals it looks more like a backward-bending knee than a heel. Make the cut in the thin part of the leg between the Achilles tendon (which comes from the muscle above) and at the leg bone that runs parallel to the tendon. You can use a spreader stick to keep the animal's legs spread by placing it between the hind legs so that it forces them apart. If the spreader is strong and is placed in the holes that you made in the back legs, you can lash the legs to it to keep them apart; then use the spreader stick to hang the deer from a branch.

The easiest method for lifting heavy game is to cut a strong, ten-foot sapling that has a Y in the upper portion. Trim off all other branches and place the sapling over a strong branch of another tree, about five feet off of the ground. With the Y end of the sapling on the ground near the carcass, lash the spreader stick to the fork in the Y and, seesaw-like, pull the raised end downward and tie it to a stake in the ground. If you have help, you can lift the deer and fasten a piece of cordage to the spreader stick, tying the other end to a sturdy branch.

In temperatures above 40°F, all meat that is not to be consumed immediately must be dried to be preserved. (See "Drying Meat" under "Preserving Food" in Chapter 9.) To preserve meat in

Hanging deer

freezing temperatures, the carcass can be cut into meal-size chunks.

I remove some of the best cuts first, like the back strap on either side of the spine. These long muscles are very tender and easy to remove. Start by making cuts down either side of the center ridge of the spine. With your fingers in the cut, slide your hand up and down the incision while pushing them into the carcass. A second skin or membrane covering the back strap should now be evident and can easily be pulled and cut away. Work your fingers into the flesh along the initial incision until you reach bone, then pull the muscle away from the carcass. Carefully tear or cut any flesh that is still connected to the rib cage.

The legs can be divided easily by cutting them at the joints or separating muscle groups. Portions of the carcass with little bits of meat still attached can be cooked and eaten within a few days (temperature permitting) or pulled from the bone, rolled into a ball, and frozen for later use.

Utilize the Bones

Bones for tools (if you don't want the marrow) can be broken open with rocks to allow access for

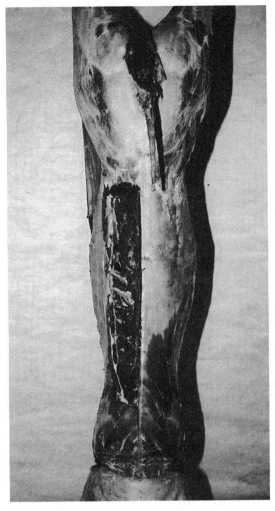

Back strap

bugs and placed on an anthill for quick cleaning. But their chance of being taken by scavengers is very high. I often place bones in trees or hang them with cordage, and within a month they are pretty clean. If I am in a rush to use the bones, I break and boil them to quickly remove the oils and marrow. (The broth is highly nutritious.) If time is not an issue, leave them out up to a year, because this allows the oils to break down and gives you a solid, white piece of bone (as opposed to an oily, translucent one).

CHAPTER 14

RAWHIDE, TANNING HIDES FOR BUCKSKIN, AND SINEW

When you are living off of the land, tools such as rope, fabric, and thread are very useful and can be employed in a great variety of ways. Rawhide—animal hide that has been fleshed, degreased, and dried (either with the hair still on or removed)—can be soaked to a flimsy, stretchable material and be used to lash anything from knife handles to footwear. Sinew, the tendon, is so strong that, even when it is separated into individual thin strands, it can be used for anything from sewing thread to reversed-wrapped bow strings (see "Cordage and Cloth," Chapter 15). Buckskin, the finest fabric of all, is soft. It is treated animal hide that makes great clothing for any occasion, from weddings to hunting trips. Its versatility and comfort to the wearer are of great value.

RAWHIDE

Rawhide is animal skin that has merely had the flesh side scraped to remove any fat and flesh left on during the skinning process. Often the hair is removed as well. Rawhide is great for making lashings; hard cases for items like bone hooks, needles, or pemmican; shoe soles; cordage; and more. The great value of it is that, when it is wet, it

is elastic and can be tied around objects like stone hammerheads, snowshoes, etc. As it dries, it shrinks and hardens. Of course, the reverse is also true. When it gets wet, it softens and stretches. Methods for protecting rawhide from the effects of moisture will be addressed shortly.

To make rawhide, you will need a green (fresh) or soaked wet hide, which can be prepared using either of the two methods below.

Racked-Hide or Dry-Scrape Method

Matt Richards, author of *Deerskins into Buckskins* (see Appendix), told me that dry-scraping hides for rawhide or buckskin was practiced by very few native peoples. It is significantly harder than the wet-scrape method when you are using nonmetal tools, and its only advantage as far as I am concerned is in the freedom to let the hide sit and work on it fifteen minutes here and ten minutes there (although wouldn't you rather just finish it?). For larger and tougher hides to flesh, like moose and bison, Richards says that it is a reasonable approach, although for smaller animals, deer included, the wet-scrape method is the way to go. That said, it can be done and therefore is included here for rawhide, but not in the tanning section later in this chapter.

Racking a hide is merely a way of supporting a hide within an external framework, like an artist framing a canvas. Most commonly, four poles are laid out on the ground in a rectangle (a one-foot margin around the hide allows for stretching) and lashed at the corners. The hide, while still green, is placed in the middle of the framework, and holes are made in the edges about every three to five inches or less and about one-half inch in from the edge, although with some thinner areas I'll inset them up to one and one-half inches. All holes should be a one-half-inch slit parallel to the nearest edge.

One method of racking the hide requires that it first be centered in the rack. Tie the four corners first—not tight, just snug for now. Lace the hide to the rack by starting at the bottom. Tie the lacing or cordage to the frame, then run it through the corresponding hole in the hide and back to the frame again. Continue this process all the way around the hide, lashing each side tighter than the last one so that the fourth side tightens the hide like a drum.

I find this to be overly labor intensive, however. I find it more efficient to first lace the top of the hide (the neck area) to the top of the rack using one piece of cordage, then to lace the bottom with another. These are snugged up, and then the two sides are laced. The whole hide is then adjusted to remove wrinkles. Be careful not to overtighten or the holes in the hide may tear out.

Due to the hide stretching while wet and shrinking while drying, you will need to snug up some of the lashings during the scraping process. It is also advisable, when you are lacing, to run all ties from the back of the hide to the back of the frame, around the frame to the front, and then through the hole in the front of the hide. This will keep the hide on a single plane rather than having one tie pulling the hide toward the back of the frame and the next pulling toward the front.

Lean the racked hide against a tree and, starting with the stake scraper (see Chapter 16) perpendicular to the hide, scrape downward from the neck. All flesh and fat should peel away and run down the hide. Be careful not to slide the scraper sideways and slice the hide.

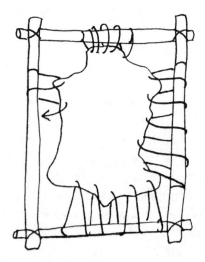

A racked deer hide

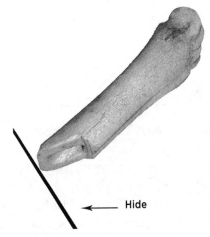

Working position for using a bone scraper

To remove the hair on a dry hide, soak the hide until the hair "slips" (comes out when gently pulled). Soak times vary. In cold, clear, flowing water, it can take three weeks. In a bucket of water, changed once daily, it takes half that time or less. Warm water makes the time even shorter still—three or four days. If a few big rocks are used to weigh down the hide, make sure to shift them periodically, because their weight compresses the hide and does not allow it to fully absorb water, thus preventing the hair from slipping. Once the hair slips, the above process can be repeated for the hair side of the hide.

I prefer to soak hides until the hair slips prior to fleshing and thus avoid having to rack the hide twice. This is OK if the hide was skinned well and no chunks of fat remain. (I skin any hide that I want to use, and in the case of deer, I use a knife only for the primary cuts.) The hair can be removed while the hide is completely dry, but it requires a lot of elbow grease and, in my opinion, may only be worth it if you use a sharp, metal scraper. Once the hair is removed, the hide can be dried and stored indefinitely. It's rawhide ready to go.

Fleshing a hide on the beam

Skinned-Log or Wet-Scrape Method

You will need a smooth, peeled log and a broad scraper (see Chapter 16). Place the hide, hair side down, on the log, leaving a bit of the hide hanging over one raised end. Leaning against the log, and pinching the overhanging hide between it and your body, scrape downward, using the scraper like a squeegee. All fat and meat should run down the hide.

Another setup that I find easier on the back is to lean the log against a tree in a more vertical attitude. In this orientation, I call the log a

Vertical beam setup

"beam." The hide is held by pinching it between the top of the beam and the tree. Work your way from side to side (not neck to tail) on the top portion, then pull the hide farther up the beam and continue until you are finished.

Soak the hide as described earlier. Once the hair slips, the hide can be placed, hair side up, on the beam and scraped in the same direction as the hair until all is removed. The hide can be spread out to dry and then stored indefinitely. It should be noted that a thin layer of skin often comes off with the hair; it is not the grain that must be removed for tanning the hide, so don't get excited.

Working with Rawhide

To make lashings or laces, a circle can be cut from the hide and a continuous spiral can be cut into it, like when you peel an apple, without breaking the skin. One method I have found to be effective is to stick a razor-sharp knife in a log and, while grasping the dry disk in both hands, pull it into the blade where the blade enters the log, moving the disk in a spiral until you have turned the whole thing into a thin strip. To use the lace, soak it for a few hours until it is elastic, then make your lashings and let them dry.

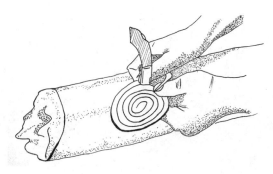

Coil method for cutting rawhide

Stretching the lace before using it will reduce the loosening and softening effects of moisture on lashings. To do this, tie one end of the wet rawhide lace to a tree, stretch it taut, tie it to another tree, and let it dry. You can also waterproof the lashings on items like hammerheads that do not need to flex: Cover them with a light layer of pine pitch and sprinkle them with ash. Too much pure pitch can penetrate the hide on hot days and soften the lashing, so mix in plenty of ground-up charcoal.

TANNING

To turn a hide into leather, you must take it a few steps beyond rawhide. As with rawhide, there are wet and dry methods, but I will not address the dry-scrape method for reasons mentioned previously. Read through this entire section before you try your first hide, because there is some advance preparation required for time-sensitive parts of the tanning process.

The goal of scraping the hide is to remove the membrane, fat, and flesh on the inside of the hide and to remove the hair, epidermis, and grain on the outside. The epidermis, a very thin layer of skin, comes away easily with the hair, while the grain is a thicker and more stubborn layer requiring more coaxing and/or brute force and determination to remove. The removal of these parts of the hide opens the door for the penetration of tanning agents that are introduced later in the process.

Once the flesh side has been cleaned of meat and fat, the wet, green hide can be scraped right away. If the hide has been dried for storage, it should be soaked either in a container or a body of water until the hair slips and the hide is swollen. Graining a hide that has been dried at some earlier point is harder than working with a green or bucked hide (see below). If the water you are using is in a container, or you placed the hide in a stagnant pool of warmer water, the process will go pretty fast—three or four days—but the hide will also get pretty ripe. In flowing or cold water, this can take much longer—even weeks. Another option is bucking the hide.

Bucking the Hide

Bucking (steps 1 through 7 that follow) consists of soaking the green hide as a way to ease its preparation for becoming buckskin. Richards (*Deerskins into Buckskins*, 1997) is a strong advocate for bucking in a white ash and water solution. While this is not exactly necessary, it reduces the number of times you must repeat step 11, and it reduces the chance of taking the process partly through step 12 and then having to go back to the beam. It is well worth the effort, because it makes the grain more visible and hence easier to remove; in addition, it eases the penetration of oils into the hide at a later time.

For bucking in primitive settings, Richards says that coating the flesh side of the hide with an ash slurry and burying it in a hole in the ground for three days works well. Dug- or burned-out logs or stumps can also provide an adequate container for soaking.

The alkali nature of the ash mixture can cause rashes and excessively dry hands and affects some people more than others. I keep it off of the insides of my arms, but my hands fare OK, although they get very dried out. Hardwood ash makes for a more alkaline slurry than softwood ash.

I have seen eggs used as gauges of the specific gravity of the solution to ensure a good mix without having it become too alkaline. The solution, once mixed, is left to sit for about fifteen minutes while you let the ash settle. A chicken egg placed in the water without being supported by a layer of ash should show a circle at the waterline at least the size of a quarter. If the egg floats on its side, the mixture is too strong; if it sinks or rests just at the surface, it is too weak.

I use whatever is in the firepit, which usually is a mixture of hard- and softwood ash. Given the lesser alkali content in the softwoods, I haven not bothered with the egg test on the grounds that finding a chicken egg in the wilderness is pretty unlikely. (And if you're thinking, "Why not use wild turkey eggs?" think back to the last five times you found a nest full of newly laid wild-turkey eggs.)

Here is the drill for tanning the hide.

1. Dampen three to four gallons of white ash.

2. After there is no more dry ash, continue adding water slowly while stirring with a stick until the consistency is thick and soupy. I try for a mixture that is wet enough to allow pouring without being lumpy—like pancake batter. The solution needs to be liquid enough to penetrate the hide easily.

3. If your containers are on the smaller side, de-hair the hide first; wring it out completely, then add a little solution to your largest empty container. Place part of the hide into the container so that one layer covers the bottom. Add more solution on top of the hide and fold in another layer of hide. Add more solution and so on until the hide is covered. Note: With smaller containers, your project will require more

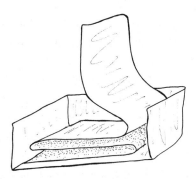

Putting in the hide for bucking

tending and more time. You may not be able to fit a hair-on winter hide into a given container, but a summer hide might fit just fine.

4. Place some wood or bark over the top of the hide, and put a weight on that. The wood spreads the weight out so that no part of the hide is compressed unduly, which can inhibit and/or prevent the solution from penetrating the hide.

5. Keep extra solution on hand to add to the hide-soaking container, because the lack of a sealing lid will allow for water loss from evaporation. Also make sure that no part of the hide is exposed to the air during this time.

6. Let the hide soak until it is very swollen, usually two or three days.

7. Rinse off the ash and place the swollen, soaked hide on the beam such that the neck is the first area worked. This is the hardest to scrape but makes your job easier for all of the remaining steps in the entire process. If you need some encouragement, choose another starting point.

8. Begin with a small area and work it as hard as you can. At first, you will get some

hide gunk, but chances are you have not gone deep enough. You want to remove the grain—a porous yet smooth, tangibly thick layer under the top layer of skin (the top layer comes off easily with slipping hair). The grain comes off leaving a distinctively different surface underneath. You may need to look closely to see the difference.

9. Once you get a spot started, keep working the hide from there and make sure to overlap each stroke. This is especially tedious for the beginner, and I clearly remember bouncing all over the hide, taking some hair from here and a patch of grain from there. Soon I did not know which areas I had done and which ones I had not. This meant that if I wanted leather, I had to go over the entire hide again systematically, scraping as if I had never touched the hide.

10. Be careful around holes and scores or knife marks. To deal with holes from arrows, bullets, or bad skinning, scrape the hide toward the hole only. Do not pass over the hole; just bring the scraper up to the edge or you will, in all likelihood, tear the hide.

11. Do a careful once-over of the flesh side. I usually am a bit lax on this portion if I've been thorough the first time through, but it did cause a problem one time when I left a large area with membrane intact.

12. Rinse the hide well in a pond, creek, or bucket of water. This step is key to getting good results. Warmer, moving water rinses the hide faster than cold, slow-moving water. When you are soaking the hide in a pond or creek, just tie some cord-

age through a hole and anchor the hide to a rock for twenty-four hours or more, and stir it around occasionally. If you use a container, the water must be changed often (every three or four hours) for the better part of two days to ensure that the alkali in the hide has been neutralized. To check for proper rinsing, look for any swollen or rubbery areas on the hide: There shouldn't be any. The hide should look as it did before, with its white/blue color.

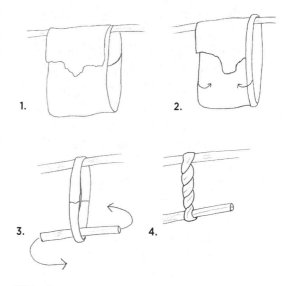

Wringing sequence

13. To wring out the hide, place it over a two-inch-diameter branch, neck down, with the hind end falling six inches on one side while the rest hangs on the other side. Spread it out along the branch, and then bring the neck end up and over the hind end, overlapping it by about six inches so that it makes a sleeve of sorts with the branch inside of it. Starting on one edge, roll the sleeve up as you would on a shirt until you reach the midpoint of the hide. Do the same on the other edge. Insert a rabbit stick or smooth, sturdy branch into the bottom of the loop that has been formed by the rolled hide, and twist in one direction until you are unable to twist any farther. Hold the twist until the drips slow, then reverse the twist. Untwist and grip the hide at the point where it contacts the branch, and pull downward, sliding the hide around the branch until the point is midway between the branch and the lowest part of the hide. Wring it again. Follow the same procedure for a total of four different wringing positions.

14. Open the hide and check to ensure that it has been wrung out well. The color should

be translucent white with a few grayish soggy spots; a few soggy spots are manageable, but too many may require another shot at the wringing station. Stretch the hide by hand over your knee, over the end of your fleshing beam, or over the wringing branch. As it stretches, it should turn an opaque white and look more like leather. Any wet spots should be squeegeed out. I stretch those spots on the stake and, with a cloth, soak up any moisture that has been forced out. The next step should be ready to go, because you don't want the hide to dry at this stage.

15. With the brains of the animal in a container, add an equal volume of hot water (not too hot for your hands or you risk cooking the hide), and knead the brains with your fingers. Crush up any lumps and make as smooth of a soup as you can manage. Add another third of a gallon of

hot water and thoroughly mix up the solution.

16. Dangle the hide into the brains with one hand while, with your other hands, ensuring that all of the hide entering gets a good coating. The hide's edges (to include the edges of holes) usually need special attention; i.e., take hold of an edge with one hand and grab the same edge a few inches down with your other hand, and pull. Stretch the hide in different directions to really encourage solution penetration.

17. Make sure that the hide is totally saturated. With your fingers kneading and stretching the hide, work your way over the whole thing, ensuring that there are no stiff, nonflexible areas. It should feel just like it did when it was fresh.

18. Ring the hide out thoroughly before repeating steps 16, 17, and 18 so that the hide has been in the brains three times and is well wrung out before you proceed to step 19. After the final wringing, open the hide and check for wet spots; deal with them as before. If you have not bucked the hide, repeat the braining and wringing steps eight times. This will afford you the greatest chance of success.

19. From this point on, the hide must be stretched and worked continuously as it dries. Any area of the hide that dries without being worked may have a tanned-leather feel to the outside, yet it will be stiff and papery on the inside. I prefer, when working a hide alone, to use a stake. This is made by cutting a three-inch-diameter sapling off at about three feet off of the ground and leaving the trunk with a wedge-shaped top. Round off the corners and sharp edges, but only slightly. The hide is worked on the stake by throwing the hide over it and pulling, pushing, and stretching it against the tip—really force it and push hard. I'll go from the stake to sitting on a log with the hide stretched over my knees and continue working it by both forcing my knees apart and stretching the hide over one or the other of my knees. An overhanging branch can also be used to good effect if all branch nubs have been removed. Place the hide over the branch as you would hang it to dry on a clothesline, grasp each overhanging edge, and, pulling hard, slide it back and forth over the branch. Rotate the hide frequently to hit all parts.

While it is best to use a systematic approach to ensure that every part of the hide gets worked, you must be flexible and tend to the areas that dry faster (like the edges, the belly skin, and the leg areas) while not neglecting the thicker parts. Except when you are working around holes, don't worry about tearing the hide—it is very tough. If you have a helper, the process will go much faster. Cold, damp days are worth skipping unless you want to be at this stage all day. Optimally, you should aim for a dry, warm day or shelter out of direct sun to work your hide. I have found that direct sun can dry the hide faster than I can work it. Stiff spots on the outside need to be addressed, usually by rubbing them with something rough like sandstone. Interior stiffness requires a trip back to the stake for a hard working over. Pull the hide in every possible direction to stretch out that spot.

A stake and staking

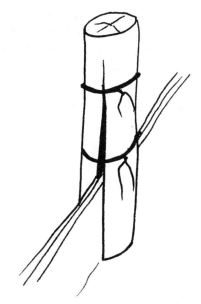

Hide pin

Smoking the Hide

Once the hide is dry, it will feel light and fluffy, and, if it is clean, it will be totally white. To finish it, it must be smoked. This process will preserve all of the work you did in the tanning process when the hide gets wet from washing or through incidental wettings.

1. A pit must be dug about two feet deep and hardwood kindling gathered, along with some punky wood. If you don't want to build a tripod, dig the hole beneath a branch that is about six feet off of the ground. Light the fire and let it burn down to make a good bed of coals while you prepare the hide.

2. The hide must be sewn into a sack. The stiff hide edges are trimmed off, and then the hide is folded in half lengthwise, with the edges matched up as best as can be managed. Stitch, or pin, the matched edges together all the way from the top (neck area), which needs to remain open, to the bottom.

3. A skirt, which is to be attached to the open end of the sack, can be made from old hide or cloth. To make the skirt, sew a piece of fabric to form a flared sleeve and attach it to the open edge of the hide sack. If the circumference of the skirt is greater than that of the hide sack opening, merely stitch all the way around and fold the remaining fabric over against the skirt, and stitch.

   I have smoked two hides without the benefit of a skirt, but doing so entails the risk that the lower hide may get too hot, stiffen, and end up brittle and basically useless. Smoking of the lower part of the hide without a skirt requires special attention or it will not receive adequate amounts of smoke. If you forgo the skirt, do not trim off the stiff hide of the neck; instead, let those edges touch the ground, and anchor them to stakes with cordage that has been run through holes made in the lower edges of the neck. Gaps between the ground and the hide can be blocked with any debris or sod available.

4. With a bed of coals thick on the floor of the pit, tie the hide to the overhanging branch or tripod, and adjust the height so that about three inches of the skirt touch the ground. Pull the skirt away from the hole and secure it.

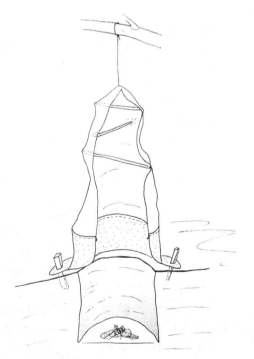

Smoking a hide, cutaway view

5. Insert three or four sticks or spreaders (less than pencil thickness) up into the hide sack so that the walls are held apart and there are no folds or sags.

6. Cover the coals with shredded, punky wood, making sure that the edges of the pit have as much punk as the middle of the pit (too often, the edges get neglected and the wood flares up and damages the hide). You should be able to hold your hand over the pit at the height of the bottom of the hide without burning it. If not, the fire needs to burn down a bit, or you need a longer skirt or deeper hole.

7. Once it is clear that a flare-up is unlikely, spread the skirt over the pit and seal the edges to the ground with weights. Give the hide about four minutes before grasping the point of a spreader through the hide (from the outside), and reposition the other end in a different spot on the far wall of the hide. Repeat the process until all spreaders have had both points moved. If they are left in place, little white spots will remain white and unsmoked.

8. After ten to fifteen minutes, remove the hide, turn it inside out, and, if the color goals are met, repeat the process for the unsmoked side.

Different woods will give different colors, from the greenish of the spruce to the yellow of the aspen, but there are always many contributing factors that will cause variations from one smoking to another. With too much time on your hands, you may find joy in making a tie-dyed sort of buckskin or perhaps loincloths patterned with leaf prints . . . or perhaps not.

You're done! The hide can now be used to make a variety of clothing items.

Grease Tanning

A cat once killed a weasel and left the carcass in the driveway, so I skinned it. Once the hide was free of the body, I wanted to flesh it, so I put it on my leg, flesh side up, and, using my knife as a squeegee, scraped down its length and watched a little wave of oil run before my blade. Eventually the oil was harder to see, and I put the skin away. Weeks later, I came across the dried-out little thing and found that, upon handling, it softened up. I buffed it between my hands and found I was holding a grease-tanned hide.

I have been playing with this method on bobcat, fisher, and mink: all have oily skin that is conducive to this process. A good indicator as to which hides you can grease tan is when you see so much oil you are at a loss as to how to get rid of it all. I have heard that fox and coyote are too dry to grease tan, but I have not attempted this method with those animals.

The area in which much of the work needs to happen is in the staking or stretching department, especially if you wish to keep the hair on. The fibers need to be well stretched to allow for penetration of the oils. The risk in learning this technique is the possibility of damaging a hide permanently. If there is too much oil or grease, you end up with grease burn, where the hide becomes stiff and translucent and sometimes almost transparent—great for primitive windows but lousy for anything else. If too much oil is removed, then you end up with a crinkly, dry hide that needs to be tanned with the brain-tanning method.

SINEW

Sinew or tendon is found on the legs or along the back straps of animals (the long muscles on either side of the spine). In the legs of deer, it is a white, flexible bundle on the backside of the leg bones. Smaller bundles can also be found on the front side. Leg sinew just needs to be cut out and have the clear sheath removed (done by slicing lengthwise, opening the bundle and pulling out the fiber bundles).

The sinew is on the surface of the muscle on the deer's back. The sinew here is more silvery in color and flat instead of in a bundle. Harvest the back sinew as you would skin a section of hide.

Hang harvested sinew, and let it dry in a spot out of direct sunlight. When it is dry, the sinew should be beaten between a smooth rock and a piece of wood or chewed to separate the fibers. Once it is partially separated, rub it briskly between your hands to finish off the job. The fibers are now ready to be twisted into cordage or used as thread.

Deer leg showing sinew location

CHAPTER 15
CORDAGE AND CRUDE CLOTH

Cordage is the nuts and bolts, the nails and screws, the very twine in the yarn of the land. Cordage is used, among other things, for bowstrings, snowshoe bindings, basket handles, bolas, snares, nets, fishing line, lashings, bags, and belts. It is also used for sewing, weaving, making a fire with a bow drill, and building shelters. Some fibers are softer and better for skin contact, while others may be scratchy yet incredibly strong.

Of the many cordage options available, most fit into one of three categories:

- Annuals such as milkweed, dogbane, stinging nettle, and hemp have a pithy center and strong fibers that grow on the outside of the stalk. Harvesting the fibers is done when the plant is dead in the fall but has not yet had the chance to start decomposing. I have harvested stalks in the winter and spring from still-standing plants, but the fibers were weak.
- Good-quality fiber can be found in the meaty leaves of yucca and agaves and in the bark of basswood (American linden), cedar, aspen, cottonwood, ash, hickory, tamarack, willow, and juniper. Fibers within this category can be harvested at any time yet require more work to gather and prepare.

- Cordage can be made from almost any plant, although the quality will vary considerably. Velvet leaf, fireweed, evening primrose, cattail, wild grape, bullrush, grasses, conifer rootlets, and green sapling bark (pounded with a mallet) are a few plant materials that lend themselves to this. Cordage can also be made from animal products like sinew, rawhide, and hair.

HARVEST AND STORAGE

Many fibrous annuals, including milkweed and dogbane, tend to grow in large patches and, once recognized, can easily be found during the summer and early fall when they are still alive and easy to distinguish from other similar plants. Harvest the dry, dead stalks in late fall by breaking them off at the ground and bundling them together for transport and storage. I prefer to harvest after the seeds have dispersed (or I sprinkle them myself) to ensure that the following year I am able to harvest in the same area. Keep the stalks in a dry place out of direct sunlight until you need them.

Raw cordage materials

Basswood and yucca offer up their fibers in different ways. When you are harvesting yucca and agaves, carefully cut a few leaves from the base of the plant (the tips are very sharp). If you are traveling, wrap the cut ends in wet towels or paper and cover them with plastic. If you are going to work with the fibers nearby, then they can remain uncovered.

Basswood trees can be found from eastern North Dakota south to eastern Texas and east to the Atlantic. The bark can be peeled easily from a live tree or branch, although it is easiest to do during spring and fall when the sap is running. Large trees (eighteen inches or more in diameter) can have bark removed, apparently with no ill side effects. (I am not a tree surgeon, so please check with one prior to removing bark if you are concerned about parasites or about adversely affecting a given tree.) My rule of thumb is to take a piece no wider than one-quarter of the diameter of the tree; e.g., if you have a tree with a twenty-four-inch diameter, you can take a six-inch-wide strip of bark.

Cut the width of your intended strip horizontally through the bark, then pry the cut section upward with a stick. Once you have enough bark freed from the tree, take hold of it with your hands and pull while walking backward from the tree. The strip will run up the trunk, getting narrower as it climbs, until it tapers to a point and breaks. In general, the longer the strip, the better, as this will define the length of the fibers with which you will be working.

Prepping milkweed

thumb down one of the cracks until the stalk is lying with the inside up and open to the sky. Remember, the fibers you seek are on the outside of the plant and now sit in your hand, facing the ground.

With the stalk under your right arm, and your right palm supporting the plant, extend the open stalk three inches past your palm and break downward. Should you break upward, you may sever the fibers. Pull off the woody portion. This should leave you with a papery, fibrous material, the skin still attached to the stalk. Extend the stalk another three inches beyond your hand and repeat. Once the stalk has been treated thus, rub the weak and wispy bit of "skin" between your hands until it feels softer and the woody bits and outermost skin crack away. You're now ready to spin the fibers into cordage, as described later in this chapter.

Preparing Plants with External Fibers

The stems of annuals like milkweed or dogbane can be crushed with your fingers or between two hard objects. Then open the stem by sliding your

Preparing Plants with Internal Fibers

The fibers of some plants, including yucca, are on the inside, and the meat of the plant must be crushed in order to access them.

A smooth, round stone the size of a dinner plate near flowing water is optimal for the task of extracting the fibers from a yucca plant. You will also need a wrist-thick stick. Dip the yucca in the water and place it on the rock. Pound on it for about twenty strokes before dipping it in the water again. As you alternate between pounding and dipping, you will notice that you are making a frothy mess of natural soap on the rock and that all of the green meat of the plant is dissipating, revealing white fibers. Soon, the fibers are all that will remain. These fibers can be left attached to the very sharp point of the leaf and stored for later use, or you can cut all but three or so fibers and use the pointed leaf tip as a natural needle and thread. Proceed to the section below on spinning the fibers into cordage.

Basswood

There are also fiber-producing plants that keep the desired fibers neither outside nor inside but just between the two. Some trees, including basswood, keep the fiber just inside the bark yet not in the meat of the tree.

After the bark has been harvested, as described above, it must be *retted*, or soaked—submerged in water. Soaking the bark in running water, such as a cold creek, will require a longer ret time (four to six weeks) than soaking it in a warm pond (two to four weeks). The soaking begins the breakdown process in the bark, which is made up of many layers of fine, paperlike material. Pieces left too long in the water are still useful, but the exposed layers may have rotted; plenty of good material may remain underneath them. Pounding the bark while dousing it with water will provide you with cordage material immediately.

Pull the retted bark from the water and peel up layers of fibers. Stiffer sections can be pounded in a fashion similar to that of yucca (see above), or the bark can be left to ret longer. The fibers are now ready to be worked into cordage.

SPINNING FIBERS INTO CORDAGE

Once the fibers are prepared, they must be spun into cordage to be useful. Here are two methods.

1. Hold the fibers near the middle of their length, with the thumb and forefinger of each hand about four inches apart. Begin twisting the material by rolling it between your right thumb and forefinger while holding firmly with your left thumb and forefinger.
2. This twisting will cause a loop or kink to form in the area between your hands. Grasp the loop or kink between the left thumb and forefinger, letting both "bundles" of fiber hang down.
3. With your right thumb and forefinger, twist the strand on the right (strand A) counterclockwise, or away from you, then wrap the twisted strand A toward you, or clockwise, around strand B.
4. Releasing strand A, grasp strand B and repeat what you have just done with strand A. This method, while slow, will make for a tight and consistent string that is suitable for bows and snare lines.

The second method is faster and is especially useful for rapid production of weaving materials or for making string that is not intended for heavy work.

1. Hold the fibers near the middle in your left hand, and place them across your right thigh with the two strands separated by a few inches.
2. Place your right hand on the strands, with the pad of your middle finger on the forward strand and the other strand just below it closer to your palm.
3. Slide your right hand forward, rolling both strands, still independent of each other, until the near strand reaches the base of your palm.
4. Now pull your hand back, bringing both strands together, where they will wind about one another. Grasp the strands where they meet, then repeat the process.

For bundles of long fibers like basswood, one end can be attached to an object, and a large loop of thin cordage, placed at the center point, can be attached to another object, such as a tree.

With the bundle forming a straight line from the anchored end through the loose loop, the free end is twisted until a kink is formed in the middle. Then, while some tension is maintained, the free end is brought to the anchored end, which is freed. Both bundles are allowed to wrap around each other. The loose loop is untied and removed from the cordage.

SPLICING

Often, the fibers used are not long enough to create a rope of a usable length. Therefore, you'll need to splice in additional fibers. Two techniques are commonly used, and I have found both satisfactory.

Making long cordage

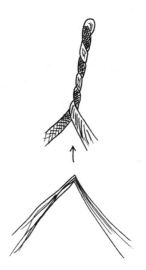

Splicing

1. If both fiber bundles below the spun cordage are of the same length, then a "full lay-in" is an option. To clarify, when two inches or more of unspun fibers are left remaining to be wrapped, a new fiber bundle is grasped at its center and placed with the center point at the last wrap. The new lengths are now wrapped along with the old ones. To avoid the bulge that the full "lay-in" leaves in the cordage, you can trim one of the unspun fiber bundles hanging below the cordage by five inches, then proceed as described below.

2. If the fiber bundles below the spun cordage are uneven, a splice is required. When two or more inches are left on one fiber bundle, a new bundle is placed on the remaining two inches, and you continue to reverse-wrap once again.

There is no substitute for practice when you are making cordage. Your speed and quality will improve quickly once you have the basic concept down. Pay attention to how tightly or loosely you are wrapping, then note the quality. Too loose of a wrap will result in weak cordage, and too tight of a wrap will compromise the flexibility and therefore the longevity of the cordage (tight fibers rubbing hard against one another will weaken and break). Try for an even width, and don't get discouraged if it takes you ten or more feet to produce a nice section of cordage.

WEAVING

A simple loom can be made for weaving long fiber bundles into blankets or robes. This method is best suited to fibers like basswood, which can be collected in long sections.

1. Lash a crosspiece that is two feet greater than the desired width of your blanket between two trees that are about three feet above the ground. This is the anchor piece.

2. If your fiber length is ten feet, then lash two more crosspieces (guide supports) to saplings or posts that are nine feet away, one above the other, and parallel to the anchor. These two should be at one foot and six feet off of the ground.

3. Attach horizontal guides every two to three inches to the vertical guide supports. These are straight saplings or branches, one-half inch in diameter, that are placed vertically on the guide supports.

4. To attach the warp, tie fiber bundles to the anchor, making sure that they are snug next to each other. I like to tie an even number of bundles. For this example, I'll tie on twelve bundles.

5. From here on, I'll call the bundles collectively the "warp" and individually the

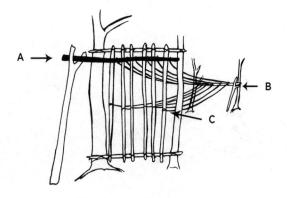

Loom

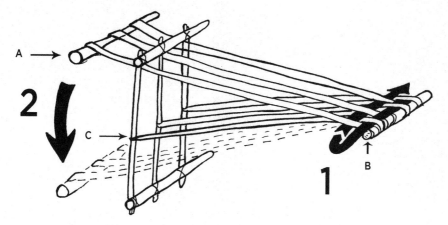

Loom in use

"warp ends." Run the warp ends from the anchor to the guides. Every other warp end is tied to a guide that is three feet above the ground. The others are passed between the guides and tied to a heddle stick, an unattached stick the width of the anchor. (In modern looms, the heddle is a frame of vertical wires that lifts and lowers the warp to allow interweaving of the weft or woof).

6. The weft is tied to one side of the anchor or an outer warp end and then fed between the stationary warp and the warp attached to the heddle stick.

7. The heddle stick is then raised up and held by Y sticks or hooks attached to the guide supports, and the weft is again passed between both warps.

8. When a weft runs short, add in another by overlapping the end of the last one by two warp ends.

9. As you progress, the weft may become uneven unless you manually snug each one up to the one previous to it.

10. To leave an opening—for example, the head hole in a poncho—simply run the weft to the middle of the piece rather than all the way to the other side and then back to the edge. Let us say that you are working on a blanket with forty warps and you want to leave a slit in the middle for your head so as to allow the blanket to double as a poncho. The weft would run through the warp until the point at which you wish to have the slit. You now work the weft through twenty warps, and then, instead of continuing on, you turn around and take the weft back to the edge again. This is repeated until the desired length of the slit is reached, at which point you repeat the process with the other side taking the weft through twenty warps. Once the wefts on both sides of the slit are lined up again, you take the weft through all forty warps, edge to edge. You will have to do this from each side.

CHAPTER 16

OTHER TOOLS AND MATERIALS

The indigenous people of North America had fairly extensive tool kits to make their lives easier. Some tools, like digging sticks, were simple and are easy and quick to replicate. Others—including almost anything made of stone—require special skills and the use of other tools to make. For short-term survival, the time and skill needed to manufacture some of the more complex tools are better spent in other ways. However, for long-term stays in the wild, such tools are invaluable, and the time used in crafting them is time well spent.

WORKING WITH STONE

Flint knapping is an art, a highly specialized skill developed through many hours, lacerations, "almost masterpieces," and loads of handmade, individually crafted pieces of gravel. Not having grown up in areas rich in flint or obsidian left me with little opportunity to play with making cutting edges from such fabled materials. I did, however, forget my knife on many an impromptu fishing excursion and needed to scrounge, not only for something with which to gut the fish but with which to make a bow drill or hand drill for cooking purposes.

A cutting edge has great value in wilderness living. Can you get by without one? Not for any extended period. In wilderness living, the need always arises to part or divide materials, to shape and adjust items. While some shelters can be made with no cutting edge, making fire, processing animals, fashioning most containers and clothing, as well as myriad other chores, cannot.

Crude stonecutting implements are appealing because they are often easy to find and simple to modify. The downside is that they don't last as long as modern cutting edges, nor are they as versatile. They probably won't tempt you to whittle a stick just for the heck of it.

Many areas in North America have little great stone with which to work, so I would pick up what I could find and literally take a crack at it.

1. Find stones that, when tapped together, make a high-pitched "clack." (If you tap a piece of quartz against sandstone, you get a "thud.") Creek beds, washes, and cuts are good places to look.

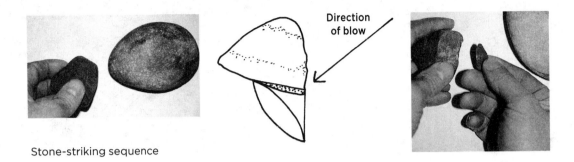

Direction of blow

Stone-striking sequence

2. Grasp the stone to be worked in your non-dominant hand, facing the stone up at an angle, and hold a hammer stone in your other hand. If the workpiece is too large to hold, place it on the ground or on another surface.

3. Strike downward onto the platform with the hammer stone and look at the flakes.

Such flakes are often adequate for gutting fish. Some rocks provide a razor-sharp, yet very brittle, edge that will break as you cut the fish. Others may break along seams within the rock, giving you a sharp, ninety-degree angle—not great, but sometimes serviceable. Still others break off rough and not sharp enough to complete anything other than abrading work.

Experiment with the rock in your locale. Look for different types of rock, or look in your local library for information on the geology of your

Different cutting edges

area. Be creative and ask around. You might be surprised how many closet experts can be found once word gets out about your interest.

Stone Pecking

Pecking can produce simple yet very useful stone tools with little skill and a lot of patience. Pecking is simply hitting a softer rock with another, somewhat harder rock. Tiny fragments of the softer stone break off, and eventually you can form a bowl or a groove for holding an axe handle. This method is not quick but is well suited for rainy days around camp.

Walking any streambed will illustrate how many kinds of rock are available for use in a given area. Some are very hard and work well for smashing bone to get the marrow or to make shards that can be made into spears or arrowheads. Some are soft like sandstone, which can be used to smooth handles or other articles. Some of the best rocks to use for bowls are soft stones like soapstone and alabaster, although I prefer the medium-grain sanding stones such as basalt, found in riverbeds and elsewhere all over the country. Not to be confused with sandstone, medium-grain sanding stones are hard enough to use as a bone-hammering stone yet are soft enough to be worked.

Stone pecking

Hafting a hammer

White quartz rock is hard enough to use as a hammer stone for working the rocks mentioned above. It is also easy to find a piece that fits comfortably in your hand and has a fine enough tip to allow precise strikes. With such a hammer stone, tap on the rock that you have selected and there should be a little mark where each strike occurred.

With your quartz hammer stone, tap other stones and listen to the sound. A dull sound comes from softer rocks. A higher pitch is an indicator of a harder rock. Try chipping pieces off of various rocks. The flakes may be sharp enough to use for small tasks. I'll often use such flakes for gutting fish.

When you are selecting a stone for a hammerhead or a bowl, look for rounded stones that have a slightly coarse feel to them. Look them over carefully for any variation in their appearance. They should be uniform, with no lines or cracks, because these will likely be breaking points.

If you are making a bowl, start pecking away. Always work on a soft surface like your lap, your hand, or in sand. Otherwise, you will likely crack your piece. I love pecking. I find a comfortable position, leaning against a tree in the sun or lounging in the foyer of my shelter while the rain

pours down, and I'll work for hours at a time. Tapping on my project becomes a meditation of sorts. It is my rhythm, matching that of my heart, and it is somehow soothing. Two or more people working projects at the same time will, in short order, all be pecking the same rhythm.

Wetting the stone seems to make the work progress faster. Striking hard will, in all likelihood, break your stone project. Thin-walled bowls are very tricky, not so much in the making, but in the keeping—they break easily. One to one and one-half inches thick is pretty good. Just remember to heat the bowl slowly and evenly or it will crack.

For a stone hammerhead, a groove can be pecked around the center of the stone. The groove is to receive a bent, wooden handle made in the same fashion as in tongs. (See the section "Tongs," later in this chapter.) Additionally, a one-inch-diameter branch or sapling, sixteen inches long, can be split all the way down its length, and the split sides of one end can be shaved down. These can then be placed in the grooves on either side of the hammerhead with at least three inches extending above the hammerhead. The split sticks are then bound above and below the hammerhead with wet rawhide (see Chapter 14).

Stone Lamps

In times not so long ago, man rose and set with the sun. Why get up two or three hours after first light and go to sleep hours after dark? This practice required more work in keeping a source of light available, used often valuable fuel in colder months, and meant working in poorer light. With the advent of electric lighting, man could rise and sleep when he wanted. When the days get shorter as winter sets in, it is nice to have the option of staying up later and working on projects by firelight, but when fuel must be conserved for potential rough times ahead, a better option is the oil lamp. This is a very simple system requiring a depression or reservoir in which fuel, in the form of rendered fat, can be held. A short wick of cordage, with one end in the fat-filled reservoir, is either placed in a trough leading up and out of the depression or pinched in a split, green twig (the "tender"), resting on the rim. About one inch of the wick is left protruding above the tender. When the wick is lit, it heats the often congealed fat and pulls it up the wick, where it burns and provides light.

The lamp base may be made of stone, shell, or clay (see "Primitive Pottery" in Chapter 17).

To make a stone lamp:

1. Place some fat in the reservoir; if you can warm it first so that the wick can easily suck up some fuel up, do it.

Stone lamp

2. Take a short section (three or four inches) of loosely made cordage, like basswood, cedar, cottonwood, or other tinder or cordage material, and dip it in the liquid or hard fat. With congealed fat, I put a glob on the tip of the cordage that I intend to light because it will drip down the wick as it burns.

3. Split the tip of a green twig (tender), and wedge the wick in it with the flame end protruding an inch. The tender can then be rested on the rim of the lamp.

4. Place a second tender nearby, or pinch the wick an inch below the first tender. When the flame begins to sputter as it burns up the wick above the first tender, simply remove it and place it below the next one.

These lamps tend to burn quickly, although the tenders slow it down somewhat. Placing too much wick in the oil at one time can result in the flame getting past the tender and igniting the whole lot.

I had read a book with information on wicks, and while I was testing different kinds of wicks, I would see how often I was interrupted by the need to tend the light. A pinch or wad of cattail set down at the edge of the reservoir provides a very long-lasting light that needs little tending and is easily made and set up. Other materials that work to varying degrees are small chunks of punky wood and compressed pinches of tinder, from dust to fibers, with additives such as cattail or milkweed down.

Animal fat does produce black smoke, so keep ventilation in mind and don't keep your head in the highest part of your shelter or you'll have trouble breathing.

WORKING WITH PITCH

Conifer pitch is a tremendous asset when you are living in the woods, and I collect it whenever the opportunity arises. It can be used as an adhesive or as a waterproof coating in applications such as:

- Fixing (hafting) stone or bone spearheads and arrowheads to their shafts (see "Hunting Weapons," Chapter 12).
- Waterproofing seams on canteens or canoes (see "Bark Canteens," in Chapter 17).
- Making engraved bone ornaments. These look great when charcoal or colored stone dust is mixed with the pitch and is then smeared into the engraving; this can be a brittle mix.
- Making temporary tattoos by drawing a design on your skin with small amounts of sun-warmed pine pitch and dusting it with charcoal or colored stone dust.
- Securing knots or lashings that will not need to be untied.

- Making buttons. This is simply a matter of tying a knot in a piece of cordage and dipping it in a pitch mix with a lot of ash. Build it up to the desired shape by adding daubs of pitch with a stick. While the pitch is still warm, it can be patted with a flat stick into the desired shape.
- Coating knife handles, wrapped in cordage, with pitch containing a high ash content.

In the applications covered here, pitch is used with a hardening agent, either white wood ash or ground charcoal. A high density of these agents hardens the pitch to a brittle state, and a lower density keeps the glue softer and more flexible.

Collecting Pitch

When I'm on a pitch-collecting mission, my tools of choice are a container and a stick that has been sharpened to a point at one end and a flat, screwdriver-like point at the other. As I walk through the conifers, I look for branch breaks at the trunk as well as those farther out, and, with my stick, I prod the areas that are healing over on the trunk or that have burst bubbles in the bark. Looking up into trees for woodpecker holes, broken branches, and other wounds is a good way to locate a pitch cache. Creating a wound to provide sap is another option, although it is often unnecessary, as so much is available at old wounds.

Preparing and Using Pitch

Often pitch has impurities in it, such as tiny pieces of bark. Some of this should be removed while you are cooking it, although a *low* density of fine impurities does not seem to have a negative effect on the pitch when it is used as glue. I pick out the larger impurities by hand. If the concentration of fine impurities is too high, however, it will result in weak and brittle glue.

The best way to work with pitch is to heat it slowly in a stone or pottery bowl until it has gently boiled. Have your projects—such as canteens, knives, spears, or arrows—ready to go. Add white ash to the pitch in small, measured amounts—up to 5 percent by volume at a time, keeping in mind that even with heavy amounts of ash (up to 50 percent), the pitch will still be very workable when it is hot. Yet, when heat is removed, pitch will harden very quickly. Ground charcoal also works well—some say better than white ash.

Depending on your intention, you may need the pitch to maintain some flexibility. A case in point is the canteen. In my first attempt, I used about a 50:50 pitch-ash mix, which became so brittle that gently squeezing my canteen caused the pitch to flake and chip off. Spears and arrows need to have stone or bone heads firmly affixed, yet pitch that is too brittle will often shatter when the spear or arrow impacts anything hard, such as the ground or a tree.

To prepare pitch for use:

1. Heat a stone bowl (see "Stone Pecking," earlier in this chapter) slowly to avoid cracking.
2. Add the pitch. Remember, pitch is flammable, so keep some dirt or a lid handy to smother flare-ups.
3. When the pitch is simmering, add some ash or charcoal in small quantities, up to about 5 percent at a time. Mix it in well.
4. Test the hardness by smearing some hot pitch onto a piece of cloth, leather, or a flexible green twig. Let the pitch cool, then bend the substrate and see if the pitch flakes off too easily. If it does, you likely have too much ash. If you can bend the cloth or twig over on itself, there is not enough ash.

If you are working with a smooth gluing surface, you may need to score it prior to applying the pitch.

Pitched products that will have a lot of contact with hands or clothing need to be well coated with ash. If they are not, when they warm up from the sun, your hands, or the fire, they will become sticky and might weaken. As a general rule, keep pitch products away from fire and other heat sources.

I recommend experimenting with plenty of caution. Hot pitch is like natural napalm. If it touches you, it will stick, and it will burn!

HAND TOOLS

Even the simplest of tools can greatly ease the task of eking out an existence in the wilderness. Do not underestimate the value of the stick and stone, worked or unworked. Both are stronger than your fingertips and fingernails and can prove invaluable in survival or subsistence living situations.

Digging Stick

A digging stick is a superb tool for all manner of tasks, from digging up edible roots to digging out a food-storage pit. Digging sticks are best made from a piece of green hardwood like beech or oak, although softer wood will usually do the trick. The piece of wood should be one and one-fourth inches in diameter and twenty-four inches long.

Digging sticks

One end can be carved or ground to a round point and the other to a flat, chisel-like point. Fire harden both ends (see "The Rabbit Stick," in Chapter 12), and you are ready to dig.

Scrapers

Scrapers for working hides can be tough to make. There are two types, the broad scraper and the stake scraper.

THE BROAD SCRAPER. The goal in making a broad scraper is to create a square edge. This can be done by removing much of one side of a straight leg bone from a deer or larger animal and sharpening one edge to at least ninety degrees.

1. Score two parallel lines that are one inch or more apart for the length of the bone (not including the knobs at each end).

2. With a stone, carefully knock out the length of bone between the lines. To be precise with your strikes, hold a smaller stone or chisel stone in place with one hand, then strike with a larger stone in your other hand. You should now have a bone missing a strip from its longitudinal axis.

3. A little abrading work is required to smooth the edges. This is a rather tedious process but is worth it if you plan on tanning many hides.

THE STAKE SCRAPER. The stake scraper is far simpler to make and is well suited to removing flesh and fat from a hide strung on a rack.

1. Starting with a straight leg bone from a deer or larger animal, score a diagonal line around one end to form a chisel-like tip.

2. Break the bone along the score line. This is tricky because scoring bone takes time, but the more you score, the more predictable the break will be. Impatience often leads to early attempts at breaking the bone and disappointing results. A well-scored bone can be tapped on a rock corner or edge of a rock so that the score lines

Broad scraper

Stake scraper

fall directly upon the stone and abrade it to remove any barbs that might damage the hide.

3. Tie a loop of rawhide or cordage to the unworked end so that the loop can pass around your wrist and add support while you are working the hide.

Tongs

Tongs are used to pick up hot rocks when you are rock boiling, to pick up coals for coal burning, and to move hot food items in or out of the fire. To make a pair of tongs:

1. Cut a straight branch that is twenty inches in length and about one-half inch in diameter.

2. In the middle of your stick, shave a four-inch section on one side, thin enough so that you can bend the stick in half fully without breaking it. The shaved section acts as a spring, holding the tongs in the open position. To aid in the bending process, submerge the shaved section in hot water or steam, then bend it slowly over a round, one-inch-diameter form or stick.

3. Once the stick is bent, tie one arm to the other while the tongs are opened about three or four inches.

A Y stick can be used for tongs to provide better stability for lifting rocks or food. Cut a three-inch-long section of sapling a couple of inches in diameter, and bend the longer Y stick around it. The short piece reduces strain on the hinge area and helps the tongs last much longer.

Camp Vise

A simple locking pair of pliers is great for working on small projects such as projectile heads or bone hooks. To make a camp vise:

1. Cut a one-and-one-half-inch-diameter hardwood branch to a length of six inches.
2. Taper one end, and then split the branch in half lengthwise.
3. Pinch a one-fourth-inch-diameter branch between the two split pieces so that the ends stick out on either side at the middle.
4. Lash the quarter-inch branch in place.
5. Carve a wooden wedge, and you are ready to work.
6. Place your project in the tapered end of the vise, and then force the wedge into the other end, pinching and securely holding the workpiece.

Tong preparation, tongs, and tong variation

Camp vise

Pump Drill

The pump drill allows the user to drill holes or create coals for fire with relative ease.

A spindle is rotated by means of downward pressure applied to a horizontal handle with a hole in the middle through which the spindle runs. Cordage attached at its midpoint to the top of the spindle has its ends tied to the handle ends. A counterbalance or flywheel is attached to the spindle below the lowest point that the pressure plate reaches to increase the spindle's momentum. Tips can be interchangeable to allow the pump drill to be used for drilling or fire making.

The process begins by holding the pressure plate and rotating the spindle by hand to wind the cordage around the spindle. Applying downward pressure to the handle then causes the spindle to spin as the cordage unwinds, and the spindle's momentum causes the cordage to rewrap around the spindle in the opposite direction, automatically setting the device up for another downward thrust. The pressure plate is thus pumped continuously, and the spindle spins in one direction, then the other, without a pause.

Pump drills can be of any size. The one described here is great for fire making and is easy to put together.

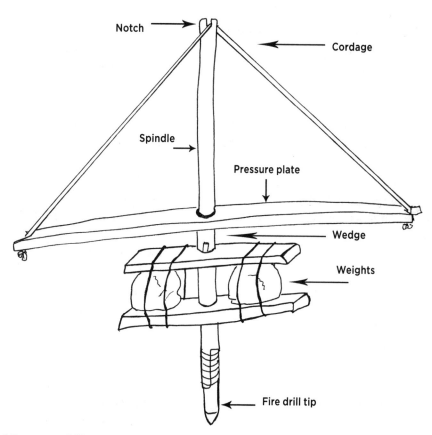

The parts of the pump drill

1. Harvest or prepare the following components:

   - A straight stick about two feet long, thumb or nickel size on the thick end, and fairly sturdy is needed for the spindle. Green wood works best if you plan to attach tips for drilling or fire making. If you want to make a fire without adding a fire-making tip, you will need to use a good piece of dry wood like that used for the spindle of a bow drill (see Chapter 8).

   - Two sticks about eighteen inches in length and at least one inch in diameter. These will make up the crosspiece or pressure plate. If you want a cleaner, tighter apparatus, a single piece of wood with a hole for the spindle drilled at the midpoint will work well. See the pump drill illustration.

   - One stick about twelve inches in length and at least two inches in diameter. This will be split lengthwise and hold the weights.

   - Two evenly weighted stones that are at least one pound each. Another option is to gather two lumps of clay to custom form your weights as described later in this chapter.

   - Two wooden spacers that are wider than the spindle by half. A two- or three-inch section of a dead branch will do the trick.

   - Wood for a fireboard, if you will use the pump drill to make fire (see Chapter 8).

   - Cordage (see Chapter 15).

2. Strip the bark from the spindle, and carve or abrade a notch in the thin end, which will be the top of the spindle. The notch needs to be deep enough to hold your cordage well.

3. Place the two eighteen-inch pieces for the pressure plate on the ground parallel to each other, with the spacers two inches apart in the middle between them. The spacers should be notched to help ensure secure binding.

4. Bind the longer pieces together at the ends and around the spacers, being careful to leave the two inches between them free of cordage.

5. Slide the spindle, thin-end first, two thirds of its length through the gap between the spacers.

6. Tie a length of cordage to one end of the pressure plate, run it up through the notch at the top of the spindle, then run it down to the other end of the pressure plate. Tie it off. (Adjustments will happen later.)

7. Attach the weights as described in the sidebar "Attaching Pump Drill Weights."

8. If you are using a dry spindle for fires, then you are ready to carve a point on the spindle.

9. Place the spindle tip in the socket of a fireboard and, resting a little weight on the pressure plate, rotate the spindle by hand until the cordage is all wound up.

10. Apply downward force on the pressure plate and count the number of revolutions. (Having trouble? Make a mark on the spindle and count how many times it goes around.) If your count is over five, chances are your setup is not as efficient as it could be. Shorten the cordage to bring the revolutions below five and see how it changes.

11. With a strong but gentle downward push on the pressure plate, the spindle should

Attaching Pump Drill Weights

There are three methods to attach weights to the spindle for the pump drill.

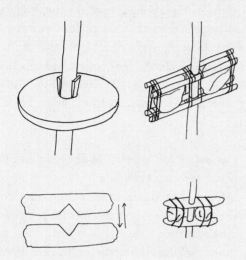

Weight options

and the weight bars. One fairly expedient method is to flatten two sides of the spindle where you wish to attach the weights. Use two twelve-inch-long, three-fourth-inch-diameter branches as clamps. Lash the clamps firmly to the spindle and the weight bar to the clamps.

Method 2

1. Hack out two eight-inch sections of heavy hardwood that is two and one-half inches in diameter. It may not be a lot of fun, but it makes for some good weights.

2. Flatten two sides of the spindle where you want the weights, then do the same to the balance point of the weights. Or, you can carve out notches that mirror the flat section on the spindle.

3. Lash the two weights to the spindle.

Method 1

1. Split the twelve-inch stick. Attach the weights by pinning them between the two pieces and lashing them tightly together. The weights can be fairly close together or father apart. I usually separate them by about six inches.

2. Attach the weight to the spindle. The goal is to have the weight securely fastened to the spindle so that it will move with it and not loosen and twist free. Chances are high that your weights are wider than your spindle, which requires that spacers be inserted into the gap between the spindle

Method 3

1. If you have easily accessible clay, pick the bigger grit out of two fist-size lumps.

2. Mold them into a compact shape like a block or sphere, and press the weight bar into them or otherwise form them to make attaching them easy.

3. Set the clay weights aside to dry.

4. Once they are dry, the weights can be brittle, depending on the quality of the clay, but they should be serviceable. Firing such weights is tricky due to their thickness. (See "Primitive Pottery," Chapter 17.)

spin smoothly around until it is completely unwound. As the pressure plate reaches the bottom, let up on the pressure, because this is when the weights kick in and wind it up again.

12. More adjustments can be made and should be played with to get the most out of the pump drill. If it spins and lurches, you need to even out the weights either by adding or subtracting material from one or moving one weight closer or farther from the spindle. Try a longer pressure plate, or move balanced weights closer to or farther away from the spindle. Experiment.

DIFFERENT POINTS. A sturdy joint must be created to allow the spindle to receive different points for different tasks. The most field-expedient way is to cut the end of the spindle at a clean, forty-five-degree angle and to do the same to the tip that will be attached. The two are mated and bound tightly. I found that a smooth spinning drill will abide this method of joining a new tip far better than one that is out of balance.

Another, somewhat more secure, joint can be made by cutting the forty-five-degree angle, and then tapering it to make a wedge on an angle. The tip has a corresponding groove in its angled face, which helps in preventing the tip from skewing.

You do not have to be a highly skilled flint knapper to be able to produce rock shards that will be serviceable as tips for drilling. See "Working with Stone," earlier in this chapter, for the basics.

- Cut or abrade a notch in the spindle into which the stone tip will fit.
- Shave down the sides of the wooden tip along the notch enough so that the stone protrudes out beyond it a little.
- Blunt the edges of the stone bit where it protrudes from the side of the notch.
- Insert the stone and lash it in place, reinforcing it with pitch if you wish.

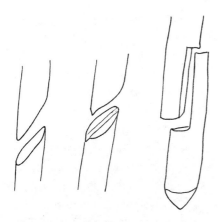

Pump drill point joints

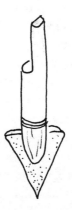

Pump drill bits with stone

Pump Drill Refinements

A weight can be made out of a round cake of clay with a hole through it. Make the hole by sliding your spindle through the clay to just below where you want the weight to sit. The clay shrinks as it dries, making the hole a little smaller. If you really want a great weight setup, make a groove on the inside of the hole in the clay before it dries, and make a corresponding hole in the spindle. Once the weight is fired and put in place, it is prevented from spinning freely by inserting a key into the two grooves that are lined up.

For a longer-term, finer-looking pump drill, the pressure plate can be split out of some straight-grained sapling, as can the pieces to hold the weights. These are then bow-drilled through so that the spindle passes through them. In such a setup, tightening the weight bar to the spindle can be done with wedges tapped between the spindle and weight bar. Be sure to add wedges only where they will push against the end grain or you will likely split your wood.

CONTAINERS

The value of a container is often overlooked until you have none. How to carry, cook, or hold the items and foods that we need for survival with no container does not at first glance appear to be a pressing question. Roasting is a fine way to cook many wild meals, but what about drinks and soupy meals? Containers are worth a lot, and knowing how to make them for whatever your needs is worth the time.

BASKETS

Baskets are useful for a variety of tasks, such as carrying firewood, catching fish, storing foods, and holding fruits, seeds, and water. Many materials are available to make baskets of all shapes and functions. They can be loosely or tightly woven, rigid, or pliable. Loosely woven baskets can be lined with grass, leaves, or hides so that small objects can be carried without the risk of loss through the holes. Skins can be draped in the basket for rock boiling or carrying water. There are more basket types, weaves, shapes, and materials than I can cover, but here are two basic baskets that can be adapted for many uses.

Basic Rootlet Basket

Any pine, oak, or hemlock tree has many fine roots just below the surface of the soil. The rootlets are very flexible, making for easy weaving. The real bonus is that, after a day or two, they dry and stiffen up, and the basket becomes fairly rigid.

1. By carefully working your hand into the dirt, you will find in the first half inch or so of soil roots as thick as sturdy shoelaces. These can be dug and pulled up in three-foot lengths (or more), and when a quantity has been collected, the weaving can begin. Any time you find exposed rootlets, as in the case of storm-downed trees, make a point of collecting a supply.

2. Place three two-foot-long rootlets parallel on the ground and three more perpendicular to and on top of the first three at their midpoints. This spot is called the "hub," and the rootlets are called the "warps" or the spokes. The warps will be woven around by "woofs" of the same material.

3. This is the hardest part of making this basket. Place a rootlet under the bottom

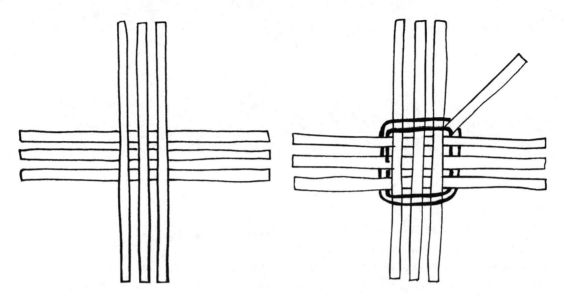

Placing the warps

Adding the odd warp and starting the weft

set of three warps. Moving clockwise around the hub, weave the woof over the top set of three and under the bottom set of three for two complete circuits. This will hold the warps together for the next step. Add in an additional warp by weaving it into the newly placed woof so that there are thirteen warps radiating out from the hub. An odd number is required so that the woof falls first on one side of the warp and in the next circuit falls on the other side.

4. From here, it is just a matter of weaving around the hub by going over one warp and under the next with the woof. When a woof runs out, simply add another, making sure that it overlaps for a few warps.

5. To finish off, stop weaving when about one and one-half inches of the warps remain extending above the woof. Bend each warp

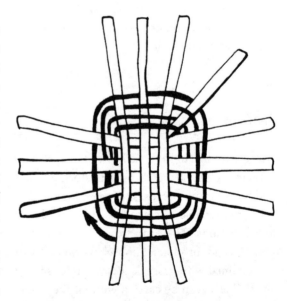

Spiraling up

over to the right, and insert it into the woof alongside the neighboring warp.

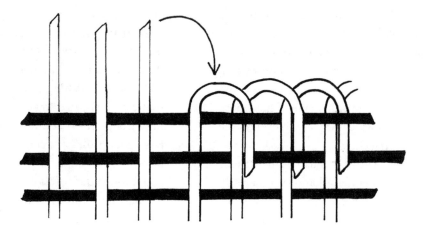

Burying the warp ends

Bark Baskets

The beauty of bark is that it folds like paper when it is fresh, then hardens as it dries. Birch, tulip poplar, cedar, white pine, and elm are some of the best barks of which I am aware. A fairly quick and functional bark basket is the "one-piece" or "single-fold basket." First, see "Bark Containers," later in this chapter, for information on harvesting and processing bark.

1. Spread out a piece of bark, cambium side (inside) up. The dimensions are not important, but for the sake of clarity, I will use a piece that is ten inches wide by twenty inches long with the grain running along the twenty-inch axis. Draw a line *across* the center of the piece. The line marks the center of an ellipse, with the points ending just shy of the edges, as shown in the illustration "Bark basket folding lines." The wider you make the ellipse, the rounder the basket will be.

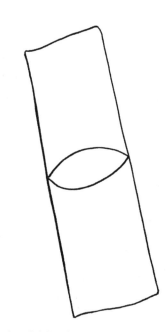

Bark basket folding lines

2. Score along the ellipse line no more than one-third of the way through the bark. You can make baskets with score marks on the outside when you are using bark that is more rigid, as in the case of rougher

pine bark and elm. With more pliable barks, I often will *not* score the bark at all, because it seems to bend into the desired shape without the risk of compromising the fibers.

3. Fold the bark on either side of the ellipse upward, allowing one piece to overlap the other by an inch.

4. Holes for stitching must be drilled or burned with either a hand or bow drill. (Either can be fitted with a bone or stone tip for boring through, or you can simply use a thin, pointed spindle to burn through.) Making holes with an awl will often create a split. The placement of the holes depends on how you want to stitch the basket. Parallel holes, an inch from each edge, allow for a number of stitch patterns.

5. The rim piece is important in preventing splits from the top during regular use. Bore holes an inch from the top around the whole edge. Tie a knot or twig to the end of your stitching material (cordage, rootlets, sinew, etc.) to keep it from passing through the holes. Run your cordage from the inside out; come over the rim piece and top edge back into the basket and through the next hole. Continue until you have gone through the last hole. Then, with the aid of a thin, blunt awl, push the cordage through the next hole from the outside in, and tie it off.

6. Adding a strap makes this basket far more useful. This can be done by threading a thong or cordage through the existing stitching on the sides and tying off.

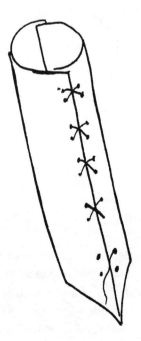

Bark basket getting stitched

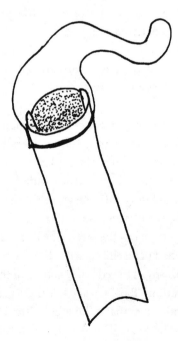

Bark basket with carry string

BARK CANTEENS

I used to walk all over the land near my childhood home, drinking from streams whenever I was thirsty. I was never made ill by these waters. With the prevalence of pollution today, however, water must often be boiled in order to purify it for drinking. This means that any hunting trip or hike is limited by your ability to go without, acquire, or carry drinking water with you. To carry purified water from camp, you can make a pine bark canteen.

1. Strip an eight-by-ten-inch piece of smooth bark from a live white pine with the grain running the long way. (See "Bark Containers," later in this chapter, for more on harvesting and processing bark.) Be sure to utilize all of the bark from the limb or tree you fell, or take a piece that doesn't reach all the way around the tree.
2. Trim bark, as indicated by the pattern in the diagram.

3. Gently fold the bark, without creasing, as indicated.

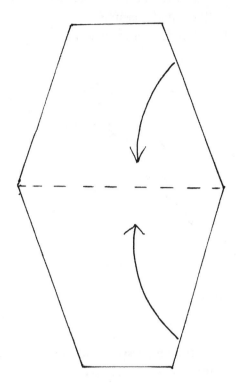

Folded pattern

4. Carefully curl one side within the other.

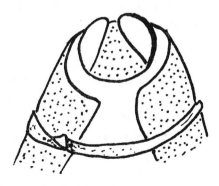

Canteen in a holding shape

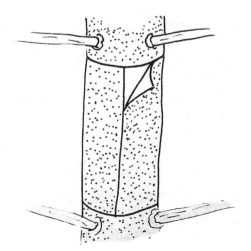

Pattern of canteen on the tree

5. Whittle a wood cork or stopper (make it round and slightly tapered so it will seal against the mouth of the canteen), and place it in the opening.

6. Lash with some remaining bark.

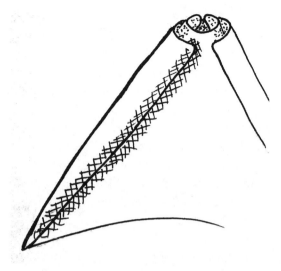

Scored seam

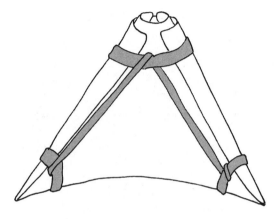

Lashed to dry

10. Attach a bit of cordage like you previously did for the lashings. This time, leave enough for a strap.

11. Acorn caps or hickory nut halves are a nice touch and add further protection to the corners.

7. Let the canteen sit a day or two. This allows the bark to dry out a bit and "remember" the shape desired. Leave it where it will get copious amounts of smoke to discourage bark-dwelling parasites, which may drill holes in your unfinished canteen. Many are often in the bark already but can be killed with a careful application of heat and smoke.

8. Once the canteen has dried, remove the lashing and score, scratch, or otherwise roughen the areas that overlap as well as those areas that are adjacent to the seams when they are closed. The score lines will help the pine pitch and ash mixture adhere (see "Working with Pitch," Chapter 16).

9. Apply pitch.

Finished canteen

To ensure the durability of your canteen, do not let the canteen get too warm, because the pitch may become too soft, thus allowing the seams to split. No hot beverages!

Holes from insects can be plugged with a little bit of pitch that has very little ash mixed in. Periodically, allow the canteen to dry out, put some coarse sand inside, and gently shake it to scour it out.

COOKING CONTAINERS

Myths are plentiful about possible cooking containers if metal ones are not available. When you are in the outdoors, four materials are available with which to make cooking containers.

- **Hide.** Unfortunately, hide is not a durable cooking container and is good only for a maximum of five to eight meals. It requires a successful hunt and seems like a waste of time. Hides are not easy to come by.
- **Stone.** Stone cooking containers are time consuming to make and hard to lug around. Your best stone option is a pothole in a stone riverbank, if you can find one. Even then, it needs to be cleaned and, during the cooking process, the surrounding rock will absorb plenty of heat.
- **Clay.** Clay is a good option, yet it requires a lot of work and extensive processing, and the results are not guaranteed. It is, however, an excellent choice for a long-term stay.
- **Bark or wood.** Of the options listed, bark and wood are often the most accessible and are definitely the fastest choice.

Bark Containers

Of all the barks I have tried, the eastern white pine has proven to be the best by far. Others are birch, tulip poplar, cedar (eastern and western), and elm, but you should experiment with others. Birch bark was widely used because the bark could be harvested and dried in flat sheets. When it was needed, it was merely heated to regain its pliability. It also has a natural preservative in the bark.

A suitable tree or branch for harvest is one that has smooth bark and can provide enough material in one piece for your project. Bark can be harvested from a live tree with little chance of killing it as long as you do not remove so much that you girdle the tree. Harvesting a whole tree and making a good many containers is also an option. When you are looking for a tree to harvest, it is a good idea to seek out one that makes ecological sense to remove. This would mean finding a tree that is either going to die in the next few years or one that is crowding out more desired plant species. A tree that is going to die could be one that will clearly be crowded out in the next few years or perhaps has begun to fall, toppled by heavy winds or stream-bank erosion. Whatever the case, look over the surrounding area, and think about how the removal of the tree will affect the area over the next few years. When it lets more light in to other plants, how will they respond? What would happen if the tree were left? Would it survive? The goal in tree selection is to be as sure as you can that the tree's removal is more beneficial to the area than if it were left standing.

Some bark, such as that of cedars and elms, takes more care to bend. These must be scored along the fold or bend lines. Scoring the outside is beneficial for two reasons. First, the outside bark is often less flexible and is liable to break or peel away from the inner layer, thus weakening it. This can lead to leaks. Second, the flexible fibers are on the inside of the bark, not on the rough outer portion, and scoring on the inside cuts some of them and reduces the number of effective fibers.

On the other hand, scoring on the inside is more common, the idea being that the tough outer bark will protect the fold lines. Of all the books I've read mentioning bark containers, only one speaks of scoring the outside, and this was only in reference to an undated museum piece. Both ways seem to work well, so see which one suits your needs.

1. Fell the branch or tree.
2. Make cuts, and be sure to make them all the way through the bark.
3. Gently peel up one corner of the piece of bark with a knife or fingertip. Then, with your fingers sliding up and down the straight cut, separate the bark from the log. If the bark is removed from a fresh-cut tree or limb, it will come off easily and have the pliability of green hide.

Small strips of the inner bark of the pine work well for tying and stitching. Care must be taken when making holes for stitching. Due to the

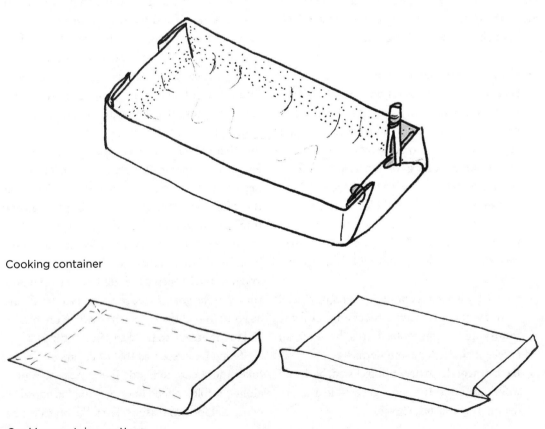

Cooking container

Cooking container pattern

straight grain of the bark, ripping is a threat. I use a small, blunt twig as an awl, twisting as I push it *gently* through the bark. When you are stitching and tying, do not cinch down too tightly, because tearing can result.

Any container that can be folded from paper can be made with pine bark. The container will stiffen within a few days and can be used regularly for both cooking by rock boiling, and eating. It is possible to cook directly on the coals once or maybe twice. The bark will burn to the waterline and will also burn off the outer bark, leaving a very thin, fragile layer.

Wood Containers

Finding a piece of wood suitable for making a bowl is a trick in itself. In the absence of a saw or an axe, large pieces of wood can be found and burned down to a workable size. This is done by slowly burning away unwanted material, frequently removing it from the fire and scraping away the charcoal to prevent your piece from cracking. If the process is rushed, large cracks can appear and ruin the project. Cracks are not always bad, however; sometimes they can be exploited by driving a wedge of stone or hardwood into them, then splitting the log in half and saving yourself time.

Once a manageable piece is secured, it can be hollowed into a bowl by placing a small heap of hardwood coals on the area you wish to hollow out. By blowing softly on the heap, either with your mouth or through a hollow tube, the coals will burn into the wood. Blowing on the coals is optional when you are working with a small pile of them; however, if a breeze is blowing, make sure to turn your bowl now and then to avoid burning out one side. Periodically remove the

coals and scrape out the charcoal. Add more coals and continue. If an area is becoming too thin, place sand, stone, or mud over the area to prevent further burning. If you see flames, dump the coals in the fire pit and scrape the bowl. Flames indicate too much heat and are a sure sign that cracks will soon appear if you don't act quickly.

Spoons can be made in the same manner. Carve out a spoon blank—a piece of wood made to look roughly like a spoon—and place a single coal on the bowl section. Hold it in place with a stick and blow with long, slow breaths on the coal. Periodically dump the coal in the fire pit and scrape out the charcoal. Use a blunt stick as a scraper to avoid scoring the inside of the project. A little sand placed in the bowl and rubbed around works well as sandpaper. Once you're satisfied with the bowl, finish carving the spoon to your liking.

PRIMITIVE POTTERY

Pottery as a primitive living tool is invaluable. Getting to the point where you are able to actually make serviceable pottery, however, is frustrating to say the least. If you want to learn how to make serviceable clay from the raw material you find, be prepared for a lot of trial and error. While the process is gratifying, it is a challenge, because there is no recipe for preparing all clays. When I started, I read whatever I could get my hands on, went to workshops, and played with clay in its various forms. When I read accounts of people firing clay and protecting their pots with potshards from unsuccessful firings, I scoffed and thought, "I don't have shards. I am not making shards, I'm making pots!" Make no mistake about it, you will make pot shards! They are great teachers and tools, so get used to having them around if you want to make pottery.

Most skills seem to have a crux, a particularly tricky part—a back that must be broken or a knot that must be loosened—after which the rest seems to come more easily. Primitive pottery is different in that it has many of these critical steps and each one must be nailed or all previous work on a given piece will be for naught. These are:

- Finding good raw material
- Getting the right temper
- Getting the right mixture of clay and temper
- Building an adequate pot capable of withstanding primitive firing
- Setting up and completing a primitive firing

By far the best way to learn about this art is to work with someone who has already built a good base of knowledge. Countless hours can be saved and much skill gained in this way. It is important to note that many potters, primitive and modern, have hard-and-fast rules that they follow with an almost religious zeal. Some of these rules apply to their area, their clay, and their firing technique. I have seen potters break strict rules of their peers and have great success. Keep an open mind and observe, take notes, and work off of what a process tells you.

The idea of trying to tackle everything at one time is daunting, which is why I recommend approaching it from one of a few fronts initially. Then, you can begin working on the others, or, you can find someone local who has already done some of the legwork. Here are two approaches that somewhat simplify the learning process by limiting the "primitive" component intially and

making use of modern tools or techniques as a learning aid.

- Working with purchased (low-fire) clay, build pots of various sizes and designs, and fire them through a primitive technique covered later in this chapter. This allows you to focus on the building process while affording you the greatest chance of having a successful firing. I have a very high success rate with such clays. The only real issues I have run into are with pieces that ended up nearer the fire's edge and did not receive adequate heat to give them the resilience hoped for in pottery. Although some people have told me that commercial clay is inferior when it comes to primitive firings, I have found that low-fire clay stands up very well to primitive firing.
- Working with clay that you have harvested and purified, build pots of various sizes and designs, and fire them in a conventional kiln. Converting raw clay into clay that can withstand the rigors of a primitive firing is tricky and time consuming. If you get good results from low firing in a kiln, then proceed to primitive firing techniques. I have taken clays from the land and had great luck making pots and bowls that I was unable to break with my hands. However, the evenness of heat and temperature reached is not something that you can attain as easily in the wild.

If you want to go whole-hog, be prepared to spend more time, because you are working in a situation in which every aspect is a variable. With purchased, low-fire clay, you know that the clay is good, so if the pot breaks, it is most likely a problem related to either construction or firing. If you are using a kiln and the pot breaks, it must be a problem with building or clay. Problems with building are fairly easy to determine due to the nature of the breaks; i.e., the break is along a construction line or seam in which one piece of clay was not adequately bonded to another. If you have access to a kiln, make some pots with commercial clay, fire them in a kiln, and, if you are successful, use the same technique on self-gathered and purified clay.

I recommend reducing the number of variables with each firing to the fewest possible. This allows you to pinpoint the area needing the work. For me, it was the firing process that required the most tweaking. I have played with many clays, have known them to be good, and have broken pots in the firing.

That all said, there is nothing to say that you can't have a successful first experience building and firing your pots.

Getting Clay

Looking at the landscape and trying to determine where clay is to be found can be baffling. There are ways to minimize your search time. Looking

Clay field-quality test

along streams and lakeshores is generally pretty good for a couple of reasons: (1) water likes to seep downward, so if it's on the surface, it is there for a reason—one being bedrock beneath it, the other being clay; and (2) moving water cuts through the substrate on which it flows, and in so doing, it exposes different layers of strata, some of which may be clay. I have found clay mixed thoroughly with rocks and gravel. I also have found clay of such purity that it needed only enough water added to make it workable. It comes in many colors—reds, grays, purples, blues, browns, greens, and shades of white or cream. I have even played with black clay. Their raw color does not let the potter know, however, what color they will turn out to be when they are fired. Most of the clays with which I regularly work fire from a light peach color to a dark red, rusty tone.

Two clay quality tests that I have used to determine the plasticity of the raw material are as follows: Roll out a piece of damp clay to a uniform pencil thickness, and gently tie it in a knot. Do not try to cinch it down by pulling hard on the loose ends; just check it for cracking. If it holds together, it should be workable. The other test is to make a ring (roll some clay between your hands so it is half an inch thick, and form this into a ring with a two-inch diameter), set it on edge, and see how much the ring slumps. If you get little slump, you likely have some good, workable material.

Purifying

Getting the stones, from fist size down to sand, and the organic matter out of the clay can be a relaxing yet time-consuming process. The satisfaction I get when I have a good load of pure clay is almost pathetic; it's worth every minute of work, although I am pretty miserly with it if I've done it with no modern aids. There are generally two types of purifying techniques used, wet and dry.

The dry purification is my least favorite because it is very labor intensive. It basically involves picking anything you don't want out of the clay. This is after you have spread out wet clay, let it dry (unless you found dry chunks initially), and pounded it to dust with a stick. If you happen to have a large sheet or a bunch of large hides, you can winnow the clay by pummeling it to dust and gently tossing it up on the windward side of the sheets or hides. As the light clay is carried gently by the breeze to fall on your sheet, the sand falls straight down, and there you have your clay. Another option is to make a sieve with grasses bunched to form a crude basket. No thanks, I choose wet purification.

Wet purification offers a few choices. My preferred method is to:

1. Submerge wads of wet clay into a container of water (bark container, hide bag, pothole, tarp or plastic bag, or bucket), and knead it until the clay particles separate and the heavier sand and gravel sink to the bottom, leaving the clay suspended in the water. Keep adding and kneading clay clumps until the water takes on a milkshake consistency and all of the clay is suspended in the water.

2. Giving the mix a good stir, let it stand for about fifteen to thirty seconds, and then gently pour the liquid out into another container, being careful not to upend the first container. The goal is to leave one container with grit and the other with clay

juice. If you have used a pothole, move on to steps 3 and 4 of the alternate wet-purification method described below.

3. Using your fingers as strainers, run them through the liquid and pull out grasses and other organic matter.

4. Set the container aside and let the clay settle out. As it does, there will be an increasing layer of clear water on top; this can be removed with a dipper.

5. If you want to speed up this process (it can take about a week), the liquid mix can be poured through a porous material like a shirt. Another method is to pour a thin layer onto a blanket or a hide with the edges slightly raised. The increased surface area will promote a short evaporation time.

6. At this point, the clay needs to be monitored closely to ensure that it does not get too dry. If it does, all is not lost—merely let it dry completely, powder the clay, and move on to "Adding Temper," below.

ALTERNATE WET-PURIFICATION METHOD. Here is another option for wet purification of raw clay.

1. Follow step 1 in the previous method.

2. Let the clay settle out in its original container. It will settle out slower (particles are smaller and lighter) than some of the other material like pebbles and small grains of sand and, therefore, make up the top layer of the material on the bottom of the container.

3. Remove the water with a dipper as the water above clears, or once the mixture is made, stir or agitate it in the container,

then pour it, water and all, into a hole dug in the ground. What will happen is that the settling out of materials from the water will happen in the ground rather than the container. Due to the porosity of the ground the water will soak in faster than the other methods mentioned in this chapter, allowing you to harvest the top layer of sediment in the hole sooner.

4. Scrape or scoop up the clay off of the top of the sludge at the bottom of the hole or container, being careful not to go too deep and reintegrating sand or gravel back into the clay. If you have any cloth or hide that is at least the size of the bottom of the container, you can, after pouring the mixture in, let it sit for about thirty seconds, then place the cloth on the bottom. The clay will settle on the cloth, allowing less material to disappear in amongst the gravel while also preventing any unwanted material from getting mixed in with the clay.

Adding Temper

As clay is heated and cooled, not only in the firing process but also in subsequent uses, it expands and contracts. Because heat and cold are not applied evenly over the pot, one part expands or contracts faster than another part. Between these two parts, something has to give; therefore, a very smooth, temper-free clay will likely crack, while one with good temper will not appear to do so. This is because, instead of getting one large crack along an expansion or contraction border, many micro-cracks form between the pieces of temper, or a crack runs into a grain of sand, or a void, causing that crack to end or to take a different direction. These many cracks are often too small to see but provide enough flexibility to keep the pot together. Issues can arise when the temper has moisture within it and explodes or feeds steam into the surrounding clay, causing it to spall off as the steam grows in volume until it can no longer be contained within the clay.

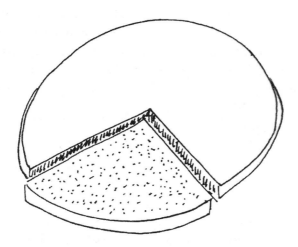

Temper and clay

Temper is often fine sand, ground-up fired pot shards (also called grog), ground-up egg- or seashells, as well as organics like cattail or milkweed down. Organic materials burn up in the firing process, leaving voids that act as insulation. Grog seems to be the best, because it has already been fired and is quite stable. To this end, I have fired sand for this use. I have had fewer issues with spalling (the cracking and flaking off of parts of the vessel wall during firing) when using it in forced drying (drying freshly made ware by direct application of heat) and subsequent firings.

Adding temper and determining how much and what to use can be tricky, and conducting tests using a variety of tempers in varying quantities is a good idea as you work on figuring out your local clay. For my initial use of clay, I make four mixes. Using either fine sand or ground-up, fired pot shards (grog), I'll make one batch three parts clay and one part temper (3:1, or 25 percent), one 4:1 (20 percent), another 7:1 (12.5 percent), and the last batch will have no temper added. I have found that some situations (e.g., with particular clays or less careful firings) require a ratio greater than 3:1 (25 percent) temper and have heard of people using a 50:50 mix, but I have not used such a temper-rich clay myself. As the amount of temper increases, it becomes readily apparent that the workability of the clay diminishes; i.e., it cracks and dries faster. This can be remedied to some extent by either presoaking your temper (especially if you are using grog) if you are adding it to already wet clay, or, if you are adding the temper to a dry mix, you can let the clay age once water has been added. I'll often add more water than necessary, mix the clay well, and let it dry to a workable consistency over a few days at the least.

To add temper to dry, powdered clay, use a container (gourd, cup, etc.) as a measure, and mix it thoroughly before adding water (or add the pulverized, dry clay to the water while you swirl it about; this prevents serious clumping). As you add water, give the clay time to soak it in, and then knead the clay well, adding water as needed. The clay can benefit from aging—being allowed to sit and really soak up all of the water it needs—although the jury is still out on whether doing this for extended periods (weeks or months) is necessary.

To add temper wet, measure out both clay and temper either by packing it into a measuring container or, better yet, make a uniform disk, cut out the desired piece of pie, and replace it with temper.

I like to then ball up the clay, leaving the temper on the work surface, and roll the clay through it. Temper will adhere to the outside of the clay and can then be kneaded and wedged in. To wedge clay is to forcefully throw it onto your work surface, not randomly, but carefully so as to maintain the clay in a lump and not let it become a pancake. Wedging not only helps to integrate the temper, it also removes air pockets in which the trapped air expands during firing, causing spalling (the flaking off of sections of your pot).

Building Pots

The building of a pot can be explained fairly simply, yet there is lots of room for improving to a high level of proficiency and beauty. Two simple pot types are the pinch pot, good for smaller objects like eating bowls, lamps, and ladle bowls, and the coil method, used for larger objects such as cooking containers, water jugs, and the like.

Flat-bottomed vessels work well where there are flat work surfaces such as tables, but these can be rare in the natural landscape. Flat-bottom pottery is also difficult to heat evenly over a fire. For both reasons, I have found it to be more prone to breakage than pots with rounded or conical bases. The rounded or cone base allows a pot to be nestled into the coals or easily supported between three or four rocks placed in the cooking fire.

In the construction of clay products, strength of the finished item is important, because it speaks to the length of time it may be suitable for use. To this end, you should know that the fewer places in which two pieces of clay are joined, the better. Poorly made joints are prone to cracking throughout the life of the pot from the moment it is made. Clay to be joined should be moist enough to stick together once modest pressure has been applied to both pieces. The most common issue in my experience is when one or both pieces are too dry. The solution is to score (scratch little lines) in a crisscross pattern on both surfaces to be joined and then run a wet finger over them. Pressing both pieces firmly together usually creates a dependable bond. This situation also illustrates the value of a pot molded from one lump of clay. There are no joints.

PINCH POT METHOD. Pinch pots are exactly that—vessels whose shape is pinched out of the initial ball of clay.

1. Form a sphere with your prepared clay.
2. Plunge your thumb into the sphere deep enough so that the tip comes within one-fourth inch of going through the far side.
3. With your thumb in the hole and your fingers outside, pinch them together, squeezing the clay to about one-fourth-inch thick.
4. Continue pinching in this fashion as you rotate the sphere so that your "pinchings" spiral up and around from the initial pinch to the lip of the pot.
5. Go over the pot and focus on acquiring an even thickness. Squeeze or smear lumps into depressions or into the surrounding body of the pot. Don't worry about dressing up the lip at this point; this can wait until later.
6. Set the pot aside to dry out of direct sunlight and not too close to a heat source. It should dry slowly and evenly.
7. Before it gets bone dry, it goes through a "leather hard" stage. It still has the darker look of wet clay, yet it has lost its malleable quality. This is a good time to trim the lip and scrape down thick areas with a shell, a wooden or bone knife, or any other tool you have for the task. This hardness is also the time to burnish, a process in which all of the clay particles are aligned, resulting in a very shiny surface. The burnishing process requires a smooth stone, pebble, or piece of polished bone that is large enough to hold in your hand but not so big as to be cumbersome. (In modern pottery shops, the backs of spoons and kitchen cabinet knobs are often used.) Sliding the smooth pebble over the leather-hard clay leaves a noticeably glossy trail in its wake. Whether you choose to burnish with no pattern, horizontally, laterally, or diagonally is up to you, but be careful around the lip, and don't push too hard. It would be a pity to break your pot at this point. If

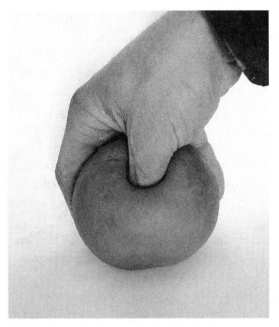

Making a pinch pot

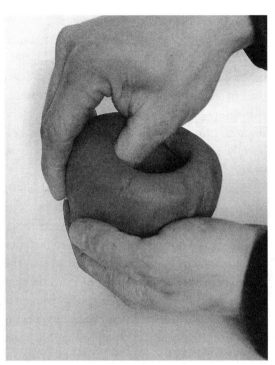

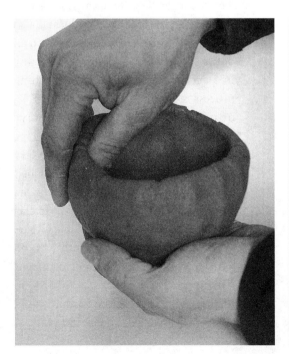

you want a really fine finish, burnish the pot when it has gone just beyond the hardness of leather, then let it dry completely. Dampen small areas at a time with a rag or brush, and burnish it once again.

Burnishing, however, is far from essential. Many old pots and shards that I have seen either in the field or museums have a rough or textured outer surface. Speculation on the rationale for this is that the increased surface area promotes a faster heating of the contents when the pot is over a fire. I like the texture on some pots, not only for the beauty it adds, but also for the increased grip you have while handling these pots when they are hot, either with mitts or more often with sticks.

Narrowing coils

COIL CONSTRUCTION. The coil construction method allows potters to build larger pots than the pinch pot method. Within this method are many techniques for building a jug, vase, or cooking pot. Here is one with some variations:

1. Begin with a pinch pot, but not one that is as thin as that described above (material can always be scraped away later).
2. Roll clay between your hands to create "ropes" of clay; these can be left round or be flattened slightly.
3. Coil the ropes onto the top edge of the pot. If you wish the pot to widen, place the ropes more to the outer edge; to narrow the pot, place them more to the inner edge.
4. If the lip of the pot is on the drier side (the new clay does not readily stick to it), score and dampen it with a wet finger prior to applying the new clay. To slow the drying

Smearing coils

process, you can cover the lip or top edge with damp leaves. If the pot is too moist and the clay wants to slump, allow it to dry somewhat before you add more clay.

5. After you add a few layers, the new coils must be smeared, or feathered, into the pot below. I often smear the coils downward on the inside of the pot and upward on the outside. This helps to maintain an even wall thickness. Always maintain a supporting hand or finger on the opposite side of the wall on which you are working.

6. It is a good idea to finish the inside of pots as you build them, because access to the inside can be tough once the pot is completed. I also try to imagine what would happen if I filled the pot with oatmeal and then tried to clean it. Is the interior smooth enough to allow for a good cleaning, or are there lots of little holes and knobs that will catch and hold food?

7. You may burnish the surface as described above, under "Pinch Pot Method." Or, while the clay is still wet, you may texture the outside of the pot with a paddle, which can be wrapped with cordage. You can etch a design in when the clay is closer to being dry.

Prefiring

The goal in preparing ware for firing is to get it as dry as possible while preventing cracking. This usually means letting it dry slowly at first. When I am drying ware and it is very hot, I will place a large leaf or two over the pieces to slow the initial drying. If you have a cloth or a piece of plastic, it can be draped over your work (the cloth should start out slightly damp) instead. On the other hand, if your ware has an even thickness and is on the thinner side, you may have success force drying pieces near a fire or between two fires. The air should be warm but not hot, and nothing in the vicinity of the pot should become too hot to touch. With the fire on one side, the ware requires constant attention, and even then it is not always enough and pots can be lost.

Firing

When you are going to conduct a firing, it is important to have all of your ducks in row. In a perfect world, the pots are placed near a fire, and the temperature is slowly brought up until the pots become too hot to handle with your bare hands. They turn dark as the organic matter in the clay is burned up. The ware is then covered with wood, which is left to burn down to ash. The ash is brushed off, and the finished pots are taken out, blown clean, and held up for townspeople to marvel at, awed by your masterful craftsmanship. You are then welcomed in every home as an honored guest . . . as I said, in a perfect world.

Let's take it step by step.

1. Create a twelve-inch-deep pit by excavating it out of the ground, building up a berm, or using a combination of both. The overall shape does not matter, but the size should be large enough to accommodate your ware in the center and still have a fire in the pit anywhere around the periphery without danger of the flames hitting the pots. The site should be located in an area that is sheltered from the wind.

2. Collect plenty of firewood, including a lot of kindling. Small hardwood sticks get a great fire going and produce good coals; softwood kindling can really crank up the

Pit fire setup

Pit fire setup with ware in place

heat, but you will need much more of it in order to keep the fire going long enough. Have a few heftier logs handy. I prefer to have more wood than I'll need just to be on the safe side.

3. Make a fire in the middle of the pit, and let it burn down to coals. This fire should have some heftier logs in it, although not all wood needs to be reduced to coals. While the fire burns, preheat your pots by leaving them close enough to become warm, and rotate them to promote even heating.

4. When the ground has been dried and heated, rake the coals from the center, creating a ring of coals.

5. Place either green-wood sticks or previously fired stones in the cleared area such that the ware can be rested on them (upside down) without touching the ground.

6. Place your pots on the rocks or rests, and let them heat slowly.

7. Add sticks as necessary to the coal ring. Slowly let the fire creep in, bringing up the temperature in the ware, but do not let the flames touch the ware. Eventually (one to three hours, depending on your experience and a million other things), the clay will darken as the organic matter within the clay is burned (some people call this "smoking"). This darkening indicates that the pots are ready for direct, even heat. Another test that some potters use and one that I have adopted is the spit or water test. If spit or water bounces off of the hot ware, the pottery is ready; if it sits and sizzles, it is not.

8. Quickly and carefully stack wood around the pots until they are well covered. Use smaller wood and kindling, and add larger stock on top. At this point, flames may touch the ware.

9. Let the fire burn for about two hours, then let it die down. Some clays are able to handle thermal shock much better than oth-

Pit fire, finished ware

ers. I have heard of pots being taken from the coals and put into a bucket of water and faring fine, while others break when a wind pops up and cools one side too fast. The choice is yours.

10. If you see a crack in your pot, it may not be the end of the road for it. Some pots have been used for years with a crack that formed during firing. Dry goods can be kept in the pot, or the pot can be sealed with pitch. Cooking in it may make the crack run and, sooner or later, end the pot's life.

Many sources that I researched when learning about pottery referred to cow dung as the fuel of choice. Not everyone has cow dung available to them, so in searching for substitutes, I tried punky wood as a fuel in the following way:

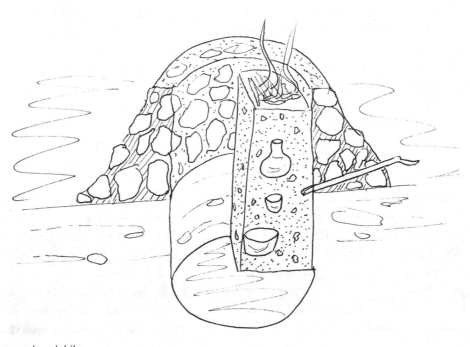

Punky wood rock kiln

1. The "kiln" can be a simple pit or, better yet, fired stone held with a mixture of raw clay and dried grass with one-fourth to one-half-inch gaps throughout. A third option is a loose pile of stones (preferably prefired) with a void or pit in the middle (the size of the pit is determined by the amount of ware you intend to fire).

2. Put down a four-inch layer of dry, punky wood on the bottom of the "kiln."

3. Fill and cover the ware completely with fuel.

4. Cover the surface of the fuel completely with very flammable materials like wood shavings, dried grasses, and tinder—fuels that ignite easily and will get the whole surface burning evenly downward.

5. Once the punky wood is burning, cover the pit with a rock slab that can span it or other materials that will reduce the amount of oxygen available to the surface. Bundles of green grasses, prebundled green-wood faggots, and slabs of bark are some of the options.

6. Let the fire burn down until the pots have cooled completely. Sometimes this can take about twelve hours, but it depends on how much air is able to get to the burning fuel.

7. Remove the pots and rinse them with water.

If you want to add some color or character to your ware, the fire can be smothered with earth or debris when it has reached maximum heat and left to cool about three or four hours. This prevents the pots from re-oxidizing and often produces some pretty neat effects. If you are intent on cooking with your pot, don't bother making it too pretty, because it soon turns black from use. Also, don't plan on making any family heirlooms, because the life expectancy for ware such as this is not too impressive.

Kilns

A rudimentary kiln requires some work but can greatly enhance your ware quality as well as your success rate. The following are two simple kilns.

DUAL FIREBOX KILN. The dual firebox kiln is built using your local clay mixed with grasses.

1. Harvest a few armloads of vegetation like grasses, goldenrod, sticks, and/or logs.

2. Place them on the ground at your kiln site so that they form a long, rounded mound about twelve inches high and five feet long. If you have found a straight, smooth log or are using sticks, make sure to fully fill all larger voids in the pile and cover all wood

Punky wood rock kiln, finished ware

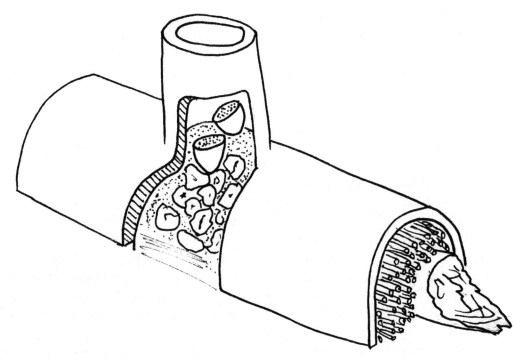

Cutaway view of kiln

with grasses or leaves as a gasket to ease removal once the kiln is dry.

3. Cover the mound with a 50:50 mixture of clay and grasses. Leave both ends open and a circle in the middle of the top. This hole is where the chimney will be and where the objects will be fired.

4. Using the coil technique, build the chimney up from the central hole.

5. In the edge of the central hole and in the wall of the chimney, pottery shards and/or prefired stones should be embedded. Allow them to jut out in a way that will allow the ware to be rested on them. More large, prefired rocks will sit on the ground below the chimney opening to support the lowest pot while allowing heat to get under the ware.

6. Let the kiln dry. Grasses can be tossed over it to retard the drying process and prevent cracking.

7. Once the kiln is dry, the grasses making up the form can be pulled out, freeing up any wood that was used in the process.

8. To fire this kiln, place preheated ware in the lower chimney and light fires in both open ends. Start them small, and slowly increase the heat, being careful to keep both fires burning at the same rate. Flames rising out of the chimney eighteen inches or more is a good thing and something that you want to maintain for about an

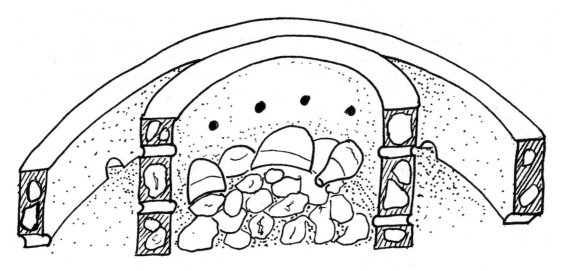

Cutaway of kiln

hour and a half before letting the fire die down and the ware cool.

I have heard of people wet-firing (firing the kiln while the material used to make it is still wet) this type of kiln with no real cracking. Because it is dried from the inside out, water is able to leave through the moist, outer surface.

DOUBLE PIT KILN. This kiln requires more experimentation but has great promise and is used in large scale in parts of Africa. As with any primitive firing method, the kiln master must pay close attention to the process and make adjustments while learning all the nuances of operating that particular type of kiln. It may not be rocket science, but it is no walk in the park either.

1. With previously fired stones (from a sweat lodge or done expressly for this purpose), build an enclosure or box that is large and sturdy enough to accommodate your ware.

2. Build a ring of stone or other type of reflector around the firing box but far enough away so that the fire can burn in the "moat"—the area between the reflector and the firing box.

3. Burn a small fire in the box and in the moat to preheat the stones, and warm the pots as you do so. Leave a section that has no fire in the moat or the heat may prevent you from getting your ware in the firing box.

4. Load the box with your ware, resting it on stones to keep it off of the ground, and block *any* side door with stones.

5. Spread coals around the entire moat and add kindling to further heat the pots.

6. Because the firing box helps to even out the heat, ware of an even thickness should be able to reach temperature fast with no

ill effects. I do recommend getting your pots very hot (smoked) before moving on to step 7, however. It is tough to know when this point is reached if the ware is not visible.

7. Place wood all over and around the kiln.
8. Fire it up and keep it burning for about an hour and a half.
9. Let it cool, and *carefully* remove any door stones.

Pottery Use and Care

Pots fired without glaze are porous and will sweat if they are filled with water. The advantage of the sweating is that, in the heat of summer, water in these vessels will remain cold as the moisture on the outside evaporates. I used sweating water containers in Australia, and even when the temperature had been more than 120°F, the water contained within them was refreshingly cool (a container was often hung on the porch, getting some sun). If you wish to cook in the pot, cook some porridge in it first, because this will help clog the pores and reduce sweating, although any cooking in it will eventually do the same thing.

Some pots can handle getting put in the fire and rapidly brought to cooking heat, and others cannot.

- Take the time to preheat the pot before cooking. If you want to really see what the pot can withstand, put it through its paces and see how it fares.
- I suggest filling a room-temperature pot with room-temperature water. Most ware, in my experience, does not do well with thermal shock, like that caused by pouring hot water into a cold pot.
- Building a blazing fire around a partially filled pot may result in cracking at the waterline, because the clay above heats quickly while the clay below heats more slowly.
- Stir your food regularly as it cooks, and clean it before the food residue has dried onto it.
- Package your ware carefully for travel.

CHAPTER 18

COMFORT AND CLEANLINESS

Comfort is not a frivolous pursuit in the wilderness. Especially during an extended wilderness sojourn, certain amenities greatly contribute to the effective performance of tasks and help you remain physically and mentally healthy. Because wilderness living takes a lot of effort, compared to living in society, a certain level of comfort seems to be virtually essential to maintain a good attitude. If you're feeling miserable, you're probably doing something wrong, and you should ask yourself why you're doing it at all.

CAMP LAYOUT

The layout of your camp is important for general comfort, efficiency, and health.

- Make sure that your latrine area is downhill from your camp and well away from any water source to avoid contamination.
- Having your food storage and cooking areas separate, clean, and away from your sleeping quarters is a good way to avoid animal visitors both large and small.

- A common mistake among camping parties is gathering firewood and food that are close to camp, slowly depleting their closest supplies. Keeping a buffer zone—an area surrounding your camp in which you don't harvest food or firewood—is a precaution that can save your life. In the event of an injury, heavy snows, or other factors inhibiting movement, you will have a good supply of materials and food nearby.

Grass Mats

Grass mats can be comfortable and can help you sleep in a warmer environment by insulating your body from the ground. Loose grass is not bad to sleep on, but there is something quite nice about a firm, yet soft, mattress to sleep on. It has been my experience that loose bedding can take some getting used to but soon firms up. If that is not your bag, make a grass mat. They are simply made as follows:

1. Gather an armload of grasses; these can be cut with almost any cutting edge. I have used lower jaws of deer, serrated wooden and bone knives, as well as steel.

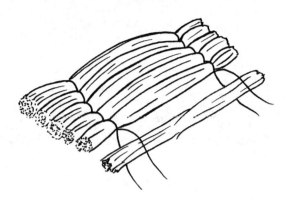

Grass mat lashing

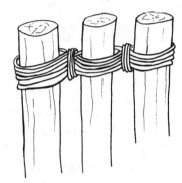

2. Divide the grass into equal-size bundles that are at least the diameter of your palm, and place them on the ground with the bundles parallel one another.

3. Lash the bundles tightly together, as shown in the illustration "Grass mat lashing."

If the mats are to be stationary, the cordage can be of a lesser quality, such as cattail, grass, etc., rather than milkweed, basswood, yucca, nettle, and the like.

Backrests

When you are working on projects around camp, it is often nice to lean back against a tree or rock; however, with minimal effort and materials, a custom backrest can be made in little time.

Backrest detail

1. Find three sturdy saplings, branches, or dead wood pieces that are at least three feet tall and an armload of branches that are the thickness of your thumb.

2. Place the three structural pieces on the ground, parallel and close together.

3. Wrap cordage around one end of the pieces at least ten times.

4. Wrap cordage around the initial lashing between each piece and cinch it down.

5. Stand the three pieces up, with the lashing topmost, and pull the base of the middle stick away from between the outer two.

You should now have a freestanding tripod.

6. Lash the thumb-thick branches to the two outermost sticks; this is easier to do when the backrest is lying on the ground.

7. Stand it up and lean back.

Sometimes you may find it necessary to tie one or more of the legs to an anchor peg or protruding root. A grass mat draped over the backrest with enough extra length to provide a cushion to sit on completes the backwoods recliner.

HYGIENE

Keeping clean and healthy in the wild is not as tough as it might seem. Once your diet of natural foods has pushed out all of the toxins and other superprocessed food of society, you will find that your body odor and oily hair fade away and plaque appears less on your teeth.

Defecating

This is a tender subject for many people, yet an important one. Many nervous poopers have refused to give in to the urge due to their lack of comfort with primitive toiletries. Holding a bowel movement back results in constipation and, if not tended to, can lead to impaction, a condition requiring medical attention. It is liberating indeed to walk into the woods and know that, at any time, in any environment, *you* can drop your trousers and comfortably take care of business. With that in mind, most public lands have strict guidelines concerning this very subject, so be sure that you familiarize yourself with local protocols.

Most people who defecate in the woods will dig a six-inch hole, complete their business, fill it in, and cover it with a rock. After years of pooping in the woods, I have come to the conclusion that leaving poop on the surface allows it to disappear far faster than if you put in the ground, given that store-bought toilet paper is *not* used. Additionally, if poop is visible, you are less likely to step in it; if it is cleverly "buried" under two inches of soil, you end up with something akin to a minefield and will develop a fear of picking up rocks. When you are in areas that receive few visitors, and you leave your poop on the surface, defecate in out-of-the-way places where people are not likely to go, such as thickets, next to thornbushes, and the like. In dry and/or hot climates, spreading or smearing your excrement will speed drying time, thus making it unappealing to flies.

The following are eight ways in which to wipe yourself. The position you use can minimize the need for extensive wiping, so it is best to poop in a squat. It helps in voiding the bowels, as well as in spreading your buttocks, keeping them safely out of harm's way. Sitting over a log, straight or forked, is more comfortable for some, while others prefer to partially squat while holding onto a tree to keep from falling over backward.

- Snow is a tad chilly, yet very effective, because it melts and conforms to your personal shape, allowing for a good cleaning.
- Sand works very well, too! While squatting, wipe lightly with a handful of dry sand. The second wipe can be a little harder. The sand soaks up any moisture, sticks to other remnants, and is then easily brushed off with a final handful of sand. This method is not as uncomfortable as it may sound.

- Stones, rounded and slightly rough, are very effective. Be careful in temperature extremes. It is possible to injure yourself with very hot or very cold stones.
- A pinecone should be first checked for pitch. If any is found, discard it. If not, wipe from the stem to the tip. Pinecones are comfortable to use and are effective.
- Sticks can be used, although they're not the best choice. They require a little more effort to get yourself really clean.
- Leaves are better if they are doubled up, but don't press too hard or your fingers might "pop" through. Use the rough side of the leaf—the ribbed side—to catch all "wipeables." Watch out for poison oak, poison ivy, and stinging nettle leaves. These would cause *great* discomfort.
- Grass and moss are fantastic for wiping. Wad them up into a clump like a little green scrub brush and wipe away.
- Water, of course, is great, but it's best to use it after first using one of the above. If water is to be used, carry a container away from the water source to avoid contamination.

Be imaginative—mix and match, start with a stick, and finish with leaves. Nature is full of potential toiletries.

Brushing Your Teeth

A black birch twig with one end chewed to a frayed tip works well as a toothbrush and tastes good, too. Oak twigs are also popular, because the tannins help kill bacteria and remove their cavity-causing by-products.

Washing Your Hair

One of the best hair washes that I have encountered is mud from a hot spring. Clay does a somewhat inferior job and requires a second wash with a deodorizing soap or plant such as soapwort or mashed mint. Clay should be mixed with water until it is a just pourable mixture. Apply it to your head, working it in so that it thoroughly soaks your hair. Leave it in for ten minutes or more and rinse well.

Cleaning Your Body and Clothing

Sand and stones are great washboards for scrubbing out clothes and scouring hands.

Soapwort, sometimes called bouncing bet, is found in disturbed soil, on riverbanks, and in streambeds. It has leaves that can be briskly rubbed between your hands, creating a green lather that works very well as a soap and deodorizer. Yucca leaves and roots can be dipped in water and beaten with a stick alternately to create good washing suds.

Do not use agaves, because the sap is acidic and will give you a burning rash. It will also burn holes in your clothes. When I was out in central Arizona, I thought to reduce my armpit odor and, finding no yucca for washing, I settled on agaves, assuming that they were similar enough that they would produce a serviceable soap. Never assume! I got a pretty impressive red rash that welted up and, after washing off the "soap" with my cotton T-shirt, I stowed the shirt in my pack. A few days later I removed the shirt to rinse it off and noticed that the area I had used as a washcloth looked like Alpine Lace Swiss cheese.

RECOMMENDED READING

Although this list is far from comprehensive, here is some recommended reading to further enhance your knowledge of survival and wilderness living skills. Some of these resources are best used in conjunction with others.

Alloway, David. 2003. *Desert Survival Skills.* Austin: University of Texas Press.

Blankenship, Bart, and Robin Blankenship. 1996. *Earth Knack, Stone Age Skills for the 21st Century.* Layton, UT: Gibbs Smith.

Bowman, Warren. 1998. *Outdoor Emergency Care.* National Ski Patrol Systems, Inc.

Brill, Steve. 1994. *Identifying and Harvesting Edible and Medicinal Plants in Wild (and Not So Wild) Places.* New York: Harper Paperbacks.

Brown, Tom, Jr., with Brandt Morgan. 1983. *Tom Brown's Field Guide to Wilderness Survival.* New York: Berkly Books.

Childs, Craig. 2000. *The Secret Knowledge of Water.* Boston: Back Bay Books.

Coon, Carleton. 1971. *The Hunting Peoples.* New York: Nick Lyons Books.

Couplan, François. 1998. *The Encyclopedia of Edible Plants of North America.* New Canaan, CT: Keats Publishing.

Dunmire, William, and Gail Tierney. 1997. *Wild Plants and Native Peoples of the Four Corners.* Santa Fe: Museum of New Mexico Press.

Easton, Robert, and Peter Nabkov. 1989. *Native American Architecture.* New York: Oxford University Press.

Edholm, Steven, and Tamara Wilder. 1997. *Wet-Scrape Braintanned Buckskin.* Boonville, CA: Paleotechnics.

Elbroch, Mark. 2001. *Bird Tracks & Sign.* Mechanicsburg, PA: Stackpole.

———. 2003. *Mammal Tracks & Sign.* Mechanicsburg, PA: Stackpole.

Elbroch, Mark, and Michael Pewtherer. 2006. *Wilderness Survival.* Camden, ME: Ragged Mountain Press.

Elpel, Thomas. 2002. *Participating in Nature: Thomas J. Elpel's Field Guide to Primitive Living Skills.* Pony, MT: HOPS Press. (Also published as *Primitive Living, Self-Sufficiency and Survival Skills.* Guilford, CT: Lyons, 2004.)

———. 2006. *Botany in a Day.* Pony, MT: HOPS Press.

Foster, Steven, and Christopher Hobbs. 2002. *Peterson's Guides: A Field Guide to West-*

ern Medicinal Plants and Herbs. New York: Houghton Mifflin.

Ganci, Dave. 1991. *The Basic Essentials of Desert Survival.* Merrillville, IN: ICS Books, Inc.

Goodchild, Peter. 1984. *Survival Skills of the North American Indians.* Chicago: Chicago Review Press.

Graves, Richard. 1972. *Bushcraft.* New York: Shocken Books.

Hamm, Jim, Steve Allely, et al. 1992. *The Traditional Bowyers Bible,* Volumes I, II, and III. New York: Bois d'Arc Press.

Hart, Carol, and Dan Hart. 1976. *Natural Basketry.* New York: Watson-Guptill.

Irwin, R. Stephen. 1984. *The Indian Hunters.* Blaine, WA: Hancock House.

Jamison, Richard. 2006. *The Best of Woodsmoke.* Springville, UT: Cedar Fort, Inc.

Jamison, Richard, and Linda Jamison. 1994. *Woodsmoke, Collected Writings on Ancient Living Skills.* Birmingham, AL: Menasha Ridge Press.

Jamison, Richard, et al. 1985. *Primitive Outdoor Skills.* Bountiful, UT: Horizon Publishers and Distributors.

Johnson, Mark. 2003. *The Ultimate Desert Handbook.* Camden, ME: Ragged Mountain Press/McGraw-Hill.

Kochanski, Mors. 1987. *Bush Craft.* Edmonton, Alberta, CA: Lone Pine.

Lundin, Cody. 2003. *98.6 Degrees, the Art of Keeping Your Ass Alive.* Layton, UT: Gibbs Smith.

McPherson, John, and Geri McPherson. 1993. *Primitive Wilderness Living & Survival Skills.* Randolph, KS: Prairie Wolf.

———. 1996. *Primitive Wilderness Skills, Applied & Advanced.* Randolph, KS: Prairie Wolf.

Mears, Raymond. 1992. *The Outdoor Survival Handbook.* New York: St. Martin's Press.

Nelson, Richard. 1969. *Hunters of the Northern Ice.* Chicago: University of Chicago Press.

———. 1973. *Hunters of the Northern Forest.* Chicago: University of Chicago Press.

Nestor, Tony. 2003. *Desert Survival Tips, Tricks and Skills.* Flagstaff, AZ: Diamond Creek Press.

Newman, Sandra Corrie. 1974. *Indian Basket Weaving.* Flagstaff, AZ: Northland Press.

Olsen, Larry Dean. 1997. *Outdoor Survival Skills.* Chicago: Chicago Review Press.

Patten, Bob. 1999. *Old Tools—New Eyes.* Denver: Stone Dagger Publications.

Peterson, Lee. 1999. *A Field Guide to Edible Wild Plants: Eastern and Central North America.* New York: Houghton Mifflin.

Richards, Matt. 1997. *Deerskins into Buckskins, How to Tan with Natural Materials.* Cave Junction, OR: Backcountry Publishing.

Schofield, Janice. 2003. *Discovering Wild Plants: Alaska, Western Canada, the Northwest.* Portland, OR: Alaska Northwest Books.

Scully, Virginia. 1970. *A Treasury of American Indian Herbs.* New York: Crown Publishing Group.

Stewart, Hilary. 1977. *Indian Fishing: Early Methods of the Northwest Coast.* Seattle: University of Washington Press.

———. 1995. *Cedar.* Seattle: University of Washington Press.

———. 1996. *Stone, Bone, Antler and Shell: Artifacts of the Northwest Coast.* Seattle: University of Washington Press.

Thayer, Samuel. 2006. *The Forager's Harvest: A Guide to Identifying, Harvesting, and Preparing Edible Wild Plants.* Ogema, WI: Forager's Harvest Press.

Waldorf, D. C. 1984. *The Art of Flint Knapping.* Branson, MO: Mound Builder Books.

——. 1999. *The Art of Making Primitive Bows and Arrows.* Branson, MO: Mound Builder Books.

Watts, Steve. 2004. *Practicing Primitive: A Handbook of Aboriginal Skills.* Layton, UT: Gibbs Smith.

Wells, Darran, and Jon Cox. 2005. *NOLS Wilderness Navigation.* Mechanicsburg, PA: Stackpole Books.

Wescott, David. 1999. *Primitive Technology: A Book of Earth Skills.* Layton, UT: Gibbs Smith.

——. 2001. *Primitive Technology II: Ancestral Skill.* Layton, UT: Gibbs Smith.

Wheat, Margaret. 1967. *Survival Arts of the Primitive Paiutes.* Reno, NV: University of Nevada Press.

White, George. 1969. *Craft Manual of North American Indian Footwear.* White Pub.

INDEX